STUDIES IN ENGLISH AND AMERICAN
LITERATURE, LINGUISTICS, AND CULTURE

VOL. 1

# STUDIES IN ENGLISH AND AMERICAN LITERATURE, LINGUISTICS, AND CULTURE

## Vol. 1

CAMDEN HOUSE
Columbia, South Carolina

# Romanticism and Culture

# Romanticism and Culture

## A Tribute to Morse Peckham
### and
## A Bibliography of His Work

Edited by
H.W. Matalene

CAMDEN HOUSE

PN 36
P 4
R 6
1984x

Set in Garamond type
and printed on acid-free paper.

# TABULA GRATULATORUM

Wilbur T. Albrecht
Department of English
Colgate University
Hamilton, New York

Adelheid M. Atkins
Department of Languages and Literature
Augusta College
Augusta, Georgia

J. Leeds Barroll III
Washington, D.C.

George C. Brauer, Jr.
Department of English
University of South Carolina
Columbia, South Carolina

Irvin L. Child
Yale University
New Haven, Connecticut

Department of English
The Citadel
Charleston, South Carolina

Claudette Kemper Columbus
Department of English
Hobart and William Smith Colleges
Geneva, New York

Robert Combs
Department of English
The George Washington University
Washington, D.C.

Georgia and David Cowart
Department of English
University of South Carolina
Columbia, South Carolina

Wystan Curnow
Department of English
University of Auckland
New Zealand

Elizabeth S. Davidson
University of South Carolina
Spartanburg, South Carolina

John H. Gagnon
Department of Sociology
SUNY at Stony Brook
Stony Brook, New York

George L. Geckle
Department of English
University of South Carolina
Columbia, South Carolina

Judith C. Gilliom
Wheaton, Maryland

Donald J. Greiner
Department of English
University of South Carolina
Columbia, South Carolina

James Hardin
Department of Foreign Languages and Literatures
University of South Carolina
Columbia, South Carolina

Gunther Holst
Department of Foreign Languages and Literatures
University of South Carolina
Columbia, South Carolina

E. Anthony James
Department of English
Lehigh University
Bethlehem, Pennsylvania

Department of English
Lafayette College
Easton, Pennsylvania

Sandra Langer
Department of Art History
University of South Carolina
Columbia, South Carolina

Steven W. Lynn
Department of English
University of South Carolina
Columbia, South Carolina

Harry Miller
College of Applied Professional Sciences
University of South Carolina
Columbia, South Carolina

James T. Myers
Department of Government and International Studies
University of South Carolina
Columbia, South Carolina

John Norton
San Francisco, California

Robert L. Oakman
Department of English
University of South Carolina
Columbia, South Carolina

Elizabeth Pochoda
Brooklyn, New York

Philip Pochoda
Brooklyn, New York

David L. Powell
Department of Literature
Evergreen State College
Olympia, Washington

Ennis Rees
Department of English
University of South Carolina
Columbia, South Carolina

Henry H. H. Remak
Department of Comparative Literature
Indiana University
Bloomington, Indiana

Jack W. Rhodes
Department of English
The Citadel
Charleston, South Carolina

William T. Ross
133 Baltic Circle
Tampa, Florida

G. Ross Roy
Department of English
University of South Carolina
Columbia, South Carolina

Clyde De L. Ryals
Department of English
Duke University
Durham, North Carolina

Peter C. Sederberg
Department of Government and International Studies
University of South Carolina
Columbia, South Carolina

Barbara Herrnstein Smith
Department of English
University of Pennsylvania
Philadelphia, Pennsylvania

Department of English
Smith College
Northhampton, Massachusetts

James Harvey Smith
Department of Languages and Literature
Augusta College
Augusta, Georgia

Robert L. Stewart
Department of Sociology
University of South Carolina
Columbia, South Carolina

William B. Thesing
Department of English
University of South Carolina
Columbia, South Carolina

Ann and Gurkan Unal
Fairfax, Virginia

Thomas A. Vogler
Department of English
University of California
Santa Cruz, California

Edward L. Wolfe
Department of English
Glassboro State College
Glassboro, New Jersey

# Preface

THIS VOLUME IS A TRIBUTE to Morse Peckham on his retirement from teaching in the post of Distinguished Professor of English and Comparative Literature at the University of South Carolina. It contains essays by a few of the people who have been close to Peckham academically, intellectually, and personally at various stages in his career.

Among them, as one might expect, are colleagues in literary studies, both at large and in departments where Peckham has taught. I recall that when Professor Ryals spoke to a gathering at the University of Pennsylvania, lamenting Peckham's departure for South Carolina, he referred over-modestly to himself as Penn's "Other Victorian." He has, of course, gone on to distinguish himself as a historical interpreter of Victorian literature in his own right, and has since taken his place in the tradition of fine Victorian scholarship at Duke University. Professor Remak, whose anatomy of romanticism is studied by every beginning graduate student in comparative literature, has brought Peckham before his students at Indiana University as a visiting Professor. Professor Smith, who came to Pennsylvania to fill Peckham's slot as a literary theorist, is one of the few scholars actually capable of doing so. Recently, she has written of Peckham that sooner or later one learns that he is right about everything. Professors Geckle, Roy, and Oakman have all been among the program heads and "Other Victorians" with whom Peckham has worked at South Carolina.

More surprising, perhaps, though not to people familiar with the breadth of Peckham's intellectual concerns, will be the presence in this volume of a psychologist, a sociologist, and a political scientist. Professor Child is one of Peckham's oldest friends and a distinguished fellow worker in the psychology of art. Professor Gagnon, an accomplished (and cultivated) sociologist, is the more recent friend who put Peckham up to writing *Art and Pornography,* in which Peckham began to emerge as a social thinker. And Professor Sederberg is one of a number of friends Peckham has made at the University of South Carolina in departments other than English. Sederberg's work in political science gives

evidence of the extraordinary impact of Peckham's precept and example on the intellectual life of the University of South Carolina as a whole. He has even gone so far as to read a paper on Peckham to the Southern Political Science Association.

Finally, there is the editor—the only contributor actually to have been a formal student of Peckham's. In soliciting contributions to a volume honoring a scholar of his breadth and depth of learning, I thought it would be inappropriate to limit the contributors as to topic or scholarly style. His great value has been that he has refused to impose such limitations on himself. The essays submitted, consequently, operate at every level of generality on which Peckham, himself, has worked: from Professor Roy's highly specialized essay in bibliography to Professor Sederberg's discussion of science as an approach to moral problems. Where their concerns overlap, not all the contributors agree either with Peckham or with each other on all points.

These are hard times for academic publishers; hence, for *Festschriften,* and consequently, for their editors. This volume has been much longer in appearing than was first anticipated. Therefore, not only the scholarship, but the patience of all its contributors, must be most gratefully acknowledged. Special thanks are due to three contributors. Professor George Geckle, Head of the English Department of the University of South Carolina, generously committed departmental money toward publication. Moreover, together with Professor Robert Oakman, Dr. Geckle guided the typescript through the initial phases of the Camden House publication procedure during the fall of 1982, while the editor was away teaching at Shanxi University in the People's Republic of China. And finally, Professor Henry Remak, having thoughtfully considered my prospectus of the volume's final contents, wrote me in China proposing *Romanticism and Culture* as an appropriate title, for which I thank him.

I am grateful to Ms. Mary Dave Denny, who typed the final manuscript—portions of it as many as three times, to incorporate editorial changes. At Camden House, Professor James Hardin has been a cheerful and tactful expediter of publication; and Professor Benjamin Franklin, V, graciously took time from his work as a Fulbright professor in Greece to help with the final copy-editing.

Above all, I am grateful to Professor Carolyn B. Matalene, my wife, for her love, and to Morse Peckham, himself, for his understanding during the vicissitudes of the venture here happily concluded.

# Contributors

Irvin L. Child is professor of psychology at Yale University and has held a fellowship at the Center for Advanced Study in the Behavioral Sciences. He is a member of the American Psychological Association, with research interests in personality and aesthetics, in which fields he is the author or co-author of many articles and books, including *Italian or American? The Second Generation in Conflict, Child Training and Personality: A Cross-Cultural Study,* and *Humanistic Psychology and the Research Tradition: Their Several Virtues.*

John H. Gagnon is professor of sociology at the State University of New York at Stony Brook. He has been lecturer in sociology at Indiana University and senior research sociologist and trustee of its Institute for Sex Research. Cultural change and human sexuality have been his major research interests, and he has held fellowships at the University of Copenhagen, in the Human Development Laboratory of the Harvard Graduate School of Education, and at Churchill College in the University of Cambridge. Among his publications are *Sexual Conduct: The Social Sources of Human Sexuality* (with William Simon), and *Human Sexualities.*

George L. Geckle is professor of English and chairman of his department at the University of South Carolina in Columbia, where he has also been head of the honors program. Elizabethan and Jacobean drama is his main research interest, though he has also published on Joyce, and, most recently, on faculty morale and development. He is the editor of *Twentieth Century Interpretations of Measure for Measure,* and the author of *John Marston's Drama: Themes, Images, Sources.*

Robert L. Oakman, professor and graduate chairman of English at the University of South Carolina in Columbia, holds graduate degrees in both mathematics and English, and is chiefly interested in Victorian literature and in the application of computers to research in the humanities. A number of essays on aspects of the latter problem have led to the publication of his standard

*Computer Methods for Literary Research.* He has also published on Henry Fielding.

Henry H. H. Remak is professor of German and comparative literature at Indiana University, where he has also been chairman of West European Studies, vice-chancellor of the university, and dean of its faculty. He has held Fulbright, Guggenheim, and NEH fellowships and holds an honorary doctorate from the University of Lille. He has been president of the International Comparative Literature Association and its co-ordinator for the comparative history of literature in European languages. His essay on romanticism is a major contribution to the standard *Comparative Literature: Method and Perspective,* and, most recently, he is the author of *Die Novelle in der Klassik und Romantik.*

G. Ross Roy, professor of English and comparative literature at the University of South Carolina in Columbia, is chairman of its comparative literature advisory committee. He holds graduate degrees in English from the University of Montreal, where he has also taught, and in comparative literature from the universities of Strasbourg and of Paris. He is a fellow of the Society of Antiquaries of Scotland, a governor of the American-Scottish Foundation, general editor of Scottish Poetry Reprints, and editor of the journal *Studies in Scottish Literature.* Among his publications is the Scottish literature section of the *New Cambridge Bibliography of English Literature.* His two-volume edition of *The Letters of Robert Burns* is now in press at Oxford.

Clyde de L. Ryals was educated at Emory University and the University of Pennsylvania. After teaching at the University of Maryland, he became professor and graduate chairman of English at the University of Pennsylvania before taking over as professor and chairman of English at Duke University. He has held a Guggenheim fellowship, and is the author of numerous articles and books on Victorian literature, among them *Theme and Symbol in Tennyson's Poetry to 1850,* and *Browning's Later Poetry.*

Peter C. Sederberg holds graduate degrees in political science from Johns Hopkins and has taught at Wellesley College before coming to the University of South Carolina in Columbia, where he is now professor of government and international studies and a former director of the honors program. His broad interests include the arts, utopian thought, comparative political systems, and political violence. Among his publications is *Vigilante Politics,* and he expects soon to publish *The Politics of Meaning.*

Barbara Herrnstein Smith is university professor of English and communications at the University of Pennsylvania, and director of the Center for the Study of Art and Symbolic Behavior. She is on the Supervising Committee of the English Institute, is a member of the Semiotics Society of America, and has held fellowships from the Guggenheim Foundation and the Princeton University

Council for the Humanities. The editorial boards of *PMLA, Critical Inquiry,* and *Poetics Today* count her as a member. Among her many publications are *Poetic Closure: A Study of How Poems End,* and *On the Margins of Discourse: The Relation of Literature to Language.*

# Introduction

I FIRST MET MORSE PECKHAM in February 1960, at what I was hoping would be a turning point in my life. And because of him, it became one. Having gone through the motions of an expensive and prestigious undergraduate French major, I was then coming from the army, terrified at my own capacity for purposelessness, fond at last of study, but still ambivalent about schooling. In college, after swallowing the bitter realization that I would never be an athlete or a social lion, I found myself befriended by most of the artistic and intellectual people in my class. But I gave the faculty a wide berth. It meant more to me that Descartes could be the subject of mirthful midnight chatter among my friends over beer than that he should be the subject of someone's unsmiling display of erudition in the lecture room the next morning. This did not, however, mean that I gave myself more than a passing whiff of Descartes. Mostly, in college, I learned the titles—not the substances—of the great monuments of my culture; and it was only in the army, out of a simple instinct for survival (although the war was then cold), that I first gave reading an important place among my vices. I was therefore both flattered and frightened when my undergraduate roommate (now Professor E. Anthony James of Lehigh University) wrote to me and suggested that I might try following his example and doing graduate work in English at the University of Pennsylvania. I knew that I was getting an education at last, but was afraid that going back to the noisome business of receiving credit for getting an education might spoil everything, once and for all.

Both hopeful and fearful, then, I went to Philadelphia to register for a full load of undergraduate English in the night school, straight from the separation center at Fort Dix. My old friend James, who accompanied me to the financial office of the University of Pennsylvania to pay my fees, was amused actually to see me salute the Pinkerton guard at the window as I presented my check. It was do or die. The graduate chairman of English had said he would admit me only if I did well in all of the courses for which I was signing up.

Two evenings later, I presented myself at College Hall for the first meeting of a course in nineteenth-century English poetry, under somebody named Morse Peckham. James had said I absolutely should not miss him. "The most controversial younger member of the department," he called this Peckham. I liked the sound of that even if (as I then thought) nineteenth-century English poetry was—what? Not Baudelaire and Rimbaud, certainly, but Wordsworth's insufferable daisies and "The Charge of the Light Brigade." Then, in strode Peckham, himself, smoking with a Dunhill holder, sporting a grizzled beard (uncommon then even among academics), lugging a tattered briefcase, bundled up in a tweed cap and Raglan-sleeved overcoat—every inch the professor, except that he seemed too vigorous for the role.

Flinging aside his winter garments, he took from the poor briefcase a thermos of coffee and the text, which he tossed down on the desk. He collected our class admission cards, fitted a new Pall Mall to the holder, clinked open his Zippo, lit up, sighed out a cloud of smoke, let his gaze settle on the window, began pacing to and fro before the rostrum, and started talking about what poetry is. I wondered what it is myself, though I was fairly sure I knew what to say if asked to discuss the matter on an examination. Poetry is supposed to be language in response to which we sense greater order, greater unity, greater form, greater meaning, and even greater truth than we can sense in response to ordinary, nonpoetic discourse. Nevertheless, on the basis of my own admittedly vulgar experience with poems, I knew that if poetry instantly transports "us" to realms of gold, I was one of "them"—the insensitive, the culturally damned. When I had read poetry, I usually underwent not meaning but an immediate inability to paraphrase to my satisfaction; not truth but a frequent sense that the poet as I understood him was wrong about everything; and not unity and order but confusion and frustration.

Almost at once it began dawning on me that Morse Peckham might be the teacher I had been waiting for—the teacher I only suspected could be possible. There he was, in an Ivy League lecture room (even if it was only night school), evidently considering his words as hard as the occasion permitted, and speaking not of poetic truth, organic unity, and significant form, but of the "discontinuity", characteristic of the experience of poems. I was hearing that there was no such thing as iambic pentameter if one pays strict attention to the sound of most verse intoned according to the actual stress, pitch, and juncture of English. The listener may rather vaguely expect an absolute alternation of unstressed with stressed syllables in English verse, but what he really gets is discontinuity, the more or less apparent violation of that expectancy. To me, everything Peckham was saying was new in the sense that I had never before heard words for it in public circulation, in or out of the classroom; but at the same time I felt that I had always known what he was talking about, even if I had never been socially encouraged to recognize what I knew as "knowledge."

The class began feeling different to me. Usually, I felt myself in the lecture hall as a body squirming on a chair, chewing its cuticles, struggling to ignore its discomfort and to give greater attention to the professorial voice in the background, which was saying the things my body would have to be able to mimic to pass itself off as well-meaning, if not educated. But as Peckham led our discussions of nineteenth-century poems, I felt myself relax. My body receded into the background, and for a time my life was the poetic print spread on the desk before me and focused on my retinas and brain, and was the voices in my ears speaking sense or nonsense about that print. I was interested at last. I could listen without having to try to listen. When the end of the class came, I could not believe that two hours had passed, and I felt as one feels after a good athletic workout. In *Explanation and Power,* Peckham himself has framed terms for the sort of shift in consciousness I felt in his class. For me, being a student has generally been a "performance," but under him, it became an "action."

Before the first evening had ended, Peckham taught us what he does when he becomes aware of reading without comprehension. It was a revelation. The classroom demeanor of most of my teachers seldom hinted that any of them could ever have nodded over the pages of the great. To be sure, they sometimes confessed needing to "reread" something for the moment obscure, but the effect of such admissions was to leave me with the eerie feeling that these people all came with an *a priori* command of all literature, and had never actually read anything for the first time. Certainly, none of them had ever taught me a procedure for coping with moments of stupidity and incomprehension, but Morse Peckham had no shame: he did. The problem we faced, he told us, was to raise ourselves to the level at which the poet was communicating, and one could begin on it as follows: one could reorganize the poet's sentence in normal word order, supplying the necessary ellipses; one could look up unfamiliar words and old usages of current words in the *Oxford English Dictionary;* one could analyze all metaphors (according to I. A. Richards's categories) by specifying the connections between their vehicles and tenors; one could make do for the moment with available reference materials in trying to fathom allusions; and one could go on to the next sentence only when one felt as safe as possible with one's paraphrase of the sentence in hand. And no matter how much simpler it might be to treat easy passages as central to the poet's meaning, while neglecting harder ones, one was always to follow Lewis Carroll's advice: begin at the beginning; go right on through to the end; then stop.

Following this procedure, with Peckham sometimes dashing down the hall to the English office for a volume of the *OED,* he and the students who cared to participate in these evenings of explication came, line by line, to substantial agreement about how some well known romantic, Victorian, and modern poems might most sensibly be paraphrased. Always, when we agreed that we had come to the end and that it was time to stop, Peckham would go back to the beginning

and read the whole poem through aloud; and always, it seemed possible, at last, to be moved—moved as people always say that poetry moves them, but as one knows it almost never does when one has simply passed an eye over the print, intoning the words, but not understanding them. And the paraphrases we settled on were revelations. The great romantics were not sentimental escapists into idealized nature, psychotic mysticism, and a never-existent past; nor were the great Victorians essentially Rotarians who wrote. Blake's "London," a couple of Wordsworth sonnets, "Kubla Khan," Shelley's "Lines When the Lamp is Shattered," the "Ode on a Grecian Urn," Arnold's "To Marguerite," "My Last Duchess," number fifty-four of *In Memoriam,* and eventually even Wallace Stevens's "Sunday Morning"—all of these evoked from us, "interpretive hypotheses" (as Peckham called them) which suggested that the romantic tradition was compounded of minds self-consciously getting to grips with what is, no matter what was officially supposed to be.

Before studying with Peckham, I had become familiar with a "sympathetic" approach to the arts of the nineteenth century in which the professor presented himself, in essence, as a sort of enlightened guide to Bedlam. Here, he implied, were all these posturing, self-dramatizing, seemingly intelligent, technically brilliant, but still fundamentally unreliable people. To speak of the content of their art, the professor did no more than read out, generally without further explication, their own grandiloquently empyreal terms of self-justification: *nature, imagination, unity, duality,* and the like. As a bourgeois adolescent, I could see nothing in these meanings to get very excited about. My undergraduate courses in the arts of the nineteenth century taught me that having a professional response to individual works was largely to have learned a fairly long list of lamely explained, perhaps unrelatable, and (ultimately) trivial themes, attributes, and movement, and to be able merely to spot particular occurrences of them. I learned to underline words like *nature* or *feeling,* but I came away with no idea why it was the part of genius in the early nineteenth century to have invested so heavily in such words. Nor did I come away believing that underlining *nature* every time I found it in a poem had much educational value for students not planning to become sympathetic professors of romanticism. In short, as an undergraduate, I never came across a professor who could justify all the bizarre interests he could point to in the nineteenth century and call by some name. Thus, no matter how sympathetic his intent, my professor's example taught me that in the end there is really no excuse for romanticism.

When I entered graduate school, therefore, it appeared to me that even though, in Bohemia, one might still try to live by romanticism, in academe, one could only hope to live off it. Peckham changed all of that. The bizarreness of romanticism, for him was not merely to be brought to archaeological light and catalogued; it was, somehow, to be taken seriously. In his class, Swinburne was not merely a self pitying rhetorical exhibitionist; he was an intelligent and

sensitive man who was suffering. His extravagance, and that of the romantic tradition as a whole, was generally plausible, and where most plausible, to be lived by, both professionally and personally. More than one person, having suffered the denial of tenure (or worse), has been able to count on the moral and financial support of Morse Peckham.

On the nights before his final examinations in the graduate survey of Victorian poetry and prose at Pennsylvania, however, even students eager to spend their lives working out the implications of his lectures were inclined to curse one of Peckham's ways of living his professional life by romanticism as he understood it. At the start of the course, when most professors would have given out a page or two of required reading and writing assignments, Peckham distributed a hefty, quarter-inch sheaf of stapled mimeograph—a sort of annals of the contents of he thickest, best annotated anthologies of Victorian poetry and prose, which we were to go out and buy. We were, it appeared, to master it all, line by line, in chronological order of publication. At the end, we were to present a term paper about it, on a topic of our own choosing. And there would be a final examination. In this exercise, we would be required to call from memory the birth and death dates of authors, and the publication dates of works chosen at random from that entire syllabus. So there were always these coffee soaked vigils, in which we gathered in various kitchens to take turns quizzing each other, hour after hour, until somehow, "as ghastly through the drizzling rain on the bald street broke the blank day," we realized that each of us could probably remember enough of the chronology of canonized Victorian writing to get by. But many were the epithets linked to the name of Peckham in these dark hours. No one else made us learn dates.

Still, through our mutterings against this bit of pedagogical perversity, we all had to admit that it was the perfectly logical outcome of everything he had taught us throughout the semester apropos of Victorian literature. Historicism was all. As he had said, there is virtually no "hard" knowledge at all in the field of English, except for he knowledge of who wrote what when. The great writers of the nineteenth century seemed perverse because (as he then put it) they wished to escape not from but into reality—to rend asunder for moments the hulls and garnitures in which custom invested reality, and look through. Learning dates was a step on the romantic escape into the real in which Peckham was trying to lead us. "It is the Obvious that eludes us," he had said, promulgating Peckham's first law. If we wanted to take romanticism as seriously as he did, there was nothing for it but to sit and learn the wretched dates.

All semester long, Peckham's lectures had been as perverse as his examination. They, too, gave evidence of romanticism taken seriously. Except for the beginning of his teaching career, Peckham has always spoken extemporaneously. I recall hearing him tell that when he was just beginning at Rutgers, fresh from his Princeton doctorate, he resolved to lecture from detailed outlines, faithfully

rewritten year by year as his relationships to the pages he was to discuss kept changing. But he found that the stresses of this discipline were not compensated by its rewards. Virtually writing his lectures out gained him slickness in class at the cost of time for reading— for laying in what I have since heard him call his scholar's "capital," an exposure to more and more of the primary materials (the "deposits of behavior," he calls them) surviving from the past, and to such secondary works of history, philosophy, and behavioral science as might suggest vocabularies for explaining these leavings of thinkers, artists, and canonizers.

Throughout the years I have known him, therefore, Peckham has lectured extemporaneously; and because he has done so, the rate of change in his spoken and (eventually) written output has been strikingly swift. The vocabulary of his work in the fifties and early sixties still presents challenges to most people trained in English studies; but, generally, these are challenges small enough that people in English are stimulated to stay with him, to tolerate his jargon, and to grant that it has some bearing on some of the discipline's concerns. Since the mid sixties, however, when he began seriously to develop a pragmatic, semiotic vocabulary, I have gained the impression that his work has become almost totally inaccessible to most literary people, while it has been more suggestive to people in the visual arts, and has been excitingly open to such social scientists as know of it. Because he has allowed himself to lecture extemporaneously, so much less of the Obvious now eludes him than eludes most of his colleagues that they constantly speak of his work as "abstract," when, in fact, it has become progressively more concrete—more capable of precisely naming what happens, or seems to have happened, than it was twenty years ago.

For three hours of lecturing about Zola's Rougon-Macquart during the semester he recently taught the history of Western high culture in the 1880s, Peckham spent nearly a month reading over all the novels and the most recent biographical scholarship on Zola. During his interval of preparation, friends dropping in on him would see books by and about Zola and his times open on the reading stands at Peckham's breakfast and dinner tables, and piled on the floor by chairs in his living room and study. Peckham would be eager to pass along facts new and interesting to him about Zola, and to try out his developing idea of the significance of the Rougon-Macquart. He would not suffer gladly the intrusion of university gossip into the conversation on such occasions. On his desk, however, one would see neither notebooks nor file cards amid the litter of correspondence and student work to be checked. And sometimes, during this month, Peckham might suddenly appear at one's back door, if the traffic at his house was not providing trial audiences enough, to have a cup of coffee and tell about Zola. Then, at the lecture itself, parties to these visits heard the points roughed out in them elaborated and integrated into the view of the 1880s as a whole which had been developing as Peckham had been considering other important figures. But the lectern remained as bare of notes as had his desk at home. On it would be only the books to which he might, or might not, wish to refer.

On the listener debauched by the exclusive reading of literature and criticism and manifesting the classical etiology of academic humanism (its pathological infatuation with wit and hatred of jargon)—on such a listener, the typical, exquisitely illuminating Peckham lecture may largely be wasted. In the terms of Ciceronian rhetoric, Peckham came to the lecture room chiefly to finish his month-long invention of what the Rougon-Macquart then could mean to him. He did not come then, nor does he ever, chiefly to stage a classical, oratorical show of arrangement, style, memory, and delivery. These matters, to be sure, are always in the back of his mind; but because he takes romanticism seriously, his joy is in the process of engaging Zola (or whatever), and not in giving these thoughts an expected public dress. He correctly judges that it is more instructive for good students actually to watch him finish this year's reading of Zola, however perplexed and hesitant he may look, than it is for the rest to be persuaded that so powerful a rhetorical presence must have been right about Zola, whenever and however he actually did read it. Peckham's is not a Ciceronian, but a romantic, Wordsworthian rhetoric. In class, it is as if he were recollecting in tranquility and contemplating his books until an emotion kindred to the epiphanies of his month of study actually exists in his mind and the successful composition of his lecture can be carried on.

Peckham lectures begin with the listing of basic, unassimilated facts: titles, editions, first performances, exhibitions, and the inevitable dates. These may be scrawled on the blackboard. There may then be a repudiation of the position Peckham took when he last had occasion to speak or write on the day's topic. "I used to think..., but now I think..." is a figure so frequent in Peckham's conversation that his friends sometimes needle him about its occurrences. These preliminaries, however, will soon give way, as I have said, to Peckham's real concern—finishing the invention of his current reading of the works in hand. His voice is resonant and audible throughout the room. He is tall, handsome, dressed and groomed for a public occasion. Nevertheless, his manner is basically inward. He is not the sincere zealot which classical rhetoric teaches speakers to portray. He is a man essentially talking to himself before a room full of eavesdroppers. Always, Peckham paces. His brow is knit, his eye contact generally desultory and unfocused. He buttons and unbuttons his jacket; takes time out for the management of cigarettes, holder, and lighter; and fidgets with coins in a pocket. The listener must accommodate himself to Peckham's startling use of "therefore" and "however," not as conjunctions, but as pause words. Though noticeable, these mannerisms do not distract his classes. Students who are moved by it pick up his intellectual style, with its quasi-philosophical, quasi-sociological vocabulary, and they may provoke smiles in debauched humanists who see them as "little Peckhams." But this sort of imitation is what good teaching is supposed to produce. It is not mimicry, but learning. Recently, I have known a number of Peckham's students who could explain why interpretation is "the perceptual disengagement of an analogically determined recurrent semiotic

pattern from an analogically determined series of semiotic matrices." But never yet have I run across anyone who could actually mimic a Peckham lecture—voice, mannerisms, and all. There is simply too much of substance being said for one to pay attention to the body saying it.

There have always been moments of panic in the middle of Peckham lectures, when he is analyzing old terms and introducing the new ones he thinks can say more about Zola (or whatever)—moments of panic when he seems to have forgotten the day's text altogether. But in the end, these anxious moments always turn out to have been unwarranted. Peckham is a Mahler, not a Mozart. His developments are long, and there are few comforting repeats. He makes demands. Our concentration may flag, but he never digresses. By the end, arid stretches of trivia and plot summary have always been given life. Amid relief and excitement, one strains to write it all down; and one goes home with high expectations for next week's good sense.

In May 1980, as time began running out on Peckham's last lecture as a faculty member in the University of South Carolina, the honors undergraduates and graduate students enrolled in his course, and the hard core of faculty members from different disciplines who had been in his audiences whenever they could get there, wondered how Peckham would take his leave of them. It was a time made for revolting clichés—for sadomasochistic gratitude to alma mater, to the community of scholars which had stimulated and guided him, and for unctuous thanks for the love of his students, from whom he had learned so much, and into whose hands he now was passing his torch. But instead of clichés, Peckham gave us a final look at the Obvious. Since most of us were planning, or were already committed to, academic lives, he asked us (having just done so himself) how we proposed to maintain our intellectual vitality throughout our academic careers.

It was a question appropriate to Peckham's situation and to the plights of the different categories of people listening to him. To stay alive, intellectually, he implied, we would somehow have to keep the modern university from working its will with us. As for him, in a moment, he would be out of it, grateful for the luck that had been his. In deciding not to be a conscientious objector at the start of World War II, he had searched his interests and decided that the art which Hitler found decadent was all that really mattered to him. Scholarship had kept him out of the front lines (he had been the official historian of a large bomber command), and universities, once he had tenure, had made it possible for him, as a single man, to follow his main interest as he saw fit. But the rest of us, he thought, were not apt to be so lucky—especially if we were married and totally dependent on an academic salary for the support of our families. We would be less able than he had been to free ourselves from the side effects of the very system by which the modern university proposed to "encourage" us to remain intellectually active. The publish-or-perish system, he said, far from succeeding in this noble objective, was "responsible for an intellectual and moral corruption unparalleled

even in American universities." As long as there were no effective alternatives to publication as means of economic advancement for faculties, economic pressures would ensure that the young professoriate would apply methods of increasing rigidity to the solution of scholarly problems of ever increasing triviality. Meanwhile, more and more of the hopelessly over-expanded undergraduate body would be taught by graduate students who (by 1980) were themselves often being taught by graduate professors whose undergraduate educations had begun at the hands of graduate students. Facing the eventual need to beat the publish-or-perish game for employment and tenure, the modern graduate student is a fool if he does not approach his courses quite cynically as the only chances he has to learn how the game is beaten. He is a fool to lavish much attention on his obligation to teach freshmen when he must learn from his professors how to mine as little primary and secondary reading as possible for as many bits of writing as he can get published.

So what about us who had done Peckham the honor of listening to him this last semester and over the years, and who would be lingering in higher education beyond him? For the faculty, Peckham saw little to be done but to press for real alternatives to publication as the means for granting tenure, promotion, and salary raises. He wished us well. For ten years, without success, he had been urging such alternatives upon every administration at the University of South Carolina. For graduate students and undergraduates aspiring to academic careers, however, there might be more hope. With luck, they might find first jobs in institutions not aspiring to "national visibility." There, in community colleges, and in such small liberal arts colleges as might survive, they would feel little or no pressure to trivialize their thinking and publish. With honor, they could study to meet the demands of a heavy and varied undergraduate teaching load such as Peckham himself had begun with, before the war, at The Citadel. They could stay interested, always, in what struck them, in their constant self-revision, as obvious and important. And in them would eventually lie the abilities to be called upon when the pedagogical failure and the scholarly demoralization of the new model American university can no longer be hidden behind a paper screen of professionalism.

Thus, in essence, did Morse Peckham take his leave of the classroom. And we rose to our feet and cheered him, and drank long life and health to him.

# Contents

IRVIN L. CHILD

# Psychology and the Writings of Morse Peckham

THE WRITINGS OF MORSE PECKHAM start from the study of literature, reach out toward the rest of our knowledge of humanity for what is most useful in understanding literature, but before returning toward that starting point they play with the varied ideas encountered along the way. I am going to comment on the relation of his writings to psychology, a branch of scholarship he explicitly draws on and contributes to. A more adequate response might come from a psychologist with a knowledge of literature comparable to Peckham's knowledge of psychology. I lack that qualification, and can comment only as a psychologist who has read most of what Peckham has published and has some amateur acquaintance with English literature and with scattered samples of the humanistic scholarship that forms the original context for Peckham's work.

Let us picture a a typical psychologist reading Peckham's books or essays. An unrealistic fantasy, to be sure; the typical psychologist would not be reading works of literary scholarship, any more than the typical professor of literature would be reading the *Journal of Experimental Psychology*. Though unrealistic, the fantasy may be instructive. The typical psychologist, if he has read widely in literary scholarship will have encountered much that seems strange, much that he will be inclined to call "nonsense," "confusion," or "rubbish." T. S. Eliot's essay, "The Three Voices of Poetry," offers an example.[1] If he asks himself what kind of discourse Eliot seems to be engaging in, he is perhaps most likely to be reminded of religious discourse. Eliot discusses poetry in abstractions that seem

[1] T. S. Eliot, "The Three Voices of Poetry," *On Poetry and Poets* (1953; reprint, New York: Noonday Press, 1961), pp. 96-112.

much like the abstractions in a sermon, apparently pointed not toward formulating and testing verifiable propositions but toward influencing the feelings and choices of the reader, and toward inducing a sense of mutuality and goodness that can be shared with others who have the same feelings and make the same choices. Such discourse may be needed, may perhaps be especially needed just now. But is it the kind of discourse to be expected at the core of scholarly writings? The psychologist is likely to feel somewhat lost intellectually, unless he manages to shift out of his role as psychologist.

Then if he turns to Peckham, he may encounter the statement that "whether we like it or not, in our culture today, the scientific enterprise is the recognized model for meaningful and valid interpretations."[2] And over and over he will find that principle exemplified in the main argument of Peckham's writings. He will feel at home. Applying a scientific model to questions of literary criticism and interpretation means (among other things) asking oneself always, "What is actually referred to? This poem means or meant what, to whom, at what time? What is the evidence that justifies the answer?" Appeal is constantly being made to concrete human behavior as the ultimate criterion of evidence. But this is just what psychology does, too. For a moment the psychologist may feel that Peckham holds literary scholarship to be properly a branch of psychology. On reflection, I think, he is more likely to see the relationship merely as one of mutual intelligibility and mutual stimulation.

Abandoning my fantasy of a typical psychologist and how he would react, I shall comment on Peckham's work from my own point ot view as one psychologist. I have two special qualifications: a specific interest over the last twenty years in many of his writings because of their relevance to my own activity in psychological aesthetics, and an even longer knowledge of Peckham as friend and informal teacher in the arts. This goes back more than fifty years. It must have been in the fall of 1928 that he invited me to go with him to a private showing, at the house of friends near the Southwest Museum in Los Angeles, of a French film based on Flaubert's novel *Salammbo*. His commentary on *Salammbo*, novel and film, was but the first of many lessons in the arts I had with him. Already in his early teens he was eagerly reaching out for broad experience and understanding of all the arts, and of the part they play in life, trying to formulate and thus to share his experience. I was an early beneficiary of the interests and skills which must later have made him a superb guide to graduate students. As this second qualification suggests, I have often read Peckham's writings not as a psychologist but as a student of the arts, depending on him as critic to open insights and point directions I had not time or acumen to have developed myself.

[2] Morse Peckham, "Literary Interpretation as Conventionalized Verbal Behavior," in *The Triumph of Romanticism: Collected Essays* (Columbia, S. C.: University of South Carolina Press, 1970), p. 370.

Now I have been re-reading Peckham's writings in my capacity as psychologist (with moments out when other interests became more dominant). I am greatly impressed by the degree of mastery he exhibits over many of the important ideas in psychology. I am even more impressed by the creative use he makes of the ideas he finds most useful from psychology and of the way he brings these together with his scholarly knowledge of the arts and the rest of his experience to offer valuable new syntheses. To give an adequate account of these would be to prepare a summary that would itself be a book. I shall attempt isolated comments on some aspects of his psychological ideas that I have rather arbitrarily selected for their relation to psychology generally. Some of his psychological ideas are major aspects of Peckham's thought, some may be mere asides. Some I have picked out for their value to psychologists, some because parallels in other psychological writings may serve to strengthen the position Peckham is arguing for; some I have chosen because I think a psychologist's view might for future readers of all sorts usefully clarify or extend the meaning of Peckham.

## Art Defined by Customary Behavior

In *Man's Rage for Chaos,* Peckham asks at the outset, "What is art?" and shows the inadequacies of several definitions that have been put forth. He then offers a social definition as a starting point: a work of art is any artifact in the presence of which we play a particular social role, the culturally patterned role of viewing something as art. This definition is realistic in allowing for the variation that can readily be observed in the range of objects or events included in the category by different people. It also shifts attention away from the artifacts themselves and toward human behavior. A useful definition of art must do this, Peckham argues, because the various artifacts labeled "art" do not in fact have any common characteristics except that on occasion this common label may be applied to them.[3]

Peckham here introduces into the study of art an approach directly parallel to one that has been found useful in other human studies. Sociologists, in recognizing that a criminal is usually defined as a person who has been caught and convicted of a crime, have cleared away earlier naive notions that a criminal could be usefully defined as any person having certain purely personal characteristics or stigmata. Psychiatric research, where it has recognized that what schizophrenics most surely have in common is the fact of having been labeled so, also clears the way for more penetrating study of various phenomena associated with the labeling. There seems every reason to suppose that where

---

[3] Morse Peckham, *Man's Rage for Chaos: Biology, Behavior, and the Arts* (Philadelphia and New York: Chilton Books, 1965).

scholars in the arts recognize the conventional nature of the concept of art, they too will be able to analyze the related phenomena with greater clarity.

Peckham's clear thinking here could have a salutary influence on psychologists as well as on humanistic scholars. We are all of us trapped by the tendency to take words as corresponding to simple realities. Researchers interested in the psychology of art may unthinkingly suppose that the substantive word *art* must correspond to a stable group of physical objects and events. Those interested in the psychology of religion may likewise suppose that religion can be defined with similar objectivity. Psychologists studying power, love, or intelligence may make the same mistake. Explicit recognition of the shifting meaning of words is a useful starting point, and a useful review point, in any research enterprise.

There are several issues involved here that are sometimes separable one from the other.

1. A category may be conjunctive or may be disjunctive. That is, the members of a category may all share some single attribute that warrants their placement in that category, or they may share only the fact of having any one of several defining attributes. Scholars generalizing about art, Peckham suggests, have often argued about whether this or that is the single defining attribute; and the arguments are futile and confusing because there is no single defining attribute.

2. The attribute or attributes that justify placing an object in a particular category may be intrinsic to the object, or may refer to a relationship with something outside. Attempts to define art have often mistakenly tried to focus on the intrinsic properties of the works themselves, whereas (as Peckham argues and as most psychologists would surely agree) the attributes that usefully define art more likely reside in the relation between a work of art and its maker or its viewer.

3. The relationships that are the defining attributes for a category may be cultural conventions or they may originate elsewhere. Scholars who have discussed the nature of art have often thought of it as a stable category of universal significance, whereas they in fact define it in accordance with the customs of art critics of their time and place. Their intention generally is to have a universally valid, noncultural definition, but their practice, being culture bound, is a barrier which may go unnoticed and be effectively insuperable. Anthropologists have in recent years been much aware of a similar distinction between etic and emic definition of particular elements of culture. The terms are borrowed from the final syllables of *phonetic* and *phonemic,* a similar distinction which had proved invaluable in linguistic analysis. (Phonetics classifies speech sounds by universally applicable physical characteristics; phonemics, by grouping together those sounds that are considered equivalent by speakers of a particular language.) The anthropologist aiming at accurate portrayal of a particular culture seeks to be sure his definitions are emic; that is, that they express the categorizations actually made within that culture. The anthropologist aiming at

cross-cultural comparisons may want a definition that can be applied equally to any culture; he might want to define adolescence as the period between puberty and full physical growth, for instance, to see how people who fall into that objective category are treated in various societies (even if some societies recognize no such category at all, and others vary in just how they define it). An anthropologist aiming to describe and interpret a particular culture as precisely as possible would want to develop clearly the emic definition of whatever categories, if any, pertinent to that period of life are recognized in that culture. There is present here, in parallel to the case Peckham is criticizing, the danger that the scholar will use as an etic an emic one of his own culture, rather than a category that emerges as useful from careful study of the pertinent emic categories found in a number of cultures. The varied cultural knowledge of an anthropologist makes this error less likely than it would otherwise be. In the study of art, a scholar might gain in a similar way through comparative knowledge of art or art criticism in diverse cultures and historical periods.

## Art Defined by Nonfunctional Stylistic Dynamism

If we start with the definition of art as what people interact with in the role of art perceiver, and consider the totality of artifacts that most consistently meet the definition, Peckham holds that an important relationship can be found among them. It is a relationship to be seen when the works of art of a single type or function, within a single culture, are arranged in a time series. Stylistic change, not explicable simply as progressive functional improvement, is found to characterize such series. Knowledge of historical sequences in the arts then justifies a second definition of art. As stated most recently by Peckham "a work of art can be identified if a chronologically arranged series of objects of the same function (such as a series of Madonnas or of ash-trays) shows an instability which is not governed by the function of the object in question."[4] This relational definition of art, Peckham argues, is not a cultural convention. It is not a special characteristic of the arts in our period of generally rapid social change, but appears to be a universal characteristic of known human cultures.[5]

The view that the arts are characterized by nonfunctional stylistic dynamism might seem to be an issue of interest to historians but not to psychologists. Peckham offers a psychological interpretation, however, which I will turn to in the next section. The point I want to make here is that the research methods of psychology can be, and in part have been, applied to this issue. Whether, and to what extent, nonfunctional stylistic dynamism is found to characterize art (given,

---

[4] Morse Peckham, "Perceptual and Semiotic Discontinuity in Art," *Poetics* 7 (April 1978): 218.

[5] Peckham, *Man's Rage for Chaos,* p 72.

of course, another definition of art as a starting point) may be a matter of controversy. Other scholars in the humanities may draw upon their accumulated knowledge to support or to disagree with this position, which Peckham initially justifies on the basis of his broad knowledge. Systematic historical studies might also be made to test specific predictions to which the notion of nonfunctional stylistic dynamism would lead. When such historical studies are made, a useful precedent to consider lies in Colin Martindale's application of psychological research techniques to this problem.[6]

Martindale, a psychologist, did not base his work on Peckham's; it grew out of different lines of thought, and his theoretical reasoning pertains to the maker rather than to the perceiver of art. He is not concerned with general stylistic dynamism, but with a specific aspect he terms "regression." His work seems to me, however, clearly pertinent to Peckham's more general account of temporal change in the arts. Martindale's study of how regression has shifted with time in French and English poetry, when compared with Peckham's views, provides a striking instance of convergence between humanistic studies and psychological research in the scientific pattern. Using computerized methods selected on grounds of objectivity and quantitative precision, he arrives at a portrayal of nonfunctional dynamism. If applied to the specific issues addressed by Peckham's theory, such methods could be an aid in resolving them.

## A Psychological Theory of Art

Peckham's theory of art stresses the presence of various discontinuities. Stylistic change through time involves a series of discontinuities; repeatedly, the perceiver of some type of art, accustomed to the style that has been current and expecting to see it repeated, encounters instead a change that violates this expectation. This discontinuity in time is paralleled by vertical discontinuities in society, between art forms simultaneously current at different levels of artistic sophistication. These two types of external discontinuity, involving the disruption of expectations the perceiver brings from outside, are paralleled by discontinuities within his experience of a specific work of art. Peckham classifies these into three general categories— implicit, internal, and modal—according to the source of the expectation and the nature of its violation. He then develops a theory about the psychological function of art that seeks to explain the prevalence of discontinuities in the experience of art. This theory proposes that the function of art is to prepare a person and society for change and other discontinuities. Cultural rules and individual routine tend toward excessive regularity, stability, and stagnation, potentially to the point of threatening the

---

[6] Colin Martindale, *The Romantic Progression: The Psychology of Literary History* (Washington: Hemisphere, 1975).

survival of both the individual and society. Art provides repeated practice in confronting varied discontinuities, and thus prepares everyone for the lability of action that may be necessary for survival in the face of the many and at times great discontinuities that arise in everyday life.

In psychology, theories of art have in recent times tended to be less ambitious and comprehensive, as part of the reaction of psychologists against the over-theorizing formerly so characteristic of their discipline. So it is not easy to compare this theory of Peckham's directly with similarly ambitious theories of art developed by psychologists. There have, however, been a number of developments in psychological esthetics which are consistent with this theory or harmonious with some part of it.

1. More than any other recent psychologist, Berlyne aims at comprehensive theory in psychological esthetics.[7] His theory is in several respects quite unlike Peckham's. He is not primarily concerned with art, but rather with some larger class of esthetically relevant stimuli that would include the arts. Nor is he primarily concerned with questions of function; he aims rather at explaining the hedonic value of stimuli. Despite these great differences, there is a striking convergence of underlying thought. The variables Berlyne thinks important for esthetics are collative variables, which by definition involve comparison between one occurrence and one or more other occurrences. Familiar versus novel, simple versus complex, expected versus surprising, ambiguous versus clear, and stable versus changeable are examples of collative variables. The implied comparison is sometimes between parts of a whole (as in simple versus complex), sometimes between parts of an objective temporal series (as in stable versus changeable), sometimes between parts of a temporal series of personal experiences (as in similar versus novel). But all of these collative variables refer to the degree to which, in Peckham's terms, various discontinuities are present. Here is a basic convergence of thought about what dimensions are most pertinent to a psychological understanding of the arts.

2. Peckham's theory of art might lead to some predictions about differences between people with a strong esthetic orientation and those with a weak one. The distinction between them might well be measured by the degree to which a person shares the esthetic preferences or judgments of people whose lives are most centered around the sophisticated art traditions of their society. Peckham does not make such predictions, perhaps because he generally tries to avoid in his theory of art, though fortunately not in his interpretive comments about art, questions of evaluation. But in his treatment of vertical discontinuities he assumes that extremer discontinuities are generally (depending on the historical epoch) characteristic of higher levels of sophistication in Western culture; this seems to be in essential agreement with a prediction that esthetic sensitivity, as

[7] D. E. Berlyne, *Aesthetics and Psychobiology* (New York: Appleton-Century-Crofts, 1971).

defined above, would be related to—or perhaps even be a measure of—positive orientation toward discontinuities. The orientation might be expressed not only in art preferences themselves but in other aspects of life. The people who choose sophisticated art may do so because their preexistent interest in discontinuities comes to be expressed in this way. Or they may do so because their greater experience with discontinuities in art makes them more tolerant of discontinuities in the rest of life.

Research I have done with college students and secondary school students in the United States amply confirms the presence of these relationships between esthetic sophistication and toleration of discontinuity. And those who have looked for similar relationships in other cultures have seen them there, too.[8] Students who like the kind of art preferred by people knowledgeable in art tend also to show tolerance of ambiguity and ambivalence, a liking for unrealistic experience, a preference for complexity, a liking for difficult problems, and various other characteristics that all seem to fit the general category of tolerating or liking discontinuities. Insofar as this correlation between esthetic preference and tolerance for discontinuities could be said to arise in the art experience— those with much experience having come to tolerate discontinuities—the correlation would be a confirmation of Peckham's theory of art. This direction of causation is not, however, established by anything about the correlation itself. In collecting the data, I had an opposite direction of causation in mind: I was considering the possibility that people who like discontinuities will prefer the "esthetically better" art because it gratifies their interests. This direction of causation is also not established by the correlation itself. Peckham's theory of art offers an alternative explanation of my findings; only research of a different kind could establish whether both interpretations, or only one, may be valid.

3. The research I have just described pertains to the viewers of art. But Peckham's theory might lead to similar predictions about the distinctive

---

[8] Professor Child has been too modest to cite any of his contributions to this work. The editor, therefore, suggests that the reader may wish to consult the following. Irvin L. Child, "Personality Correlates of Esthetic Judgment in College Students," *Journal of Personality* 33, no. 3 (1965): 476-511; Marc Cooperman and Irvin L. Child, "Relation of Esthetic Sensitivity to Psychoanalytic Character Traits," *Proceedings of the 76th Annual Convention of the American Psychological Association 1968*, 3, 439-440; Marc Cooperman and Irvin L. Child, "Esthetic Preference and Active Style," *Proceedings of the 77th Annual Convention of the American Psychological Association 1969*, 4, part 1, 471-472; Irvin L. Child and Sumiko Iwao, "Personality and Esthetic Sensitivity: Extension of Findings to Younger Age and to Different Culture," *Journal of Personality and Social Psychology*, 8, no. 3, part 1 (1968): 308-312; Sumiko Iwao, Irvin L. Child and Miguel Garcia, "Further Evidence of Agreement between Japanese and American Esthetic Evaluations," *Journal of Social Psychology*, 78, no. 1 (1969): 11-15; and Mah P. Anwar and Irvin L. Child, "Personality and Aesthetic Sensitivity in an Islamic Culture," *Journal of Social Psychology*, 87, no. 1 (June 1972): 21-28.

characteristics of those who produce art, and of generally creative people. They, too, should exhibit to a higher degree than the average person various characteristics that imply a liking or tolerance for discontinuities. Perhaps from Peckham's theory one would predict that early experience with art is one factor that would lead them to such a tolerance, which would then prepare them for a creative life. Perhaps from Otto Rank's theory[9] one would view the artistic interest itself as an end point rather than a beginning. The prediction, in any event, seems amply confirmed. Most pertinent, perhaps, are the studies of architects[10] and writers[11] at the Institute for Personality Assessment and Research, and of art students by Barron[12] and by Getzels and Csikszentmihalyi.[13] A tendency for greater artistic creativity to go with various characteristics that could be summarized as tolerance or liking for discontinuities seems to emerge in each of these studies. Again, the research does not permit a distinctive test of Peckham's hypothesis as against other hypotheses that would stress different sequences of influence. But the results are generally harmonious with his ideas and offer no hint of a contradiction to them.

## A General Theory of Behavior as a Theory of Meaning

In the complex *Explanation and Power*,[14] Peckham presents a general theory of human behavior based on theory of meaning. Though the argument might be difficult in any event, it is not made easier by Peckham's formidable vocabulary used in a somewhat idiosyncratic manner that is hard to keep separated from other more common usages. Like his other books, it includes many thought-provoking comments on a variety of topics, and a discussion of a few of these could easily become as long as the book itself. Any attempt at extracting a single main thesis is bound, therefore, to be oversimplified. Yet I will try to state briefly what I see as the main thesis, in order then to make some comments on it in relation to psychology.

Meaning consists of some kind of response. This is seen most clearly in the case of language. Printed or spoken texts obviously have no meaning except as a person is able to interpret them—to assign meaning to them. The printed or

---

[9] Donald W. MacKinnon, "Personality and the Realization of Creative Potential," *American Psychologist* 20 (April 1965): 273ff.

[10] Ibid., 273-281.

[11] Frank Barron, *Creativity and Personal Freedom* (Princeton, N. J.: Van Nostrand, 1968).

[12] Frank Barron, *Artists in the Making* (New York: Seminar Press, 1972).

[13] Jacob W. Getzels and Mihaly Csikszentmihalyi, *The Creative Vision* (New York: Wiley, 1976).

[14] Morse Peckham, *Explanation and Power: The Control of Human Behavior* (New York: Seabury, 1979).

spoken texts are instructions for an internal performance, just as a musical score
is a set of instructions for a performance with instruments or singing voice. What
is true for language is also true for any other kind of environmental impact on a
person; perception and understanding of it involves interpretation, the creation
of meaning.

People can communicate readily with each other only if they have a common
language and give approximately the same meaning to what is uttered in it.
Interaction is greatly facilitated, moreover, to the extent that nonlinguistic
objects and events are given similar meaning by different people. Efficient
maintenance of a community or society depends not only upon a shared language
but also upon shared interpretations of the physical and social environment.
Community life places great pressure upon individuals to interpret events in the
generally shared way.

A human community might easily stagnate, and be unable to adapt to changed
conditions, were it not for a tendency toward randomness that is characteristic of
human beings. Random variations in the interpretation of events produce
altered meanings, and these are a potential source of change. Institutions or
individuals that can influence the tenacity of standard interpretations, or can
influence the spread of new interpretations, are able thereby to exert power over
human actions, since what people do is controlled by how they interpret events.

To me, this main thesis of *Explanation and Power* is a compelling and useful
synthesis. I do not know how scholars in the humanities will respond to it, but I
think the response of psychologists would generally be similar to mine. Most
elements in the main argument are not novel to psychologists and do not
challenge generally accepted modes of thought in psychology; but the novel way
in which they are joined together is impressive and valuable. Psychologists will
also be interested in the fact that an analysis of human behavior so similar to
their own should have emerged from so different a source. Literary criticism—
the interpretation of texts, especially those produced by writers of long ago—
seems superficially far removed from most psychological experiments and
counseling sessions. Yet trying to understand what is being done in interpreting
a poem is the starting point from which Peckham develops his general theory. It
is reassuring that such diverse aspects of human activity lead to such agreement
in ultimate theory.

I shall comment on the relation to psychological thought of several features of
*Explanation and Power.*

1. Peckham shows here an admirable ability to transcend the explanatory
customs of his own discipline. Looking at this book from the framework of my
own discipline of psychology, I note some ways in which this achievement is not
complete and where Peckham's theory might be usefully modified or extended by
further transcendence of its origins. One instance lies in the emphasis on words.

In his work as a literary critic, the material to which Peckham applies his

interpretative skills consists of printed texts. They are language, and they are language represented as a series of printed words, plus punctuation marks. In this broader theoretical work on human behavior, in speaking as he so often does of the meaning of words, Peckham is holding to this starting point. A linguist, whose work is more centered on spoken language, might be more likely to speak of the meaning of utterances, and less likely to leave his reader able to think of meanings as responses to single words.

One who starts from considering the meaning of music, of the visual arts, or of nonverbal communication in ordinary social interaction, might arrive at a different formulation of a theory of meaning, which could be different from a theory based on either words or utterances. A notable fact is that linguistic meaning is almost entirely conventional. How about facial expressions, foods and other useful objects purchased in the market place, or the signs of which music and the visual arts are composed? In the interpretation of all these types of sign, the sign itself is much more likely to limit the possible meaning in ways not completely dependent on convention. While any community's conventional definition of food may exclude many nourishing substances, it is not likely to include many substances that are completely worthless as nourishment. Perhaps Peckham's great emphasis on the lability of meaning is a product of his starting with words. The emphasis may be overdone; but on the other hand, it may be a distinctively valuable contribution. Some scholars who likewise start with words fail to appreciate the implications of the fact that the meaning of language depends on convention. How much more likely, then, that those who start with other kinds of sign might fail to appreciate the importance of convention, which surely remains almost everywhere one influence on meaning.

A separate issue from that of conventionality is precisely that of verbality. The tradition of logic and of analytic philosophy encourages us to suppose thinking to be perhaps always verbal. Many behavioristic psychologists make this assumption explicit. Peckham does not seem to share it. So I infer, for example, from his account of the meanings with which people respond to music and dance, an account which does not seem to imply that language is necessarily involved. But when presenting a general account of explanation, and of the explanatory regress that may lead up to God as the most general explanation, his theory seems to be shaped rather more about the nonverbal aspects of perception and understanding. A greater emphasis on the nonverbal might produce an account that would differ in important ways. Verbal aspects of perception and understanding, for instance, are easier to think of as hierarchically organized, with clearly defined logical relations, than are nonverbal aspects. And we commonly suppose that what is verbally expressed can be more easily changed; Freudian psychoanalysis is not alone among therapies in making this assumption. Attention to verbal explanation may produce a stress on the possibility of change, and on the person's readily becoming subject to external control. An emphasis on nonverbal

aspects of meaning, on the other hand, might produce a stress on the stability of the individual's habits of interpretation once they have been formed. The nonverbal is not neglected by Peckham; indeed, he devotes a major chapter to it in *Explanation and Power*. Nor is he unaware of the distinctions I have mentioned; they are explicit or implied in his discussions of the relation between the verbal and nonverbal. He argues for a certain priority of the verbal in human behavior as a matter of fact rather than as a choice by the theorist because of the extent to which the verbal comes in human beings to control the nonverbal. He may well be right. But there may be an element of choice here, too. Though the stress on words is less emphatic than it might be in most literary scholars, what remains may still be traceable to the dominance of the literary components in the origins of Peckham's thought.

2. The general theory presented in *Explanation and Power* implies acceptance of the view that Peckham calls "transactionalism" in *Man's Rage for Chaos*. This is the view that what is experienced at any moment emerges from the influence of environmental output and internal processes, that experience is a transaction between person and external reality. The term has been used in psychology of perception, and in the earlier book Peckham uses it in that context. In *Explanation and Power,* however, he extends the view of experience, but the term itself is not used. Here Peckham's choice is paralleled in psychology. *Transactionalism* is no longer a term often used, yet the idea it represents is widely accepted.

There are in psychology two main currents that might be thought of as opponents of the broadly transactional interpretation of experience. One is the perceptual theory of James J. Gibson,[15] which stresses the information contained in the external stimulus complex. Though the organism is given an active and organized role in this theory, the organismic contribution is limited to somehow getting out of the situation the information that is really there. The other and more complete opponent of a transactional view is the naive objectivism of the behaviorist tradition. Here the psychologist, unreflectingly, takes his own experience as a given, places it in the external world, and speaks of its components as "stimuli" which are assumed to be equally present for anyone else similarly situated. This naive objectivism is also the commonsensical assumption of the layman. It seems too obviously inadequate to offer any real challenge to a transactional view. The Gibsonian theory may, of course, to the extent it is justified by advancing knowledge of perception, restrict the organismic contribution to the adaptive uniformities of general perceptual processes. But a transaction seems still implied—a transaction which for simple perception is better understood the better our knowledge of those general processes and

---

[15] James J. Gibson, *The Senses Considered as Perceptual Systems* (Boston: Houghton Mifflin, 1966).

which, for more complex phenomena of interpretation, classification, and inference must implicate also processes of greater variability. In any event, the predominant assumption in recent psychology is interactive or transactional, and thus thoroughly consonant with this aspect of Peckham's theory.

3. "Randomness" plays an important part in the theory Peckham presents in *Explanation and Power,* and this concept is more controversial in psychology than the others I have commented on. The basic status of the concept is itself disputed. The many psychologists who argue that psychology must assume perfect causal determinism are, if they demand logical consistency of themselves, required to reject the concept of randomness. On the other hand, the concept of randomness seems essential for the many and widespread uses of statistical inference by psychologists—often the same psychologists whose deterministic position should require them to reject the concept. The difficulty may be resolved by regarding randomness as merely an illusion resulting from ignorance. At any stage of our developing knowledge the many unknown factors operating in a given situation (together with factors that are known to exist but are not measured or controlled) combine to produce an appearance of random variation. The presence of this pseudorandomness might sufficiently justify the use of statistical reasoning based on assumptions of randomness.

Peckham, however, seems to postulate a more genuine randomness. He speaks of "the brain's capacity to produce random responses." This, he argues, is a fundamental condition of human behavior, the condition that makes semiotic behavior possible. Capacity for randomness of response has increased, he suggests, through evolutionary development; its high level in human beings has been established because of its survival value in human life, and is of course genetically transmitted.[16]

Controversy about the position Peckham gives to randomness is likely to center on two questions: Is the concept of randomness compatible with a scientific, causally-oriented analysis of behavior? Is the concept of randomness, employed in this way, compatible with the observed facts of planfulness, integration, and appropriateness of invention and creativity? The first of these questions emerges from the deterministic, mechanistic side of psychology; the second, from the humanistic, holistic side, with its emphasis on spontaneity in the service of conscious intention. To each of the questions, though they come from opposite positions, a potential answer is available in the sage writings of Donald T. Campbell, a psychologist who, like Peckham, is interested in making the fullest possible use of evolutionary biology in interpreting psychological events.[17]

---

[16] Peckham, *Explanation and Power,* 164-166.

[17] Donald T. Campbell, "Blind Variation and Selective Retention in Creative Thought as in Other Knowledge Processes," *Psychological Review* 67, no. 1 (1960): 380-400.

Campbell's answer to the first question, whether postulation of randomness constitutes necessarily a departure from causal analysis, is that the question arises only because of ambiguity in the term *randomness*. It is often used to include the meaning "uncaused" or "in principle not subject to causal analysis." But that element in its meaning is not necessary for the way randomness appears in Peckham's (or in Campbell's) theory. What is needed can be well expressed in the term *blind variation,* and Campbell favors substituting it for *randomness* (in this psychological rather than statistical context). Blind variations may have their causes, but they are independent of the circumstances that pose the problem that occasions the variations. A more detailed explication of the meaning of *blind variation* is offered by Campbell on page 381 of his article. If in speaking of *randomness* one holds steadily in mind this restricted definition—equivalent to that of *blind variation*—then Peckham's position is equivalent to the one Campbell is arguing for.

The question raised here by the humanistic tradition in psychology is not so easily disposed of. Does blind variation characterize human thought processes, and is it fundamental to even the directed, voluntary, insightful steps in creativity whose occurrence makes one doubt the appropriateness of a blind-variation theory? Campbell devotes almost the whole of his paper to justifying his positive answer to this question, answering in detail the various arguments that have been put forth on the other side. The position he espouses might be regarded as a compromise; it is far from the simplistic position that might have been taken before the development of Gestalt psychology. But it is probably the position that Peckham's proposal about randomness would work out to if considered in detail in relation to the difficulties acknowledged by Campbell. And Campbell is probably right in arguing that this position remains the most promising one from which to start a more detailed search for understanding human creativity.

Psychology has profited greatly from innovative ideas introduced by investigators from other fields who have turned their attention to basic psychological theory. Pavlov and Freud brought their differing modes of medical thought; Piaget brought a style of thought derived from embryology. Is rich future development to be expected from the humanities? The writings of Morse Peckham show us how ideas developed in literary interpretation can be generalized to provide a framework of psychological thought. What will follow when such a framework—interpretation of meaning as the central problem of human behavior—is put earnestly to work in the conduct of psychological research?

PETER C. SEDERBERG

# Science and Violence

At one end of the spectrum, pure science is concerned with knowledge and truth; at the other, pure politics is concerned with power and action.

Don K. Price, *The Scientific Estate*

The only final way to prove that [a person] is indeed mistaken is to kill him. Throughout human history it has been a very popular way of defeating an opponent in arguments about meaning. Certainly it has an almost irresistible charm.

Morse Peckham, *Art and Pornography*

## The Demise and Resurrection of Ideology

TWO DECADES AGO, as the United States emerged from the quiescence of the 1950s, certain social scientists announced the "end," or at least the decline, of ideology.[1] This declaration, made with no small amount of satisfaction, proclaimed a new and peaceful *political* period, one in which conflicts spawned by the Industrial Revolution over the ultimate ends of political action would be resolved by continuous material expansion and in which political debates would then be confined to the choice of the best means for achieving consensual goals. Such optimism, of course, was unjustified. The vaunted material success of an advanced industrial economy has since proved insufficient to defuse the charges of domestic racism and foreign oppression, and now even the viability of the economic organization has been undermined by the realities of scarcity.

[1] See, for example, Daniel Bell, *The End of Ideology* (New York: Free Press, 1960) and M. Rejai, ed., *Decline of Ideology?* (New York: Aldine, Atherton, 1971) for balanced overviews of the issue.

Despite the rather premature celebration of the demise of ideological conflict, the celebrants' impulse illustrates an interesting point: their perception of science as a successful political institution. "Success" is a slippery concept; by political success I mean simply the ability to resolve conflicts through means short of force. If political disputes could be confined to the choice of optimal means to achieve agreed upon ends, then governmental decision making could use essentially scientific techniques to select the best course of action. In short, outcomes could be determined by procedural logic and empirical validation, a much neater method than either "ballots or bullets." Science for centuries has apparently managed its conflicts in just this fashion, an enviable record that understandably encourages emulation. Even though the effort to assume away differences over ends, as in the "end of ideology" thesis, and to reduce politics to the discussion of maximizing means has proven inadequate, scientific method continues to possess the appeal of success, especially in contrast with the apparent failure of other institutions of conflict resolution.

Paradoxically, science is conventionally seen as apolitical, and this characteristic, it is widely believed, enables scientists to resolve their disputes in ways short of force. Morse Peckham, however, argues that the contrast between science and other institutions is more apparent than real: not only do other forms of decision making in the everyday world use protoscientific analysis, but also science contains certain features that undercut its apolitical stance.[2] Indeed, as the scientific model is more systematically and broadly exploited, its political frailties become increasingly evident. The success of science in conflict resolution has occurred within an insulated sphere. Efforts to expand this sphere may erode its achieved credibility. Moreover, the systematic exploitation of the scientific model itself constitutes a potential source of discord and even violence.

The possibility of an intrinsic link between science and violence is an outrageous notion, at least to those inclined to defend the purity of scientific knowledge and to argue that evil consequences are the results of its misapplication. The assumption, though, that science is somehow immune from normal human shortcomings is naive and even dangerous. Only if we are aware of our limits can we hope to avoid disaster. This paper explores the limits in three stages. First, it contrasts science and politics and then delineates their essential unity. It next explores the limitations of science as a political institution. Finally, the essay suggests how science contributes to what René Girard calls a "sacrificial crisis"—a crisis that raises the possibility of unrestrained reciprocal violence.

[2] Morse Peckham, *Explanation and Power: The Control of Human Behavior* (New York: Seabury, 1979), pp. 155-62.

## Politics and Science: Contrast and Unity

Politics, broadly speaking, is the process through which meanings are established, modified, or abandoned within an organization.[3] An organization is a hierarchy of verbal and nonverbal behavior, the former subsuming the latter. Politics, then, is not an activity unique to governments but occurs in all organizations including the individual, who gives himself covert directions for a performance (either verbal or nonverbal).

According to Peckham, the meaning of a sign, whether verbal or nonverbal, can be best conceived as the response to that sign. Since meaning is not immanent in the sign, there exists no necessary response to any particular semiotic configuration. Thus, to stabilize meaning within an organization, response to external configurations must be stabilized. Conversely, to change meaning, response must be altered. The ultimate determinant of response is force, and, therefore, for Peckham, force is the ultimate determinant of meaning.

This equation of meaning with response, which Peckham shares with the tradition of American pragmatism, contributes some of the conventional connotations of the broad concept of politics suggested above. Specifically, politics thus defined implies action (response), controlled through the application of power, and the final resort of power in politics is force. The use of force, however, indicates the failure to limit response through other means. If force fails, then the effort to establish meaning fails, for there is nothing left on which to rely. Consequently, the ability to determine meaning and secure action short of the recourse to force is a measure of political success.

Peckham's view of the process by which meaning and response are determined suggests a link between politics and science. He calls the methods other than force through which meaning can be established "seduction" and "manipulation." The former involves manipulating the verbal redundancies, or ideologies, to which a person subordinates his behavior. These verbal systems, more or less well articulated, explain and validate (or invalidate) the perceived world and thus can be used to justify particular responses. Force and seduction, however, appear primary, at least in terms of precedence, for people learn ideologies through a process involving both.

Ideology, admittedly, carries a connotation of false knowledge or even delusion whereas science presumably embodies a drive to reality which, if not productive of absolutes, at least provides for a measure of security from delusion. This

---

[3] This definition is similar to, but somehow more inclusive than Peckham's (*Explanation and Power*, p. 225). The subsequent discussion of meaning and the nature of science is also drawn from his work, particularly pp. 1-42, 140-62. Obviously, I am summarizing and interpreting for my own purposes a substantially longer argument of Peckham's. Although I believe the summary is fair, the interpretation is mine.

perspective is partially accurate. Science represents the systematic exploitation of the links among explanation (theory, hypothesis), experimentation, and feedback. Experimentation is nonverbal behavior guided by the explanation (verbal behavior), the results of which are used to confirm, modify, or abandon the governing explanation.

The most interesting aspect of this description of science is that it is so uninteresting. Nothing exists in this model of scientific inquiry that sets it dramatically apart from inquiring behavior in the everyday world. There, too, experiments are continually conducted under the control of tacit explanations and consequent expectations, and the results are frequently used to correct the original predictions. The model remains essentially the same whether a person is crossing the street or crossing genes: explanations prescribe the behavior thought necessary to achieve certain outcomes. Failure to categorize accurately the position of oncoming traffic can provide impressive feedback on the adequacy of the expectations governing street crossing.

I prefer to label what occurs in everyday activities like crossing the street as *protoscientific* behavior to indicate that it resembles, but is not identical to, scientific activity. The model remains the same, but the method differs. As the preceding definition states, science is the *systematic* exploitation of the linkage among explanation, experimentation, and feedback. Scientific investigations are procedurely overdetermined; that is, they are under the control of strict codes of what constitute the appropriate methods for linking explanations (verbal signs) with experiments (nonverbal signs) and with one another. The adherence to these codes distinguishes science from protoscience and makes the product of scientific inquiry relatively reliable, at least in certain areas.

Relatively reliable, however, is not wholly reliable. Scientific knowing is not completely free from the inadequacies that afflict knowing in general. First, the facts upon which the explanation rests are not pure but perceived; that is, they are selected and categorized by the perceiver for a response. To select and to categorize, though, means to exclude, for we cannot account for everything. A residual of the unperceived and, consequently, the unexplained remains after every experiment. Moreover, the experimentally produced configurations that the scientist chooses to subsume in his explanatory system have no more inherent meaning than those of the everyday world: they imply no necessary response. In every experiment, therefore, "there is invariably a residue of data which is unresponded to and a range of responses which are not made."[4] These residuals are a source of instability in scientific, as well as everyday, explanations.

The enhanced ability of science to resolve disputes over meaning, then, is not found in either explanation or experimentation, per se. The foundation of agreement, rather, is under cultural and social control; specifically, the prevailing

---

[4] Ibid., p. 149.

procedures defining what constitutes "appropriateness" as judged by the scientific community.[5] These procedures can be termed an *ideology of inquiry* and include everything from prescriptions governing the formulation of hypotheses, through techniques for structuring experiments, to the rhetoric for reporting results. The ideology of inquiry also defines the appropriate methods for creating and manipulating explanatory hierarchies.

Like conventionally defined ideologies, the scientific ideology of inquiry is both prescriptive and validational. It is also enforced. The scientific estate may not have at its disposal the means to impose the ultimate sanction, death, but errant members will find themselves ostracized, mostly by the refusal of learned publications to distribute their opinions. Severe transgressions, such as the forging of evidence, can, if discovered, result in communal disgrace, as Sir Cyril Burt has posthumously learned. Interestingly, ostracism is an enforcement apparatus used by communities that lack a centralized enforcement apparatus. In this sense, the scientific community is politically "primitive."

The ideology of scientific inquiry, then, is a set of explanations about how to make acceptable explanations. Like all explanations, it is predictive; specifically, it predicts that if one conforms to ideological prescriptions one's results will not only be more reliable, but also will become socially current. In order to participate in the scientific community, a person must be willing to submit to its ideology of inquiry. The scientific estate, in this way, resembles other organizations in that it is under the control of a dominant ideology enforced through means that are external to the explanatory process itself. Dominant, however, does not mean unchallenged, for deviant explanations and parascientific publications that support them exist at the fringes of the scientific enterprise. Naturally, certain defenders of ideological purity devote considerable effort to demolishing, or at least quarantining, these perverted orientations.[6]

Peckham, though, notes one distinctive trait of the organizational ideology of science: its interest in innovation. Early stages of modern scientific inquiry, approximately through the Enlightenment, sought to stabilize explanation. The human mind and the world were believed to be essentially isomorphic, and only ignorance prevented perfect harmonization. Scientific discoveries, although innovative, were believed to move humanity toward this harmonization. Some members of the scientific community undoubtedly still hold to this essentially eighteenth-century view, but the dominant perspective accepts the hypothetical nature of knowledge—an acceptance that encourages scientists "to exploit

[5] Ibid., p. 157.

[6] For example, see Carl Sagan, *Broca's Brain* (New York: Random House, 1979), especially "Venus and Dr. Velikovsky," pp. 81-127. Sagan's essay is a fine example of imposing procedural controls on an errant explanation.

[explanation's] inherent instability."[7] This commitment to innovation, none-theless, is not unqualified; for innovative positions, to be recognized, must conform with the dominant procedural prescriptions and even then may still encounter resistance.[8]

Science, therefore, resembles other ways of establishing meaning; that is, other examples of the political process. The behavioral triad of explanation, experimentation, and feedback is widespread throughout the protoscientific activities of the everyday world. The manner in which these behaviors are manifested in science is under strict procedural controls—or as Peckham says, overdetermined—but these controlling mechanisms are similar to other means of ideological control in society with one difference: the scientific ideology of inquiry exhibits a greater commitment to innovation.

The willingness of scientists to submit to these controls accounts for the success of science as a political institution. In addition, at least in terms of predictive power, scientific procedures may be judged as more appropriate for conducting inquiries into the physical world than competing ideologies, such as theological or sociomythic explanations. Apparently, then, if we wish to emulate the success of science in resolving disputes short of force (or, at least, extreme force), it is not a matter of imitating *what* scientists do. We already are, or more accurately, scientists are imitating us, for protoscientific behavior preceded contemporary science. Rather, to emulate scientists we must imitate *how* they do it; we must submit more areas of social life to the procedural controls of scientific investigation. To some extent we seem willing to do just that, as the Masters and Johnson sexual research projects amply demonstrate.

Some retrogrades, though, express misgivings about this imperialist insti-tution. And well they might, for there are reasons to believe that the procedural ideology of science encounters serious problems as it expands its range of endeavor, problems that may ultimately erode the image of political efficacy even in those areas of previously demonstrated success. Moreover, the innovative thrust of the ideology becomes corrosive of an ever widening sphere of relations as science penetrates into the remainder of the social world. Scientific success, like all success, contributes to its own failure; indeed, it contributes to the failure of other institutions as well.

## The Limits of Science as a Political Institution

Historically, other institutions have challenged the political efficacy of scientific procedural controls. Most famous, perhaps, are the theological

---

[7] Peckham, *Explanation and Power*, p. 157.

[8] On resistance to change see Thomas S. Kuhn, *The Structure of Scientific Revolutions* (Chicago: University of Chicago Press, 1962), pp. 143-58.

objections to the cosmological propositions of Copernicus and Galileo. In retrospect, we evaluate this conflict with a certain amount of benign contempt for the Church, because the scientifically established proposition proved superior to the *a priori* prescriptions of the theologians. More recently, the mayor of Cambridge, Massachusetts, has assumed the theological role by questioning the wisdom of allowing genetic researchers in his city to function free from the restraints of other political institutions.

Having established the analogy between the astronomical and the biological controversy, should we then dismiss contemporary fears as quickly as we do those of 350 years ago? Perhaps not, for some significant concerns may be at work here. Biologist Lewis Thomas recommends:

> Maybe we'd be wiser, all of us, to back off before the recombinant-DNA issue becomes too large to cope with. If we're going to have a fight about it, let it be confined to the immediate issue of safety and security, of the recombinants now under consideration, and let us by all means have regulations and guidelines to assure the public safety wherever these are indicated or even suggested. But if it is possible let us stay off that question about limiting human knowledge. It is too loaded, and we'll simply not be able to cope with it.[9]

His position implicitly recognizes that certain questions are more susceptible to scientific procedural control than others. We should consequently limit science to the former and, apparently, not discuss the more intractable questions at all.

Unfortunately, this solution will not do. Loaded questions will not go away; indeed, as science expands the range of its activities, it actually generates more of them. The history of biology is an interesting example of the problem. Not so long ago botanists and zoologists poked and peeked in the background, while the achievements of physicists and chemists vied for world attention. Not so any longer. Biology now lies on the cutting edge of human inquiry, opening areas for investigation and control far more unnerving than those conferred by the power locked in the atom. Mankind has always known ways to destroy life, albeit never with such grand finality, but the power to create life was the province of the divine. One can imagine what the seventeenth-century papacy would make of this new power. Theological reactions aside, biological research is clearly penetrating closer to the level of social life, while physics and chemistry, in their explorations if not their applications, remain relatively remote from direct human experience. The investigations of the geneticists and the speculations of the sociobiologists are far closer to immediate human concerns. Pure science, operating under its own procedural controls, seems increasingly likely to produce more questions and conflicts than its own institutional devices can resolve.

---

[9] Lewis Thomas, "The Hazards of Science," in *The Medusa and the Snail* (New York: Viking, 1979), p. 69.

Beyond biology lie the social sciences. While the political efficacy and independence of scientific institutions are being seriously questioned for the first time in decades in the areas of the "hard" sciences, the social sciences have never fully established scientific procedural ideology as the sole arbiter of meaning. Why this is the case in the social sciences may help to explain why biology and even the physical sciences are increasingly attacked on extrascientific grounds.

The effectiveness of the scientific explanatory enterprise is measured most simply by the accuracy of its predictions, as they are the most direct method of provisionally validating or invalidating explanatory propositions. In order to gauge the success of a prediction, one needs accurate and unambiguous feedback. If the feedback is sparse or contains a good deal of "noise," then the ideological controls of scientific procedure will be less effective in determining meanings; that is, the range of responses to the feedback will begin to widen (a consequence Peckham calls the "Delta Effect"). Such a situation is usually not tolerable, especially in areas effecting the sensitive interests of other institutions, so other ways will be sought to establish meaning. Force is the last of these.

Thomas wants to confine the recombinant debate to "the immediate issue of safety," because it may be evaluated with minimum noise. The loaded question, however, is part of the feedback of these experiments as well. Science has generally proceeded by ignoring disturbing feedback until some resolution could be formulated, but now in these sensitive areas such "optimal ignorance" becomes increasingly difficult to maintain.[10]

The social sciences, however, have generally found it troublesome either to eliminate or ignore unwelcome noise. They are beset by at least six problems, three substantive and three methodological, that limit the capacity of scientific procedural controls to establish unambiguous meaning. These problems, to be sure, are not points of absolute contrast with the conditions prevailing in the natural sciences; in fact, the extent to which they are shared helps to explain some of the new difficulties encountered by the natural scientists. Each of these six problems contributes in its own way to the level of feedback noise.[11]

The first substantive problem concerns the complexity of individual human beings. Each one is a product of a unique genetic and biographical heritage. Although one must not underestimate the degree of sharing that exists (e.g., common needs, common cultural experiences), certainly the basic units of analysis in the social sciences differ more from one another than do members of other animal species, much less the elements of the periodic table.

[10] The phrase is borrowed from Norman T. Uphoff and Warren F. Illchman, "The New Political Economy," in Uphoff and Illchman, eds., *The Political Economy of Development* (Berkeley: University of California Press, 1972), p. 9. They define it as "an assessment of what one does *not* need to know in order to decide upon a course of action."

[11] For a more extensive discussion of these problems see Peter C. Sederberg, *Interpreting Politics* (San Francisco: Chandler and Sharp, 1977), pp. 11-21.

The limits on cultural commonality make up the second substantive problem, that of cultural diversity. Although some people share certain cultural experiences, such as belonging to the same language group, these experiences are never identical. Not only do those raised in different language/cultural systems undergo substantially different socializing experiences, but also even those in the same group have their own variants of the presumably common culture.

Third, humans can change their behavior in unpredictable ways. Peckham argues that the fundamental difficulty here is the human capacity to randomize response.[12] Not only is it impossible to determine precisely what element of a stimulus field a person selects for response, but also it cannot be known exactly how a person will respond to a particular stimulus, even if that stimulus could be identified. Of course, institutions of social control—that is, all institutions—are created to narrow the range of response as much as possible, but they have never yet been completely successful. Ironically, the success of social scientific explanations depends, to an extent, on the effectiveness of mechanisms of social control to ensure predictable response.

The three methodological quandaries partially relate to these substantive problems. First the opportunities for controlled experimentation are severely constrained in the social sciences. In part, this is an extrascientific problem, for people simply do not wish to be experimentally manipulated. Beyond such social and ethical objections, many areas of social life cannot be plausibly subjected to controlled experimentation. Some disciplines, especially psychology, have established methods of experimentation that seem to resemble those in the natural sciences. Peckham, though, has dissected these efforts, demonstrating the extent to which psychologists structure the situation to produce the desired results, a form of control, to be sure, but not what is usually implied.[13]

Due to the limited capacity for controlled experimentation, social scientists must conduct most of their investigations into social phenomena in their natural settings—a context that leads to an inevitable contamination of results. Here, too, they encounter a second methodological quandary. The scientific enterprise depends upon accurate feedback which, in turn, implies accurate measurement. Many social phenomena, however, cannot be accurately measured with interval or, better, ratio scales. Even efforts at mere nominal classification are often empirically dubious. The dilemma seems to be that in order to deal with the significant, social scientists must often be inaccurate; to be accurate, their investigations are commonly limited to the relatively trivial. Even where a reasonable significant measurement exists, overconcentration on it leads to the exclusion of "softer" elements, resulting in the underestimation of important residuals. The gross national product as a measure of national well-being exemplifies this problem.

[12] Peckham, *Explanation and Power*, pp. 261-69.
[13] Ibid., pp. 15-34.

Finally, social scientists seem particularly vulnerable to infection from extrascientific concerns. All scientists bring to their research the psychological baggage that makes up their personalities, and the direction of research itself is influenced by external sources of power and funding. Science most certainly is not value free; rather science strives to minimize the intrusion of external values and biases that might erode the effectiveness of scientific procedural controls. Social scientists, however, may well find it difficult to isolate themselves from such infection, for the problems they study more immediately involve their own lives and emotions. One conventional response is to sanitize their research through excessive abstraction, a strategy that is value-biased itself, as well as one that tends to cut the explanation away from its existential foundation. Thus, social scientists confront yet another dilemma: in order to conduct meaningful research into their subject—human beings and their social interactions—social scientists run the risk of being unduly influenced by nonscientific values and identifications; to minimize such influences they often seem to dehumanize their subjects into objects for manipulation and control.

These six problems conflate to produce two significant consequences for social science feedback. First, social scientists find it difficult to pursue a strategy of optimal ignorance, for data that "do not compute" continually intrude to subvert proposed explanations. Second, even when reasonably accurate measurements of the relationship between the explanation and the experimental results are available, the link is generally statistical. Now one can argue that all explanatory relationships are statistical, even in physics. Yet as one moves from the "hard" to the "soft" sciences, statistical relationships tend to grow progressively weaker. This, in turn, weakens, and even eliminates altogether, the predictive capacity of a purported explanation, resulting in contending explanations for the same phenomenon. In short, the procedural controls of the scientific ideology of inquiry become increasingly ineffective in establishing even provisional meaning.

The natural sciences, as suggested earlier, are not immune from these hazards. Thomas's complaint suggests that as biologists move into areas closer to the concerns of other political institutions, they will encounter reactions that can neither be ignored nor subsumed by the conventional scientific controls. Response, and therefore meaning, will become more indeterminate. Astronomy provides another interesting case. Here the limited capacity for controlled experimentation and direct observation has resulted in competition among fascinating speculative explanations. The origins and ultimate end, if any, of the universe, are sufficiently distant from the interests of other institutions so as not to excite much concern over this ambiguity of meaning. Still, it illustrates another of Peckham's observations: the weaker the control the wider the drift.[14]

---

[14] Ibid., pp. 164-65.

Any effort to confine the explanatory process to that feedback most easily managed by scientific procedural controls may well prove futile. The exclusion of powerful responses from consideration within the scientific community will only leave them clamoring at the gates of other institutions. Scientists, then, face their own unwelcome dilemma as they delve into socially sensitive and ontologically murky areas: they will generate conflicts that cannot be managed by their established means, but if they ignore this conflictual feedback, the issues will most likely be decided by other institutions without scientific input.

The possibility of extrascientific imposition of control sends shudders through the scientific community. The extreme way of posing the challenge is to question whether scientific inquiry should be restricted in some way, and specifically whether certain areas should be excluded from scientific scrutiny. Generally, such suggestions provoke paeans to man's boundless mind and insatiable curiosity.[15] One might cynically retort that the minds and curiosity of most scientists seem easily bound and satiated by whatever areas are currently being funded by governmental and corporate research monies. These incentives, admittedly, are essentially indirect means of control. The specific and conscious choice to define a forbidden area of knowledge may be a qualitatively different matter.

Biologist Robert Sinsheimer notes, however, that certain areas of scientific inquiry should at least be considered of dubious merit. One is the search for extraterrestrial intelligence. The assumption that this intelligence, once discovered, would be benign is optimistic. More importantly, "the impact of more advanced cultures upon the less advanced has almost invariably been disastrous to the latter," whatever the intentions of the former.[16] Deliberately to seek out such a consequence seems to him to be a misallocation of resources. A second example of questionable research deals with a problem of more direct concern: the efforts to prolong life significantly, perhaps by hundreds of years. "The impact of a major extension of the human life span upon our entire social order, upon the life styles, mores, and adaptations associated with 'three score and ten,' upon the carrying capacity of a planet already facing overpopulation would be devastating."[17]

The rationale for restriction, then, is not being made on theological or even humanist grounds of protecting man's already damaged self-esteem. Rather the problem is perceived as one of simple survival. Science, therefore, in pursuing such investigations (and more examples could be developed) may generate feedback that it cannot subsume and consequences it cannot contain. Other political institutions may well be tempted to move in, especially in questions of

[15] Thomas, pp. 74-75.
[16] Robert L. Sinsheimer, "The Presumptions of Science," *Daedalus* 107 (Spring 1978): 30.
[17] Ibid., pp. 30-31.

survival, and impose their own controls, by force if necessary. Rather than contributing to the resolution of disputes over meaning, science may be linked to the widening of conflict. This potential linkage, moreover, may be more intimate, for the development of the scientific ideology of inquiry has been associated with forces that have undercut the capacity of other institutions to manage conflicts short of the recourse to force and may even encourage a deterioration into a cycle of violence.

## Science and the Sacrificial Crisis

"Science," Peckham observes, "is also the model for institutions in their fullest form."[18] Organizations are set up to control behavior, to determine response which constitutes meaning. Organizations, like explanatory systems, are hierarchical; each lower level is subsumed by a higher one until some termination point is reached. The higher one's position in an organization (or explanation) the more one knows about its general structure and purpose and the less one knows about its functioning at the lowest level. This lowest level of the organization, as in an explanation, constitutes its empirical frontier beyond which lies the reality the organization attempts to subsume (explain) and control. If science is the systematic exploitation of the links among explanation, experimentation, and feedback, then a highly developed organization consists of coherent orders (explanations) being given down the hierarchy rigorously guiding behavior at the frontier (experimentation) followed by sufficient, accurate feedback concerning the effectiveness of the original directives. Organizational logic, then, resembles the scientific ideology of inquiry. Most organizations, however, admittedly fall short of this ideal type: orders downward are inconsistent, behavior haphazard at the empirical frontier, and upward feedback, especially negative upward feedback, blocked.

Modern bureaucratic organizations, or at least the Weberian typification of them, are developed precisely on this scientific model. "Bureaucracy," Richard Rubenstein notes, "can be best understood as a structural and organizational expression of the related processes of *secularization, disenchantment of the world,* and *rationalization.*"[19] These processes are also those involved with the rise of modern science; indeed, the association between modern science and bureaucracy is not coincidental but organic. Modern bureaucracy imitates the procedural controls of science in an effort to duplicate in the area of bureaucratic concern the apparent success of the sciences. As Max Weber observes:

[18] Peckham, *Explanation and Power,* p. 191. The following comparison is based on pp. 189-91.

[19] Richard L. Rubenstein, *The Cunning of History* (New York: Harper Colophon, 1978), pp. 27-28.

The peculiarity of modern culture, and specifically of its technical and economic basis, demands this very "calculability" of results. When fully developed, bureaucracy also stands, in a specific sense, under the principle of *sine ira ac studio* [without anger or zeal]. Its specific nature...develops the more perfectly the more the bureaucracy is "dehumanized," the more completely it succeeds in eliminating from official business love, hatred, and all purely personal, irrational, and emotional elements which escape calculation.[20]

If a society ever falls completely under bureaucratic domination, in that externally imposed limits on bureaucratic operations are eliminated, then all hell can break loose. Rubenstein argues that in Nazi Germany only after the "Jewish Problem" was delegated to the bureaucracy

was it possible to contemplate the extermination of millions. A machinery was set up that was devoid of both love and hatred. It was only possible to overcome the moral barrier that had in the past prevented the systematic riddance of surplus populations when the project was taken out of the hands of bullies and hoodlums and delegated to bureaucrats.[21]

The very forces, then, that contributed to the efficient operation of the death camps were also those that contributed to the development of modern science; indeed, science and bureaucracies are dominated by analogous procedural controls. A connection exists, therefore, between science and the ultimate horror of the twentieth century. The nature of their consanguinity might be best discovered by exploring the functions of the institution that the processes of secularization, disenchantment, and rationalization served to undermine: religion.

René Girard, in a brilliant and disturbing study, peels back the palimpsest of religious ritual to reveal the violence—the sacred violence— at its core.[22] His analysis is too rich to summarize fully, but certain particulars can be drawn upon to illuminate a connection between science and violence. The fundamental threat to human communities, Girard plausibly argues, is an outbreak of reciprocal violence—a violence that destroys all distinctions and recognizes no bounds, an awesome cycle of retribution and revenge. Modern societies seem relatively immune from this cycle due to the effectiveness of their judicial organizations. As Girard observes:

The system does not suppress vengeance; rather it effectively limits it to a single act of reprisal, enacted by a sovereign authority specializing in this particular function.

[20] *From Max Weber,* ed. H. H. Gerth and C. Wright Mills (New York: Oxford University Press, 1958), pp. 215-16.

[21] Rubenstein, p. 27.

[22] René Girard, *Violence and the Sacred,* trans. Patrick Gregory (Baltimore: Johns Hopkins University Press, 1977).

The decisions of the judiciary are invariably presented as the final word on vengeance.[23]

Premodern communities lack this highly articulated system of control; however, they gain some protection through religious rituals "in which sacrificial rites divert the spirit of revenge into other channels."[24] The sacrificial violence embodied in these rituals commemorates an aboriginal act of violence that ended a "sacrificial crisis"; that is, a period of reciprocal violence. At that time, the crisis-torn community divested all of its enmity upon an arbitrarily chosen surrogate, who by his death reunified the community. In retrospect such a miraculous result would appear to have been caused by divine intervention; consequently, the despised surrogate for the community's mutual blood lust would be endowed with a sacred aura. Subsequently established religious rituals substituted a sacrificial victim in the hopes of being able continuously to reconstitute the community.

Religious prohibitions also serve to protect the community. The sacrificial crisis results from and contributes to the breakdown of distinctions—the degrees upon which order depends. Reciprocal violence produces a truly vicious equality among all the participants. Equality of degree leads to equivalent desires and thus to conflict and further violence. This "monstrous doubling," Girard argues, lies at the heart of many of our violent myths, whether that of the rivalry of Achilles and Agamemnon or that among Oedipus, Creon, and Tiresias. Wherever a violent rivalry can occur, then religion promulgates a prohibition (the last seven of the Ten Commandments aptly illustrate this). Religious sanctification props up an order based upon distinctions and limits. Girard concludes:

> Religion, then, is far from "useless." It humanizes violence; it protects man from his own violence by taking it out of his hands, transforming it into a transcendent and ever-present danger to be kept in check by the appropriate rites appropriately observed and by a modest and prudent demeanor.[25]

More modern societies largely dispense with religious protection for, after all, they are defended by the judicial system. Yet Girard raises a frightening prospect:

> As soon as the essential quality of transcendence—religious, humanistic, or whatever—is lost, there are no longer any terms by which to define the legitimate form of violence and to recognize it among the multitude of illicit forms. The definition of legitimate and illegitimate forms then becomes a matter of mere opinion, with each man free to reach his own decision. In other words the question is thrown to the winds.[26]

[23] Ibid., p. 15.
[24] Ibid., pp. 20-21.
[25] Ibid., p. 134.
[26] Ibid., p. 24.

The disenchantment, secularization, and rationalization of the world—the processes from which science has grown and to which it mightily contributes—corrode the transcendental justifications for the judicial distinction between legitimate and illegitimate violence.

The complicity of science in a contemporary sacrificial crisis extends beyond its contribution to the dissolution of the sacred. Science, at least for the past century, has maintained an ideological commitment to noncommitment. As Peckham notes, such a stance leads to a remarkable capacity to exploit categorical instability. No categorization, no explanation, is adequate; all must be open to challenge, to revision, to abandonment. Modern science, not Trotsky, has ushered in the permanent revolution, a continuous structuring and destructuring of the world. This ability has contributed both to remarkable advances in the ability to predict and control certain phenomena and to a dissolution of differences as the scientific perspective spreads throughout society. Girard himself observes, "The very essence of modern society might be said to be its ability to sustain the possibility for new discoveries in the midst of an ever-worsening sacrificial crisis—not, to be sure, without many signs of anxiety and stress."[27]

In his discussion of reactions to recombinant-DNA research, Lewis Thomas notes, "Classical mythology is peopled with mixed beings—part man, part animal or plant—and most of them are associated with tragic stories. Recombinant-DNA is a reminder to bad dreams."[28] Not merely dreams, for the horror of a collapsing order is not immaterial, and myths, as Girard convincingly demonstrates, are rooted in existential experience. "A dynamic force seems to be drawing first Western society, then the rest of the world, toward a state of relative indifferentiation never before known on earth, a strange kind of nonculture or anticulture we call modern."[29] A major factor in the "force" is the innovating ideology of science.

The innovative drive of science, therefore, contributes to the threat of continual categorical disintegration, a major element of what Girard terms a sacrificial crisis. At the same time, the forces intimately associated with the rise of modern science dissolve the transcendental authority of those institutions—religious and judicial—designed to protect the community from outbreaks of reciprocal violence. What remains are those organizations that have most closely patterned their operations on the model of scientific procedural controls: modern bureaucracies. And, as the Holocaust demonstrates, there seem to be *no inherent limits* on what these organizations will do.

[27] Ibid., p. 238.
[28] Thomas, p. 71.
[29] Girard, p. 189.

## What Is to Be Done?

Science, like all other human endeavors, is tainted. Far from ushering in an age where conflicts over meaning diminish, the limitations of the scientific ideology of inquiry widen conflict and increase the potential for violence. Science, of course, is neither the only nor the most significant contributor to conflict and violence, although bureaucracy, its handmaiden, may be. Nevertheless, science cannot be expected to save the modern world from the forces that threaten it, for it is very much a part of those forces.

If this is so, then from where can some solace be sought? Ironically, one possibility might be for us to turn the argument of the essay against itself. If all explanations tend to ignore data that cannot be subsumed, then the explanation developed here can be no exception. Scientific procedural controls, after all, have been successful in establishing at least provisional meaning in many areas of inquiry. Additionally, though scientists are involved in dissolving established categories and innovating new meanings, wide areas of knowledge remain relatively stable for extended periods of time. Science, this counterargument would conclude, remains the best hope for establishing meaning short of force, at least in comparison with the other institutions available.

Such a counterargument, however, does not so much invalidate the original statement as weaken the necessity of its conclusions. Like all explanations of the social world, the link between science and conflict is not one of absolute necessity but a statistical tendency. Scientific procedural controls embody both efficacy and inefficacy, and the latter grows in significance as scientific inquiry expands into more ambiguous and sensitive areas. Concentrating solely on the accomplishments and ignoring the dangers only increases the probability of the negative consequences.

A second possible source of solace would be to "relativize the relativizers."[30] If science teaches us that cultural orientations are relative to particular times and places, then why should the scientific world view be exempt? It too, may be considered culturally specific, and from its contradictions and limits a new cultural order will emerge. Such a position is most fully developed by Pitirim Sorokin in his massive *Social and Cultural Dynamics*.[31] Sorokin believes, not without some cause, that the Western world is nearing the end of a decaying sensate era, and out of the collapse of this age would arise a new ideational culture in which transcendental values would again reign supreme. Were one inclined to seek avatars of this transformation, they might be found in such areas as the

[30] The idea is from Peter L. Berger, *A Rumor of Angels* (Garden City, N. Y.: Doubleday, 1970), chapter 2.

[31] I confess to being something of a philistine, having read only the 700 page condensation rather than the four volume original. See Pitirim Sorokin, *Social and Cultural Dynamics* (Boston: Porter Sargent, 1957).

resurgence of religious fundamentalism or the neopythagorian combination of science and mysticism of the Lindesfarne Association.

Yet the "leap of faith" to faith is a difficult one to make. The processes of disenchantment and secularization seem difficult to reverse at this point, and it certainly is unlikely that institutions of transcendental meaning capable of resolving the expanding cycle of social conflict could be manipulated into existence. Perhaps the best that could be hoped, and it is a pallid hope, indeed, would be for the sacrificial crisis to generate once again a surrogate victim capable of reuniting the torn community. In this case, though, the community is worldwide, and if a full cycle of reciprocal violence engulfs it, there may be little left to be reconstituted.

If scientific optimism is a dangerous delusion and religious revival a forlorn and necessarily unpredictable and uncontrollable hope, we are left with merely muddling through. We cannot, after all, turn our backs on science. We engage in protoscientific behavior all the time, and we might as well do it well. We cannot ignore the need to innovate new responses, for if all explanations suffer from inadequacy, then clinging to outworn ones may threaten our survival. We cannot defend order for its own sake, for any system of distinctions and degrees perpetuates its own injustices.

Yet, the scientific ideology of inquiry can handle well only those areas where substantial precision is possible. As the relations between explanation and experimentation become clouded and conflictual, then other values and limits must be imposed. If no order deserves automatic defense, no innovation merits unqualified acceptance. As Peckham points out, an innovation

> may be fruitful or damaging. If it is judged to be the first, it is validated by the word "creativity"; if it is judged to be the second, it is invalidated by the word "error." Whether human innovation is beneficial or harmful to the survival of the human species is impossible to say, for the species is neither extinct nor yet free from the threat of extinction.[32]

We must pursue, then, a fragile and fluctuating equilibrium. God, should he exist, help us.

---

[32] Peckham, *Explanation and Power,* p. 273.

H. W. MATALENE

# Material Incompetence and the Rhetorical Ethos of the *Ancien Régime*

## I.

MORSE PECKHAM HAS WRITTEN that "the great poetry of the past, if we take it too seriously, is capable of teaching us the most revolting nonsense."[1] Certainly, most undergraduates, without having engaged the great literature of the past with anything approaching seriousness, would agree; and with that sort of agreement the professor of literary history, if he wishes to remain in his right mind, need not overmuch concern himself. His problem is to reach the serious layman and to interest him in the great literature of the past—"revolting nonsense" and all. Peckham himself has done that with romantic literature— once thought to be the revolting effusion of tender-minded, obscure, and self-indulgent escapists, but reinterpreted by Peckham and by the best in recent historical scholarship so that the layman can see in the romantic tradition what it really means to be serious about human conduct in the modern world.

But literary historians now facing the problem of interesting the laity in texts that appeared before romanticism often seem condemned to failure. It is possible to give careful, historically plausible readings to post-romantic texts and to find good students who are deeply grateful for having been exposed to powerful ideas

[1] Morse Peckham, *Man's Rage for Chaos: Biology, Behavior, and the Arts* (Philadelphia and New York: Chilton Books, 1965), p. 314. Research for this paper was partially funded by a summer research grant from the Department of English of the University of South Carolina. I thank my friend in sociology, Professor Robert L. Stewart, for invaluable bibliographical pointers. And I am grateful to Peter Laslett and the Cambridge Group for the History of Population and Social Structure for their intellectual hospitality.

which are quite new to them, and which they can carry into practical life. But careful, historically plausible readings of great preindustrial texts generally turn up the sort of "revolting nonsense" to which Peckham refers: pious platitudes, truisms, and quaint, unscientific errors. Thus, one eminent historian of preindustrial literature is left to apologize for what he calls "the endless Renaissance debates on the problems and pseudo problems of friendship."[2] Another warns the modern layman not to be carried away by *Romeo and Juliet,* for the star-crossed lovers are impulsive sinners from the viewpoint of Elizabethan theology. Indeed, this scholar teaches us that Shakespeare contrived for the action of "Verona's drama of amour-passion" to take place between a Sunday morning and the wee hours of the next Friday, "exactly that portion of the week *not* occupied by" Christ's passion.[3] Or, finally, from the reading of *Tristram Shandy,* the literary historian may require his students to bring to the examination the knowledge that sperm cells once were thought to contain little men.

Unless the historian of preindustrial literature is capable of explaining how anyone who mattered could ever have taken such stuff seriously, he is not likely to persuade anyone who hopes to matter to take it very seriously now. And this failure is unfortunate, for the classics are part of the historical record, and history (as Peckham implies) is a profoundly practical discipline of knowledge. It is no less than the science of how we got into this mess—a way of getting some perspective on what the present mess is so that reasonable approaches to it may be planned and attempted. It is not enough to note that Montaigne and Machiavelli were two in an "endless" series of Renaissance figures who wrote truisms about the need to know real friends from mere patronizers or flatterers. In themselves, such truisms may no longer interest us very much, but the fact of their having seemed important enough to warrant such frequent repetition from antiquity onward calls not for apology, but for explanation. It is part of a cultural pattern which includes every mature Shakespearean tragedy—in all of which someone counts too much or too little for his own good on people who claim to be his friends. It is the pattern called "the looking-glass self" by sociologists in our own century.[4]

The best efforts at explaining to the modern laity how anyone could ever have taken the "revolting nonsense" in preindustrial literature seriously, in my judgment, have been Marxist efforts; but they have been none too good. They go close to the heart of the matter when they point out that preindustrial literature

[2] Ronald Berman, "The Ethic of *The Country Wife,*" *Texas Studies in Language and Literature* 9 (Spring 1967): 49.

[3] Roy W. Battenhouse, *Shakespearean Tragedy: Its Art and Its Christian Premises* (Bloomington: Indiana University Press, 1969), pp. 115-16.

[4] Charles Horton Cooley, *Human Nature and the Social Order* (1922; reprint, New York: Schocken Books, 1965), especially pp. 183-85.

was written of, by, and for the ruling class,[5] but they are too quick in assuming that the high culture of the *ancien régime* was no more than a conspiracy of the rich and the intellectuals against the poor, and their analysis of "class" as "relation to the means of production" sheds no very direct light on what the best-known writers of the last three preindustrial centuries said about being a gentleman, a nobleman, or a member of royalty. For those writers, owning the means of production was almost incidental to what really constituted nobility. The important thing about ownership was that it helped to buy the fullest possible access to what we might call *the culture of deference*—to the whole range of signs (the "redundancy system," Peckham would now call it)[6] that make language work, however imperfectly. Language begins to work when people shut up and listen, and the preindustrial economy, while it produced what it could to keep all individuals alive and healthy, was primarily geared to the production, for some potential speakers, of an attentive silence, respectful or resentful, in others. It was geared, in other words, to produce the signs subsumed by the term "nobility." Aristocratic behavior was designed to produce a hearing for speakers who could not talk technical sense about the basic, worker's interest in having maximum longevity, health, and well-being at a minimum cost in attention to others who would change his habits.

Insofar as the Marxism of the Frankfurt school recognizes that making language work is quite as essential to human survival as nutrition, shelter, clothing, and medicine are, it shows itself capable of understanding the economic priorities of the *ancien régime*. Still, it has not, to my knowledge, understood them. Undeniably, the ultimate evidence that one might be living in a situation of social equality would be an awareness of participating in something like Jürgen Habermas's "ideal speech situation," in which all parties are equally solicitous of being understood, of understanding all others, and of reaching a rational consensus about vital courses of collective action.[7] The Western culture of deference, however, takes it for granted that the ideal speech situation does not, in fact, exist. Its defenders, among whom are the great writers of the preindustrial West, argue, in essence, that the ideal speech situation has never existed, and cannot exist, and that the culture of deference came into being in response to this sad fact. This argument makes some use of history, but it ignores abundant historical evidence which denies that what has existed must exist, and that the hitherto nonexistent is impossible. The modern political Left, on the other hand, argues that were it not for the sad historical fact of the culture of

[5] See, for instance, Louis Kampf, "The Humanist Tradition in Eighteenth-Century England—And Today," *NLH* 3 (Autumn 1971): 157-70.

[6] Morse Peckham, *Explanation and Power: The Control of Human Behavior* (New York: Seabury, 1979), especially pp. 162-84.

[7] Thomas McCarthy, *The Critical Theory of Jürgen Habermas* (Cambridge: MIT Press, 1978), pp. 305-10.

deference, the ideal speech situation could be approached, or even attained. But it, too, in its most radical manifestations, ignores historical evidence. Rioters and organized cadres have often driven powerful speakers into exile and executed the police chiefs who helped make people listen to them. The palaces from which princes have spoken have often been vandalized or opened to the public as museums, and new holidays commemorating such revolutions have often been placed on national calendars. Post-revolutionary gains in freedom of speech have sometimes been recorded; but there seem always to have been new palaces and new police chiefs; and always there have been new speakers to receive more than equal shares of the gross national attention.

Always, in varying measures, the ideal speech situation eludes us. The question of who should listen to whom, on which topics, remains more or less open to negotiation and has never been finally resolved. Perhaps, then, in the atomic age, it is the wrong question; and we should ask not who should be listening to whom, but what ways human cultures have devised, short of threats of violence, for ending our inevitable negotiations over who will talk, and who will eventually listen and obey. The ethos of the Western *ancien régime* is of profound interest as one such set of deference arrangements.

The purpose of this paper is to try to interest laymen who are concerned with the general question of how peoples make language work in some of the "revolting nonsense" about why anyone listens to anyone else which is to be found in English and European literary texts of the last three centuries before the coming of romanticism and industrialization. In a paper of this length, much must be omitted. Real geographical and chronological variations from the general pattern I try to describe will be obscured, and many factual anthropological, sociological, and historical objections will remain unanticipated in my ignorance. These are faults. Nevertheless, as Peckham hopes at the end of *Beyond the Tragic Vision,* I hope to offer an "instrumental construct" which will make the works I discuss seem less quaint and platitudinous than they now often seem, and which will open works which I do not discuss to more vital and valid interpretations than they may now be receiving.[8]

Ten years ago, the sociologist Lee Rainwater doubted that "anyone studies the behavior of the disinherited out of solely scientific reasons." Always, Rainwater felt, the impulse to describe and explain the poor is partly an impulse to allay the explainer's anxiety over his failure of empathy with them.[9] One can just as easily doubt that a modern scholar can be any more scientific about the rich and powerful, and about the "revolting nonsense" in their literature, than he can be

[8] Morse Peckham, *Beyond the Tragic Vision: The Quest for Identity in the Nineteenth Century* (New York: George Braziller, 1962), pp. 371-72.

[9] Lee Rainwater, "Neutralizing the Disinherited: Some Psychological Aspects of Understanding the Poor," *Psychological Factors in Poverty,* ed. Vernon L. Allen, Institute for Research on Poverty Monograph Series (Chicago: Markham, 1970), p. 26.

about the poor. But unlike the modern scholar who studies the poor, the scholar who studies the aristocracy must be on his guard—as Marxism cannot be—against the unscientific impulse to be proud of the failure of empathy which impels him to study aristocratic behavior. The rich, too, are always with us, at least in the West, and they have sometimes tried to explain why. It may be instructive to listen. If one does listen, one may at least be more clear about what the political Left is attacking and the political Right defending than either side has usually been.

## II.

The first romantics often interpreted the French Revolution as demonstrating the failure of views of human motivation characteristic of the Enlightenment. Sometimes, in the hope of being scientific, these views reduced all behavior to providing for basic bodily survival. And, as the nineteenth century unfolded, European high culture began to rethink eighteenth-century senses of what human beings need and will act to achieve. As Thomas Carlyle and John Ruskin put it, falling back, for want of a better, upon an ancient bit of religious vocabulary, man is not all biological need—"stomach" or "skeleton"—but is also "soul."[10] In other words, human need is not reducible to survival in health and bodily comfort; for surviving, healthy, comfortable people still yearn for meaning—for responses to experience that seem all at once to be scientifically valid, ethically and logically coherent, and socially recognized.

Or, as Robert W. White, the psychologist of competence, has more recently reminded us, even though human beings often "act as if their nervous systems craved that utterly unstimulated condition which Freud once sketched as the epitome of neural bliss . . . if these same [people] be granted their Nirvana they soon become miserable and begin to look around for a little excitement." Even chimpanzees in laboratories will open hasps, not only when they are hungry and receive food for doing so, but also, it seems, simply because they want something to do until they grow tired of doing it. Hasp opening is a competence as well as a means to the economic end of getting food. It is enjoyable, presumably, as no more than a way of feeling alive by willing one's body to make an impact on its environment. Like interpreting literature or stamping in puddles, it can be done "for its own sake," without any productive end whatever in mind. Moreover, according to White, the college boy greeting his date with the hope of seeing how far he can get with her is, broadly speaking, not very different from the well-fed,

---

[10] Thomas Carlyle, *Sartor Resartus,* in *English Prose of the Victorian Era,* ed. Charles Frederick Harrold and William D. Templeman (New York: Oxford University Press, 1938), pp. 130-31; John Ruskin, "Unto This Last," in *English Prose of the Victorian Era,* pp. 923-24.

hasp-opening ape. His motive is not the persistence of inconvenient and uncomfortable physiological arousal, but an impulse to test his persuasive competence, and his real love is probably boasting of it among his fraternity brothers.[11]

Whether we speak of satisfying the "soul" as Carlyle does; of satisfying the need for "meaning" as modern usage both in and out of the behavioral sciences does; of satisfying the "will to power," as Nietzsche does, of expressing "competence," as White has; or of giving vent to an "instinct of workmanship," as Veblen does, we are acknowledging the irreducible aggressiveness of behavior.[12] We are acknowledging that to live is to produce an environmental impact, and we are recognizing that everything—including other human beings, and even including the human agent's own, homeostatically stable, symptom-free, idle body—everything is potentially subject to a human agent's aggression, competence, or will.

Once the aggressiveness of all behavior is admitted, one might begin a hypothesis about the way in which Western culture has channeled man's aggressive competence by noting the likelihood that every human being born experiences his first reasonably reliable competence as a newborn infant when his vocal cries bring on the attention of adults. If this is true, every human being who survives infancy controls other human beings vocally before he controls anything else by any other means. Thus, we all enter the human sphere of action—the social sphere which alone is capable of responding to language— long before we are competent to enter the nonhuman sphere—the economic sphere involving aggressive, productive control over objects not capable of responding to language, the sphere of dumb animals, and mute vegetables and minerals.[13] In short, if we escape infanticide, and if the economically productive

[11] Robert W. White, "Motivation Reconsidered: The Concept of Competence," *Psychological Review* 66 (1959): 297-333.

[12] See Ernest Becker, *The Birth and Death of Meaning: A Perspective in Psychiatry and Anthropology* (New York: Free Press of Glencoe, 1962); Murray Edelman, *Politics as Symbolic Action: Mass Arousal and Quiescence*, Institute for Research on Poverty Monograph Series (Chicago: Markham, 1971), especially pp. 31-33; Friedrich Nietzsche, *Beyond Good and Evil*, in *The Modern Tradition: Backgrounds of Modern Literature*, ed. Richard Ellmann and Charles Fiedelson, Jr. (New York: Oxford University Press, 1965), pp. 772-79; David Riesman, *Thorstein Veblen: A Critical Interpretation* (New York: Seabury, 1960), pp. 60-63.

[13] See Hannah Arendt, *The Human Condition* (Chicago: University of Chicago Press, 1958). She implies the distinction employed here between labor for the maintenance of bodily homeostasis against nonhuman objects, and work and action against human objects through speech and (if necessary) through war. Her lamentation over the passing of ancient social philosophies and of the societies presumably based upon them, and her failure to develop the idea that "speech is what makes man a political being" (p. 3), in my judgment, compromise the book.

adults among whom we are born deign to allow us a subsistence out of what they produce, we all begin life like little aristocrats—like rudimentary beneficiaries of Europe's *ancien régime,* its rulers, and their leisured symbionts; and history suggests that abandoning such a way of life to become productive, oneself, in the nonhuman sphere, is as difficult and painful for cultures as it is for individuals. Morally attractive as it might seem for each of us to choose life as a self-sufficient hermit, subsisting off the nonhuman world, and leaving the human world free of his will, no human being, at birth, has the strength, coordination, quickness, suppleness, endurance, and knowledge of how the nonhuman world works to be able to survive on his own. For the newborn, the injured, the sick, the aged, and the aristocrat, survival depends on competence in the vocal manipulation of whomever among productive individuals will listen and try to understand. For all human beings, getting the attention of others is the first matter of life and death; consequently, therefore, one of the greatest of anthropological, sociological, and historical questions is that of how speakers have gone about the task of interrupting the activities of other potential speakers and turning them into cooperative listeners.

Common knowledge of what it is to mature in different cultures reveals a variety of ways in which individuals and groups manage their biologically and socially inevitable passages back and forth between attempts at competence in the human and in the nonhuman spheres of action—between making productive people pay attention and developing one's own productive competences. Some cultures encourage or demand of every mature individual that he be competent in both spheres. The Maoist insistence that mature, urban intellectuals and planners experience periods of physical labor in the country, and that mature laborers experience periods of serious ideological debate and planning, pre-sumably so that each has felt something of the resistances faced by the other, is an attempt at such a cultural arrangement. In the West, another such attempt was the insistence of the later Habsburgs that their children, who would inherit the Austro-Hungarian empire, must learn some manual trade. As a general rule, however, things have been otherwise in the West. A mature European has not been one who can easily and contentedly pass over from verbal manipulation of other people into nonverbal manipulation of nonhuman objects. Maturing in European culture has, rather, been a process of refining the child's primal competence in vocally exploiting the attentions of others. For us, as for many other cultures, it has not been the self-sufficient hermit (from whom all others are free), but the rhetorically effective talker (who "enthralls" his listeners), who is genuinely mature. And to be not only mature, but great, in the West, is to have refined the primal child not only to the point of rhetorical competence, but to the point of military competence, at which one can find it in oneself to force bad listeners, who will not be rhetorically enthralled, to pay attention, to try to understand, and to comply; or to get out of the way or suffer in body for not listening.

Thus, for Plato, at the beginning of Western intellectual history, the willing passage from manipulating the human, social and political sphere of action to manipulating the nonhuman, economic sphere was the mark of a slave—of one who, facing death in battle, has made the craven choice to die at length, after enduring a lifetime of interruption by other humans and of the frustration, the humiliation, and fatigue of moving mute, dumb resistances, rather than choosing to risk immediate death, in battle, as a free man facing the ultimate resistance to one's will to be heard.[14] It is one of history's more macabre ironies that the West, which from the beginning could seriously consider the risk of violent death as the sole "viable" alternative to a lifetime of productive drudgery, should thus have motivated itself not only to have conquered the world, but also to dream of, and eventually to accomplish, an industrial revolution. If we have been unusually productive of labor-saving technologies, it is because, as a culture, we hate the laborious life with an apparently unique intensity. We hate it even as we hate death.

Maturing in the West, then, as I have said, was originally thought of as a process of refining upon our primal, vocal competence in interrupting the activities of others, seizing their attentions, and motivating them to produce us a surplus by laboring in the nonhuman sphere of action—the economic sphere, which no child is competent to enter productively enough to survive. Through interaction, during the first six-odd years of life, with a household and with various neighbors, the Western infant's cry has always been refined into a more or less commanding dialect of a more of less commanding European language. Then not long after the age of seven, in preindustrial England at least, formal schooling would further refine the dialects of the few children who did not immediately enter upon a lifetime of labor.[15] Rhetorically trained, the speech of the successfully schooled Westerner would take on the procedures of data collection, data manipulation, and expression characteristic of the ruling class, both when that class is defining reality among its peers (using the procedures of logic and, later, of science) and when it is interrupting others (rhetorically) to initiate labor against the reality so defined.

But preindustrial Europe never regarded logic and rhetoric as refinements enough on the primal, vocal competence to assure that potentially productive people would drop their own initiatives, pay attention to the schooled speaker, and then do as he told them to do. Our ancestors therefore required the mature speaker, ideally, to be able to appeal to the eyes as well as to the ears and to the beliefs of potential listeners. They expected him to display certain commanding

[14] *Great Dialogues of Plato,* trans. W. H. D. Rouse, ed. Eric H. Warmington and Philip G. Rouse (New York: New American Library, 1956), p. 183.

[15] See William Labov, *Sociolinguistic Patterns* (Philadelphia: University of Pennsylvania Press, 1972), p. 138; see Alan Macfarlane, *The Family Life of Ralph Josselin a Seventeenth-Century Clergyman: An Essay in Historical Anthropology* (Cambridge: University Press, 1970), pp. 205-10.

facial and bodily appearances which (as we shall see) contrasted strongly with the body types and kinesthetic bearings of people actually laboring against the brute resistances of the nonhuman. Moreover, as if to provide the mature speaker with an "overkill" of visible, nonverbal adjuncts to his logic and rhetoric, preindustrial Europe expected the greatest of mature speakers to display wealth—visible signs that all were to pay attention, but signs which did not depend on the great man's genetic inheritance or on his learned mastery of his body's potentials for speech and gesture. Thus, our ancestors clothed the great in rare, exotic, and meticulously worked materials, and they expected the great to live among liveried retinues of doting listeners in monumental works of architecture set in laboriously grown and maintained gardens. And if individuals and groups still would not listen to a speaker who displayed logic or science, rhetoric, bearing, costume, fine and decorative art, architecture, gardening, and retainers, Western culture expected the great man and his listeners to be able to force them to do so in battle.

In brief, the West, like all other cultures, has what we could call a culture of deference, which speakers hell-bent on being heard must master by learning, purchasing, or stealing as many as possible of the signs to which Westerners usually respond by keeping quiet, trying to understand, and complying, or by getting out of the way, or (finally) by resisting, rhetorically or militarily.

The perception of human potential upon which the management of interaction between individuals and their environments was first based, in the West, then, was like a child's apprehension of what spheres of action are open or closed to his competence. Like a child, our ancestors found the human sphere far more open to them than the nonhuman; for through the culture of deference, people can be taught to respond to vocal utterances far more easily than dumb nature, through technology, can be "taught" to respond to human muscle. In the beginning, therefore, as Father Ong has said, Western culture was "rhetorical culture."[16] The trivium of ancient liberal arts—grammar, logic, and rhetoric— was the basis of an education designed to help its initiates move people in a world where available mechanical advantages were relatively small, and where things had to be moved, when gravity, wind, and water proved fickle, by mortal muscles aching with incompetence—dying for glucose, oxygen, water, electrolytes, and the excretion of lactic acid while at work, and for the rest and nourishment to restore themselves. In its earliest, rhetorical phase, Western culture's common sense found it obvious that most people, most of the time, would suffer the bodily miseries of fatigue, malnutrition, disease, inclement weather, and even (though rarely) of invasion by the larger animal predators.[17] Rhetorical Europe raised its

[16] Walter J. Ong, S. J., *Rhetoric, Romance, and Technology: Studies in the Interaction of Expression and Culture* (Ithaca: Cornell University Press, 1971), p. 1.

[17] Fernand Braudel, *Capitalism and Material Life: 1400-1800,* trans. Miriam Kochan (New York: Harper, 1973), pp. 34-36.

young in the liberal arts rot wholly out of want of moral courage, but because its everyday experience told it that no one could command a hearing by offering laboring listeners a painless way to make life safe, warm, dry, clean, comfortable, easy, fat, and generally free of symptoms and of interruptions by others. Our ancestors knew that no one who claimed an easy competence over something like gravity, or distance, or disease could conceivably be worth listening to. The place of science in their culture of deference was humble indeed. Their literature, therefore, is full of mad scientists—the quacks of Webster, Molière, Swift, and Samuel Johnson come most quickly to mind—scientists whose madness consists not (in the manner of madness in modern science fiction) of using real discoveries about the nonhuman to exert military monopolies over the attentions of laymen, but of claiming to have discovered competences over the nonhuman to begin with. As late as the end of the eighteenth century, when French medicine, showing the mark of the Enlightenment, was abandoning the use of Latin and beginning to base diagnoses not only on verbal reports of symptoms but on actual examinations of the sick, the peasantry of Anjou, which had always been skeptical enough about the competence of university-trained physicians to maintain quacks and empirics of its own social standing, continued to avoid established doctors—now, precisely because the new style of doctor looked competent and refused to make sickness seem an eternal mystery involving God and the devil.[18]

Nevertheless, despite the entrenched belief that few improvements were to be expected in man's abilities to cope with the nonhuman, a long-contemplated revolution in the West's sense of humanity's alternatives achieved a sort of critical mass among the influential people of the later eighteenth century. What Fernand Braudel has called "the line of the possible" was redrawn by thinkers and men of action, and for the first time, a real, moral alternative to rhetorical culture as a means of pacifying the social process whereby those capable of production were made to produce a surplus to support those too weak or too powerful for productive labor appeared to be within reach.[19]

Things had apparently changed since Blaise Pascal, one of the great understanders of rhetorical culture, had written amid the remarkable cold, hunger, disease, warfare, and baroque grandeur of the European seventeenth century. "Concupiscence and force," Pascal writes, "are the source of all our actions." He means that in this laborious, fallen world, one can count on people to produce for others only when they fear punishment, or when they covet diversions, and superfluous, deference-producing, beautiful property as the rewards which put an end to labor. Pascal implies that, whatever God may have

[18] François Lebrun, *Les Hommes et la mort en Anjou aux XVIIe et XVIIIe siècles: Essai de demographie et de psychologie historiques* (Paris: Flammarion, 1975), pp. 283-84.

[19] Braudel, *Capitalism and Material Life,* p. ix.

meant, one cannot count on men to produce out of Christian charity. "All men naturally hate each other," he writes. "We have used concupiscence as best we can to make it serve the common good, but this is mere sham and a false image of charity, for essentially it is just hate."[20]

In the next century, however, the writers of the Enlightenment were more hopeful than Pascal had been. In the eighteenth century, death rates began declining. Populations began growing. The pain of sustaining life actually seemed to be diminishing. To the Enlightened, the eternal and unwilling economic struggle of covetous, craven, inept, ill-managed Western labor began looking as if, at last, it had won a rudimentary competence and established a beachhead in the nonhuman sphere of action. The scientist no longer seemed mad, and it seemed to Enlightened liberals that the rhetorical culture of the *ancien régime* could be swept away at last. It seemed that there was no need for speakers any longer to dazzle their listeners with rhetorical tropes and figures, with displays of wealth, and with shows of force, for now, speakers could hope to back their words with scientific demonstrations of easy new competences over immemorial nonhuman sources of pain and labor. Human beings acting on their own initiatives naturally hate to be interrupted, but the Enlightened were sure that any worker would welcome interruption and gladly fall silent to hear and see sound ways of increasing his consumption while actually shortening and lightening the productive, deferential process by which he would have to pay for increased consumption. Deferring to scientists and engineers, it appeared, would not be felt as an experience of social distance, and therefore could not be resented as such. Liberty, equality, and fraternity would characterize Enlightened, post-rhetorical interactions because insofar as these interactions remained hierarchical at all, they would subject one to deference only when a speaker was talking about the specialized field of the non-human in which he had an academically certified competence. And even then, one would listen with the love which students are commonly said to feel for their teachers. In brief, the Enlightened felt that the *ancien régime,* with its great redundancy of nonsubstantive status symbols, should give way to a new world, which would be run with displays of a single, new, substantive kind of status symbol: jargon.

Recent studies of the quality of life in the eighteenth century, however, have suggested that the grounds it offered for the unprecedented self-confidence of the Enlightenment may not have been as firm as they first appeared. William H. McNeill, for instance, has concluded that the "vital revolution" of the eighteenth century—the worldwide population explosion which began then, and which now threatens the survival of the human species—was indeed "an essential background for the popularization of 'Enlightened' philosophical and social

[20] Fernand Braudel, *The Mediterranean and the Mediterranean World in the Age of Philip II,* trans. Sian Reynolds (New York: Harper, 1972), I, 267-75; Blaise Pascal, *Pensées,* trans. A. J. Krailsheimer (Harmondsworth: Penguin Books, 1966), pp. 54, 97-98.

views." But McNeill believes that the vital revolution was "mostly due" not to eighteenth-century advances in medical competence, but to "ecological adjustments of which men were entirely unaware" at that time. He argues that "two great transportation revolutions—one by land, initiated by the Mongols, and one by sea [including the discovery of America], initiated by Europeans" brought about a worldwide "'domestication' of epidemic disease...between 1300 and 1700." Previously separate human populations, living, "after many generations," in "mutual adaptation" with different groups of "infectious organisms," came into contact with one another.[21] Four centuries of epidemics ensued as men and microbes not used to one another met. Then, but this time throughout the entire globe, the virulences of the surviving disease strains and the immunities and folkways of the surviving human hosts were mutually adapted once more.

Memorable as they are, the medical innovations of the English Enlightenment did not bring on the decline in mortality which brought about the new demographic profile of the eighteenth century. Thomas McKeown and R. G. Brown point out that the introduction of nitrous oxide as an anesthetic, in 1800, expanded the scope, but not the safety, of surgical operations. Between 1700 and 1800, the number of hospitals in England may have increased from five to "at least fifty," but in them, until there were good antiseptics, at least thirty-five to fifty percent of amputees died after surgery. In London, the first lying-in hospital was founded in 1749, but as late as 1871, Florence Nightingale could point out that mothers remaining at home to deliver their children were on the order of five times less likely to die than mothers availing themselves of the new hospitals. Since the mechanisms of disease remained unknown, the best that Enlightened English medical writers could do was to point out correlations between particular environments and particular diseases. But it was not until the end of the nineteenth century was near that (under the impetus of periodic transmissions of cholera from India to Europe and North America, and with the final evidence against the miasmal theory of contagion) governments began taking such basic actions as building plants to process urban water and sewage.[22]

Nor were the eighteenth century's undeniable advances in the production and distribution of consumer goods as revolutionary as once was thought. Many scholars, following the lead of Paul Mantoux, now point to an acceleration of technological, commercial, and financial life in England, a few conspicuous features of which (such as a growth in numbers of patents for industry and Acts of Enclosure for agriculture) can be dated near 1760. This is rather different, as T. S. Ashton suggests, from the schoolboy's conception of England as suddenly

---

[21] William H. McNeill, *Plagues and Peoples* (Oxford: Basil Blackwell, 1977), pp. 9-10, 224, 257.

[22] Thomas McKeown and R. G. Brown, "Medical Evidence Related to English Population Changes in the Eighteenth Century," *Population Studies* 9 (November 1955): 119-41; McNeill, pp. 235-91.

"swept by a wave of gadgets" in 1760. Indeed, Samuel Lilley, writing of the purely technological innovations of the Industrial Revolution, sees them "as a phase—a crucially important phase, but still only a phase—of a second Technological Revolution [in world history that] has been going on continuously from the early Middle Ages...." And insofar as the Industrial Revolution gave the Enlightenment evidence of its own success by raising the standard of consumption for all, it did not begin to do so until after the Napoleonic Wars—a full lifetime after the supposed revolution of 1760.[23]

The problem, in the words of M. W. Flinn, is that "there must [always] be entrepreneurs as well as inventors" for economic growth to take place. Both existed, contrary to Whig and Marxist views of history, in all of the *ancien régime's* social strata, yet it was exceedingly difficult for them to find each other. As Carlo Cipolla remarks, the financial problem of the *ancien régime* was to turn those with savings from "hoarders" into "investors." When William Russell succeeded his dead father as the fifth Earl of Bedford in 1641, his mother "formally handed over... the keys" to the family hoard—a "great trunk which stood in Bedford House... and served as the family bank." Paper money, lacking the aesthetic appeal of gold, was less attractive to hoarders, and was consequently one among an increasing number of goads to investment. Generally speaking, "the rise of the middle class" is an explanatory myth which obscures the obvious fact that aristocratic families which maintained the economic basis of their access to the culture of deference over long periods of time were constantly interested in making money out of their lands, and in other investments and speculations. As J. H. Hexter has said, aristocratic boozers and whoremasters have always been conspicuous, but they have never been normal, nor have they augured well for the future honor of their families. Land was the best collateral for loans in the preindustrial West, and the consequence of this fact is that in many cases an aristocrat's credit and his stylish willingness to take the great risk were the bases of entrepreneurship in the *ancien régime*. But it is not as an investor in a "process of economical heating" that modern middle-class historians are most apt to remember the likes of Madame de Maintenon.[24]

[23] Paul Mantoux, *The Industrial Revolution in the Eighteenth Century: An Outline of the Modern Factory System in England*, trans. Marjorie Vernon (1928; revised, London: Methuen, 1964); T. S. Ashton, *The Industrial Revolution 1760-1830* (1948; reprint, London: Oxford University Press, 1972), pp. 42, 99; Samuel Lilley, "Technological Progress and the Industrial Revolution 1700-1914," *The Fontana Economic History of Europe: The Industrial Revolution*, ed. Carlo M. Cipolla (Glasgow: Fontana/Collins, 1973), p. 187.

[24] M. W. Flinn, *Origins of the Industrial Revolution*, Problems and Perspectives in History, ed. H. F. Kearney (London: Longman, 1966), p. 70; Carlo M. Cipolla, *Before the Industrial Revolution: European Society and Economy, 1000-1700* (London: Methuen, 1976), pp. 38-43; Gladys Scott Thomson, *Life in a Noble Household 1641-1700* (1936;

The person of James Watt, the inventor of the steam engines that powered the Industrial Revolution after 1783, was "among the first" in economic history in whom experimental inventiveness met with administrative and entrepreneurial abilities. Before Watt, useful invention often went begging for capital or for acceptance by labor. "There were so many obstacles" to technical innovation, Fernand Braudel reports, "that we can agree with James Watt... 'that in life there is nothing more foolish than invention.'" In 1618, for instance, Jean Tardin published information about the possibility of gas lighting, but light from gas (distilled from coal or naturally occurring) is a nineteenth-century phenomenon. Or again, the principles of the electric telegraph were published in 1635, but not until rediscovered in 1819 did they become the basis for the instant communications of the modern world. Or finally, the Italian plans for the silk-throwing mill which became, in 1717, the first "true factory" in England had lain in the Bodleain library at Oxford for nearly a century before James Lombe returned to the River Derwent with them—not from Oxford, but from two years of industrial espionage in Italy.[25]

And just as the bringing together of technical competence and capital had not been as effectively institutionalized in the old world as it has since become, institutions for bringing new technologies comfortably together with the labor pool, still inadequate today, had hardly yet begun to appear. "Most people," Carlo Cipolla reminds us, "lived at a subsistence level. They had no savings and no social security to help them in case of distress. If they remained without work, their only hope of survival was charity... normally... noticeably more than one percent of gross national product." Justifiably, therefore, the laborer constantly feared technological unemployment. French printers' helpers went out on strike in the mid sixteenth century against new presses requiring fewer hands. And the preindustrial textile industry, Braudel records, because of "the elaborate division

---

reprint, Ann Arbor: University of Michigan Press, 1959), p. 41; J. H. Hexter, "The Myth of the Middle Class in Tudor England," *Reappraisals in History* (London: Longman, 1961), p. 79; Lawrence Stone, "The Nobility in Business, 1540-1640," *The Entrepreneur: Papers Presented at the Annual Conference of the Economic Society at Cambridge, England, April 1957*, ed. B. E. Supple (Research Center in Entrepreneurial History, Harvard University), 14-21; Braudel, *Capitalism and Material Life*, p. 323. See also Jerrilyn Greene Marston, "Gentry Honor and Royalism in Early Stuart England," *Journal of British Studies* 13 (1973): 28; H. J. Habakkuk, "Economic Functions of English Landowners in the Seventeenth and Eighteenth Centuries," *Explorations in Entrepreneurial History* 6 (December 1953): 92-102; and Fritz Redlich, "European Aristocracy and Economic Development," *Explorations in Entrepreneurial History* 6 (December 1953): 78-91.

[25] Ashton, pp. 24-25, 49; Braudel, *Capitalism and Material Life*, pp. 322-33; Cipolla, pp. 174-76.

of operations and the poverty of workers," experienced worse disruptions. Labor-saving innovations like the beetle (for cutting fabric) and James Kay's flying-shuttle (for weaving) were resisted because they eliminated workers once needed. As early as 1710, a century before the Luddism that followed industrialization, there was machine breaking in the English midlands.[26]

Pedagogical institutions for informing the world about new technologies were also lacking. Cipolla points out that James Lombe probably could not have learned to build a silk-throwing mill from the book that lay in the Bodleian library. He would have had to go to Italy anyway, just as today, "when a firm buys new and elaborate machinery it sends some of its workers to acquire, directly from the manufacturers, the knowledge of how to operate it." There were few professional engineers as such—Leonardo da Vinci is an example of how engineering came packaged with other competences—"Nor was there any systematic [technological] training before the eighteenth century." Technological innovations spread almost exclusively by means of the migrations of technicians, who were sometimes actually kidnapped. And while the English were very good at learning the skills of foreign-born technicians who came to live among them, other cultures, like the Turkish, have not been. Indeed, a frequent complaint of Enlightened Anglophiles in France was that the English yeoman and husbandman were infinitely more open to foreign improvements and to native experimentation in agriculture than was the stubborn and relatively unproductive French peasant. Still, despite the revolutionary character of its eighteenth-century agriculture, England in the 1880s became, and has remained, a net importer of food, and English agriculture was not effectively mechanized until the present century.[27]

If life was improving in the eighteenth century, then, it was not entirely because of Enlightened man's innovations in coping with the nonhuman. Nevertheless, as they perhaps always had been, Western intellectuals were looking for evidence that the "line of the possible" could be redrawn, and that, consequently, rhetorical culture and the whole *ancien régime* of religion, property, and force which backed it could be dismantled.

From the beginning, rhetoric, a hallmark of the educated man, had always been *faute de mieux*—a way of moving people who ought to (but who do not) listen to

[26] Cipolla, pp. 19, 22-23; Braudel, *Capitalism and Material Life*, p. 322; Ashton, p. 25; George Rudé, *The Crowd in History: A Study of Popular Disturbances in France and England 1730-1848* (New York: John Wiley, 1964), p. 81.

[27] Cipolla, pp. 176, 179-81; Braudel, *Capitalism and Material Life*, p. 322; Pierre Goubert, *Louis XIV and Twenty Million Frenchmen*, trans. Anne Carter (New York: Vintage Books, 1970), pp. 32-33; G. E. Mingay, *The Gentry: The Rise and Fall of a Ruling Class*, Themes in British Social History, ed. J. Stevenson (London: Longman, 1976), pp. 168-73.

reason. In the *Gorgias,* Plato blackens the name of the Sophists for having taught rhetoric. "As self-adornment is to gymnastic, so is sophistry to legislation; and as cookery is to medicine, so is rhetoric to justice," Plato argues. For him, rhetoric "has no account to give of the real nature of the things it applies," and is therefore inferior to logical dialectic. His pupil, Aristotle, denies that dialectic and rhetoric can be as sharply distinguished as Plato implies. Moreover, for Aristotle, "scientific exposition is in the nature of teaching, and teaching is out of the question [with some people, to whom] we must give our proofs and tell our story in popular terms." For centuries, philosophers tried and failed to agree how logic could be purged of obscurity without dwindling into rhetoric, and how "mere rhetoric" could be purged of its manipulative immorality without taking on the obscurity of logic and losing its mass persuasiveness. Thus, throughout the epoch of rhetorical culture, there was an unhappy cohabitation of logic and rhetoric, which many thinkers grudgingly accepted as inevitable, and which all would willingly have ended. In the Middle Ages, St. Augustine and many others followed Aristotle's general line of thinking on the matter. In book 4 of *De Doctrina Christiana,* for instance, Augustine asks, "who would dare to say that [God's] truth should stand in the person of its defenders unarmed against lying, so that they who wish to urge falsehoods may know how to make their listeners benevolent, or attentive, or docile [with rhetoric], while defenders of truth are ignorant of that art?" And Peter France, summarizing the seventeenth-century French Jansenist position on pulpit rhetoric, further indicates the durability of an Aristotelian pragmatism about the matter: "In a fallen world persuasion inevitably involved the use of irrational means."[28]

Meanwhile, among those who disliked rhetorical culture's manipulative quality, but who were less fatalistic about the necessity for nonrational persuasion, the naive empiricism which became a characteristic of the Enlightenment was emerging. The Enlightenment offered science as the final solution to the eternal problem of candidly getting the uncultivated, laboring masses to listen to the few speakers in possession of the truth. Late in the sixteenth century, citing the authority of Socrates, Seneca, and Cicero, Montaigne wrote that "anyone who has a clear and vivid idea in his mind" can communicate it without the rhetorician's "fine tricks [which] serve only to divert the vulgar [and which] are easily eclipsed by the light of a simple, artless truth." Montaigne here rejects what W. S. Howell has called the "stylistic" rhetoricians of his age, who took it for granted that "the vulgar" would not pay attention to anybody who

[28] Plato, *Gorgias,* trans. W. R. M. Lamb, in *Readings in Classical Rhetoric,* ed. Thomas W. Benson and Michael H. Prosser (Bloomington: Indiana University Press, 1969), pp. 3-21; Aristotle, *The Rhetoric,* trans. Richard Claverhouse Jebb, in *Readings in Classical Rhetoric,* p. 55; St. Augustine, *On Christian Doctrine,* trans. D. W. Robertson, Jr., in *Readings in Classical Rhetoric,* pp. 134-35; Peter France, *Rhetoric and Truth in France: Descartes to Diderot* (Oxford: Clarendon Press, 1972), p. 118.

talked as they did themselves. Among English stylistic rhetoricians, George Puttenham cautions not only against sounding too learned, but above all against sounding like "poore rusticall or vnciuill people [such as] a craftes man or carter, or other of the inferiour sort, [who] do abuse good speaches by strange accents or ill shapen soundes, and false ortographie."[29] Stylistic rhetoric, therefore, consisted of adorning one's truth with tropes and figures, spoken in the dialect of the court, to distinguish it lexically, syntactically, and phonologically from the way it might sound if spoken by a worker. But Montaigne implies that if one's message really is the "simple, artless truth," even "the vulgar" will be gratefully attentive and finally edified by its obviousness, no matter how one speaks it. The key to the gross national attention, in other words, is the obvious practicality and empirical demonstrability of the message—not the nonsubstantive, purely formal elegance of its style.[30]

In England, one of Montaigne's most distinguished readers was Francis Bacon, perhaps the most influential of all subverters of rhetorical culture. Addressing his sovereign about the need for an advancement of learning, Bacon was suspicious of philosophy invented to be a refuge from the material world. He wanted learning to be practical, if not downright commercial—to be "a rich storehouse for the glory of the Creator and the relief of man's [economic] estate." The Renaissance, Bacon felt, in effect, had recovered the stylistic vices of ancient rhetoric, and the theological debates of the Reformation had spread these vices everywhere:

> Because the great labour [of contending Protestant and Catholic preachers during the Reformation] was with the people, (of whom the Pharisees were wont to say, the wretched crowd that has not known the law,) for the winning and persuading of them, there grew of necessity in chief price and request eloquence and variety of discourse, as the fittest and forciblest access into the capacity of the vulgar sort.... This grew speedily to excess; for men [like Puttenham] began to hunt more after words than matter.

Still, Bacon was confident that if popularizing theology had necessarily produced an escalation of stylistic rhetoric, the advancement of science could reverse the process to the benefit of all. Working scientifically, the mind of man might "work upon matter, which is the contemplation of the creatures of God," and its wanderings might be limited by matter more obviously and convincingly than the pure logic of theology and casuistry had been able to limit them. Therefore,

[29] George Puttenham, *The Arte of English Poesie,* ed. Gladys Doidge Willcock and Alice Walker (Cambridge: University Press, 1936), p. 144.

[30] Michel de Montaigne, "On the Education of Children," in *Essays,* trans. J. M. Cohen (Harmondsworth: Penguin Books, 1958), p. 77. See also Wilbur Samuel Howell, *Logic and Rhetoric in England, 1500-1700* (1956; reprint, New York: Russell and Russell, 1961), p. 328.

the tropes and figures with which the stylistic rhetoricians encumbered theology and casuistry to make the vulgar listen would be unnecessary. In short, except in empirically unresolvable disputes about first causes, Bacon was confident that the language of science would at last end the unhappy cohabitation of logic and rhetoric of which Western intellectuals, since Plato, had constantly complained.[31] Hence, before the seventeenth century had ended, by suggesting that practical talk about the materially obvious was both possible and irresistible as a candid means of nonviolent social management, Bacon became a national and international culture-hero. Proposals like his for the advancement of empirical learning proliferated, found royal favor in England, and captured Enlightened minds on the continent.

Among the best-known indicators of the Enlightened hope that science could offer a moral alternative to rhetorical culture is Thomas Sprat's *History of the Royal Society* (1667). Sprat praises the members of England's royally sanctioned scientific organization for having been "most solicitous [of] the manner of their discourse: which [otherwise] had been soon eaten out by the luxury and redundance of eloquence [which] ought to be banished out of all civil societies, as a thing fatal to peace and good manners." For Sprat, the greatest contribution of the Royal Society to the pacification of human interaction was to have "exacted from all their members a close, naked, natural way of speaking, positive expressions, clear senses, a native easiness; bringing all things as near the mathematical plainness as they can, and preferring the language of artisans, countrymen, and merchants before that of wits or scholars."[32]

The Baconian tradition was an important part of the French Enlightenment's *anglomanie* and egalitarianism, for Baconians conceived of the advancement of science as necessarily involving an egalitarian establishment of familiarity between the concerns of the never-laboring, aristocratic, verbally oriented intellectual, and the nonverbal concerns of the despised mechanic.[33] If science were to replace logic, eliminating the hateful, eternal need for rhetoric, Western high culture would need to lose its squeamishness about physical labor, about

[31] Francis Bacon, "First Book of Francis Bacon of the Proficience and Advancement of Learning Divine and Human," in *Francis Bacon,* ed. Arthur Johnston (New York: Schocken Books, 1965), pp. 35-37, 43-44.

[32] Thomas Sprat, "The History of the Royal Society," in *Restoration Literature: Poetry and Prose 1660-1700,* ed. Cecil A. Moore (New York: Appleton-Century-Crofts, 1934), pp. 180-81.

[33] H. F. Kearney, "Puritanism, Capitalism and the Scientific Revolution," *Past and Present,* 28 (July 1964): 81-101, has argued that in fact the growth of early science was not motivated by immediate, practical, economic concerns. The major advances, he believes, "were in fact the achievement of a handful of men, Gilbert, Briggs, Gunter, Gellibrand, Wilkins, Barlow, Wallis, Wright, Oughtred and a few others. None of these were artisans, although they did find the assistance of instrument makers essential" (p. 93).

picking the minds of those who have done it, and about reasoning with them on the ground of the newfound common interest of labor and management in easing the manipulation of the nonhuman. There could be no more *dérogeance*. The Enlightened would no longer permit the French nobility to belittle those who publicly took a scientist's interest in how the world worked, a technician's interest in making science productive, or a businessman's interest in marketing the fruits of technology. In his *Essay on the Interrelations of Men of Letters with the Great,* the encyclopedist D'Alembert complains of his noble countrymen's reservations about protecting their intellectual betters. "In England," he writes, "people were content that Newton should have been the greatest geometrician of his century; but in France, we would have wanted him charming as well." The time for the technocrat to replace the aristocrat had come, and de Jaucourt, the author of the *Encyclopédie's* article on the French language, found it "shameful" that jargon should any longer be proscribed from the conversation of the ruling class—"that people today do not dare to mix French, properly spoken, with the terms of the arts and the sciences, and that a man of the Court forbids himself to know what would be useful and honorable to him."[34]

The Baconian belief that all men would willingly unite to promote relatively painless human dominance over the nonhuman, then, became an important basis for intellectual and aristocratic participation in the egalitarianism of the French Revolution. Morse Peckham's notion of the "cultural vandal" is admirably applicable to the Revolution's leaders.[35] They acted upon an ancient hope that hard, intersubjectively demonstrable, empirical facts—"simple, artless truths" (to return to Montaigne's phrase)—could move men to produce for everyone's material benefit if only rhetorical culture could be demolished.

But even before the Reign of Terror in 1793, there were those who accused Enlightened radicals of not knowing what was possible. "Already," Edmund Burke wrote in 1790, "there appears a poverty of conception, a coarseness and vulgarity, in all the proceedings of the [French] Assembly and of all their instructors [the Enlightened *philosophes*]. Their liberty is not liberal [and] their science is presumptuous ignorance...." No matter what the cultural vandals of the Revolution might claim, the attack of the Paris mob on Versailles, on 6 October 1789, convinced Burke that the masses were not alive with repressed ideas for revolutionizing production, and with it the quality of material and social life for all. They were simply alive with hatred for those with power to interrupt them and change their ways; and (much as Pascal had said of their ancestors) they still had to be approached by the insistent, Enlightened technocrat just as the benighted aristocrat had always approached them—either with violence, or

[34] Quotations from France, pp. 68, 72 (my translation).

[35] Morse Peckham, "Romanticism and Behavior," in *Romanticism and Behavior: Collected Essays, II* (Columbia: University of South Carolina Press, 1976), pp. 22-26.

with the "pleasing illusions" (as Burke calls them) of rhetorical culture. These, Burke felt, had been vandalized by speculative philosophers who lacked the experience of government necessary to bring it home to them that these illusions provided the most reliable nonviolent means of making France pay attention. Thus, "All the pleasing illusions, which made power gentle and obedience liberal...are to be dissolved by this new conquering empire of light and reason. All the decent drapery of life..., furnished from the wardrobe of a moral imagination,...as necessary to cover the defects of our naked, shivering nature, and to raise it to dignity in our estimation, [is] to be exploded as a ridiculous, absurd, and antiquated fashion." Without the pleasing, pacifying illusions of rhetorical culture, "at the end of every vista" in the academic groves of the radical Enlightenment, "you see nothing but the gallows." With these old illusions, however, Burke trusted that France "would have had a protected, satisfied, laborious, and obedient people, taught to seek...the true moral equality of mankind, and not that monstrous fiction, which...serves only to aggravate and embitter that real inequality, which it can never remove [between] those whom [the order of civil life] must leave in an humble state, [and] those whom it is able to exalt to a condition more splendid, but not more happy."[36]

These passages from Burke's *Reflections on the Revolution in France* essentially view Pascal's bleak concupiscence through rose-colored glasses. For Burke, people work not because they enjoy being productive, but because they covet the illusion that perpetual, aristocratic release from labor into apparent leisure and luxury constitutes happiness. It seems to have been clear to Burke, therefore, that either the ruling class must present itself to working people as the incarnation of labor's desires, or it must simply force labor to produce. Hence, it is not the guile of their rulers, but the imagination of the oppressed themselves, that has conjured up the odd symbiosis which constitutes the Western culture of deference—the symbiosis of conspicuous leisure and consumption with hidden managerial work. In effect, Burke acknowledges that by any absolute standard of rationality the *ancien régime* is institutionalized irrationality; but he venerates this irrationality because the irrationally concupiscent laboring poor, to the extent that they envy the idle rich and confuse them with the managerial class, resist their real rulers that much less effectively, thus making management possible.

In many of the more familiar passages of his conversation and writing, Burke's sometime associate, Samuel Johnson, also insists on the pragmatic inevitability of an irrational culture of deference in which confusion between pleasing illusions and personal merit has been institutionalized. In chatting about Rousseau, Johnson assumes (like Pascal) that hatred is at least as predictable a

[36] Edmund Burke, *Reflections on the Revolution in France,* in *Eighteenth Century Poetry and Prose,* ed. Louis T. Bredvold, Alan D. McKillop, and Lois Whitney, 3rd ed., (New York: Ronald, 1973), pp. 1158, 1156-57, 1144.

response to competence, or personal merit, as are admiration and emulation. Like Burke, Johnson grants to egalitarians that man's needs for the superfluous consumption which signals status and promotes deference are "artificial"— "nonfunctional," we might more carelessly say, today. Six pounds a year, Johnson estimates, "will fill your belly, shelter you from the weather and even get you a strong and lasting coat ... of good bull's hide." But these same six pounds leave absolutely untouched one's need for deference—for "a greater degree of respect from our fellow creatures." Nor could one supply that need, Johnson implies, by saving on purchases of luxury and ease, and investing simply in displays of productive competence. "In barbarous society," Johnson remarks during his first meeting with James Boswell, "great strength or great wisdom is of much value to an individual. But in more polished times ... there are a number of other [apparently nonfunctional] superiorities, such as those of birth and fortune, and rank, that dissipate man's attention, and leave no extraordinary share of respect for personal and intellectual superiority." This apparently inequitable confusion between achieved and ascribed "superiorities," Johnson concludes, "is wisely ordered by Providence to preserve some equality among mankind." In other words, the dissipation of attention from merit, though unjust, is necessary to the pacification of interaction in a fallen world because it can also be a dissipation of hatred from merit. The unequal distribution of status symbols which are not themselves competences mitigates the tyranny of the competent over the incompetent and acts as a sort of lightening rod. It attracts the envy of the justly unrewarded incompetent to the incompetent who is unjustly rewarded, thus providing a measure of protection for the competent, who, as Johnson writes, have "given no provocation to malice, but by attempting to excel," and who, in a strict meritocracy, would be nakedly exposed to suspicion, calumny, and scandal emanating from the incompetent, in his "torpid and quiescent state, amid the gloom of stupidity, in the coverts of cowardice."[37]

Moreover, I might add by way of elaboration on Johnson's social philosophy, the institutionalized incoherence of merit and superiorities provides a ground in actual social experience (a ground unavailable in an absolute meritocracy) upon which the unrewarded—both the competent and the incompetent—can build some measure, however imperfect, of self-esteem. If competences and rewards are sufficiently out of phase, the incompetent need not measure themselves against the obvious achievements of the competent, who alone have been rewarded. The unrewarded incompetent can see other incompetents who have been rewarded and hence, can feel not worthless but merely unlucky. Similarly, the presence of rewarded incompetence teaches the unrewarded talent that he need not doubt his own value merely because others do not recognize it.

[37] James Boswell, *The Life of Samuel Johnson, LL.D.*, in *Eighteenth Century Poetry and Prose*, p. 890, 900; Samuel Johnson, *The Rambler*, in *Eighteenth Century Poetry and Prose*, pp. 726-28.

Recognition, he can see, is only a lottery. And finally, in theory, at least, if there is enough institutionalized injustice, the rewarded incompetent is given experiential grounds for guilt—a feeling which can turn him into an aristocratic patron, who seeks to exculpate himself by investing his undeserved rewards in undiscovered talents, thus giving them, for better or worse, the power to make their marks upon the human and nonhuman spheres of action. Thus does institutionalized injustice provide some empirical grounds for all of the prejudices and rationalizations which maintain the self-esteem of the incompetent and the poor.

The Johnsonian contention that an institutionalized incoherence between productive competence and observable consumption is providential is, of course typical of an age when philosophers could still claim that this was "the best of all possible worlds," and when a poet could announce that "whatever is, is right." What distinguishes this preindustrial conservatism from today's conservatism, however, is the constant awareness that the world which was—though the best possible—was far from being the best imaginable. The best imaginable world, from the viewpoint of preindustrial high culture, was a world without an aristocracy; but one had to know the aristocratic life, from the inside, to believe that this could be so. From the viewpoint of the preindustrial laborer (as the *ancien régime* saw him) a life without labor or the hateful interruptions of bosses—an aristocrat's apparent life—was the best imaginable. To lose the leisure class, for this hypothetical laborer, was to lose all hope of earthly happiness—all evidence that one could be free of the managerial class. One needed to be not a water carrier in the streets of Paris, but a Voltaire in retirement at Ferney, to believe that the bored insatiability of Pococuranté, the Venetian nobleman in *Candide,* was the likely outcome of an aristocratic freedom from the most desperate obligations to integrate one's competences into the economy. For Pococuranté, as for the middle-class decadent of the late nineteenth century, "the flesh is sad, alas! and I have read all the books." He has known every experience that people regard as rich and rewarding: sex, literature, art, music, philosophy—everything but competent labor in the nonhuman sphere of action, about which the high culture is silent because competent labor seemed virtually unimaginable in the preindustrial West.[38]

### III.

The historical theories of the rise of the middle class and of the Industrial Revolution convince us that we are free at last of the rhetorical ethos of the *ancien régime,* but recent trends in the social sciences and the everyday

---

[38] See Voltaire, *Candide: or Optimism,* trans. Robert M. Adams (New York: W. W. Norton, 1966), pp. 61-65.

experience of millions of people suggest that we are not. Increasingly, the traditional sociological and historical terms for human relationships—terms such as *class, status, power, position, function, struggle, stratification, equality,* or even *work* and *leisure*—have come to sound like empty hypostatizations. Sometimes, the adjectives *political, economic,* and *social* are treated as synonyms; and then, sometimes, they are used to indicate ill-defined distinctions between different kinds of human conduct. Recently, however, scholars in various disciplines of inquiry have converged upon the realization that language is what makes human conduct human.

Accordingly, these pages have suggested that the driving forces in political, social, economic, and intellectual history are the needs not only to produce and improve the means of bodily survival, but also to produce and improve the means of making language work. These constitute a continuum of signs conventionally recognized in the Western culture of deference: signs that one either has or has not the right to be heard and obeyed. The categories of sign involved would appear to be these: logically or scientifically precise language; rhetoric (including dialect); kinesic bearing (including age, sex, and race); costume; setting (including architecture, fine and decorative art, and retinues of peers and subordinates who give one access to the public either through media, including the verbal arts, or through force of arms); and finally, legal access to what Peckham has called "the ultimate sanction of meaning"—the right to inflict deprivation, torture, death, or imprisonment on bad listeners.

This continuum has a "cultural" pole (logic or science), a "political" pole (the right to force), and has a range of "social" sign-categories (rhetoric, bearing, costume, and setting). Every category of sign in the Western culture of deference is underwritten by economic productivity—by labor's appropriation of nature, whether it be in support of scientific laboratories for the production of jargon, of dancing classes for the refinement of bearing, or even of such closely related deference-promoting activities as wig making and the deployment of intercontinental ballistic missiles. The political Left generally wishes to see the social range of deference signs selectively or radically discredited under cultural reinterpretation, supported (if necessary) by political force. And the political Right generally wishes culture, supported (if necessary) by politics, selectively or radically to validate the social range of deference signs.

As I have said, a hope, generally quite faint, has existed throughout the intellectual history of the West that language could be reformed so that human interaction could be guided by precise logical or scientific language alone, unsupported by the social and political range of deference signs. As scientific explanation gained official acceptance, the Enlightened often thought that it would produce such simple, artless truths that most listeners could not help being persuaded by them. Hence, rhetoric, bearing, costume, setting, and legal force would all simply wither away. But in fact, science has produced bewildering

volumes of neologisms to which most of us are at least as incapable of responding as Aristotle said the ancient masses were of responding to logic. To talk sense in the modern, professionalized world is to be greeted with the blank stares and fidgeting of listeners outside one's field, and even of some within it.

Israel Gerver and Joseph Bensman, while not stressing language in their sociology of expertise, have called speakers of the modern, professionalized truth "substantive experts," and have implied that for substantive language to have any sort of impact on mass attention, and hence on the human and nonhuman spheres of action, it must first gain a hearing among two other kinds of experts—the "interpretive" and the "administrative"—who then respeak it to the masses.[39] In the terms of this essay, the position of Gerver and Bensman is that pure logical or scientific language must be accompanied and, as it were, contaminated by rhetoric, and even by the more bluntly social and political adjuncts of rhetoric in the culture of deference, if laymen are to listen and workers are to act upon it. The category of laymen, of course, now includes most kinds of experts in substantive fields other than that of the speaker.

The characteristic of the interpretive expert is that his "stature is granted by the layman, whereas the substantive experts devalue him as a popularizer at best and a vulgarizer at worst." This means, in effect, that without the science reporter to translate for him, to wear a business suit for him, and to gain access to the visible and audible media for him, Einstein would remain, for even more people than now probably remember him as such, an incomprehensible longhair in a sweatshirt—or worse. With the interpretive expertise of the science reporter, however, or of the schoolteacher, Einstein can become a culture-hero—one of Gerver's and Bensman's "symbolic experts," who "personify and symbolize expertise in a given complex field for the uninitiated public," even if that public understands only the results, and has no grasp of the beautiful procedures of the symbolic expert's work.[40]

Administrative experts are usually substantively trained, as interpretive experts may also be, but they "co-ordinate, facilitate, recruit, and arrange the activities of [substantive and interpretive experts] in a formal association in order to execute agreed-upon policies." It is administrative expertise, in other words, which puts substantive utterances to work by translating them into job definitions and deadlines for other experts and for labor. In doing so, however, administrators tend to be seen by substantive experts as "derivative incompetents or restrictive agents, who take credit for substantive work which they both hinder and misunderstand"—especially when they press the substantive expert for results. And because the substantive expert, in post-romantic culture, basks in

[39] Israel Gerver and Joseph Bensman, "Towards a Sociology of Expertness," *Social Forces*, 32 (1953), 226-35.
[40] Gerver and Bensman, 227, 229.

the glory of symbolic expertise and vicariously enjoys the cachet of culture-heroes, the modern administrator is "in an anomalous position [in which] the established legitimacy of his subordinates is a barrier to his own." This, the sociologist G. C. Homans has predicted, is precisely the sort of situation in which purely symbolic status displays are most likely to become necessities of administration. It may be necessary for the administrator, so to speak, to call the substantive expert from his cluttered laboratory onto the wall-to-wall carpet beneath the administrator's large, expensive, and essentially empty desk.[41]

The professionalized, pedantic truth alone cannot win its way with the attentions and comprehensions of lay listeners, as Alexander Pope's *Essay on Criticism* (1711) warns:

> 'Tis not enough, your counsel still be true;
> Blunt truths more mischief than nice falsehoods do;
> Men must be taught as if you taught them not,
> And things unknown proposed as things forgot.
> Without good breeding, truth is disapproved;
> That only makes superior sense beloved.[42]

Pope's remarks are squarely in the rhetorical tradition of the *ancien régime*—the tradition of which we have already heard D'Alembert complain apropos of Newton. They suggest that whether we like it or not, the language of high culture always fails to win a good hearing unless it is supported by the social range of deference signs in which administrators and interpreters must be expert, and which begins with rhetoric.

Rhetoric, though always "mere" in comparison with logical or scientific utterance in Western intellectual history, is nevertheless unavoidable. Indeed, a cynic might say that logic is merely the rhetoric with which one must approach an audience of logicians, and that science is the rhetoric with which one must approach an audience of scientists. Rhetoric is always "mere" because it has frequently been willing to compromise the speaker's precise conviction for the sake of making some approximation of it acceptable, and, if possible, under-standable, to a particular audience with known prejudices and verbal expectations. Rhetoric is disciplined and rehearsed gossip. It is the basic activity of the modern world's teachers and administrators, if not of its laborers and academicians; and as I have suggested, in the fallen preindustrial world, rhetoric and its various social and political adjuncts virtually exhausted Western man's

---

[41] Gerver and Bensman, 227, 230, 231; George Caspar Homans, *Social Behavior: Its Elementary Forms,* revised edition (New York: Harcourt Brace Jovanovich, 1974), p. 213.

[42] Alexander Pope, *An Essay on Criticism,* in *Eighteenth Century Poetry and Prose,* p. 529, 11. 572-77.

sense of what competence could be. In those days, one began by moving people with words because words came more easily than the means of moving mute, dumb things.

How rhetoric moves people is a fascinating subject upon which the new disciplines of psycholinguistics and sociolinguistics are shedding light—or are recovering, apropos of modern society, the light shed centuries ago by the classical rhetoricians. What they seem to have sensed is that even though everyone learns to talk, most people's talk seldom makes perceptibly more sense than the talk of most others, and is seldom formally distinguished from the talk of most others by greater lengths of utterance, clearer syntactic continuity, and more apparent consciousness of segmental and suprasegmental · phonemic rhythms. Most of us find unrehearsed, extemporaneous speech hard to sustain. We quickly run out of appropriate clichés. We make false syntactic starts, abort sentences begun, and, while grunting out pause-words, we grope for a word or a grammatical pattern that might work. We are petrified at the prospect of simply falling silent while others expect us to go on; and we know that we are never far from it. Rhetoric teaches the speaker to capitalize on the normal fears of the other potential speakers who are listening to him. Where they hear themselves as stammering fumblers after words, they must hear him as spontaneous and fluent. Where they suffer poverty of expression, he must obviously enjoy what the classical rhetoricians called *copia,* the abundance of expression. And if he was drilled in the commonplaces of "invention," in "arranging" the arguments invented, in embellishing them with words chosen according to the tropes, and with sentences patterned on the figures of "elocution"—if he was drilled in the art of "remembering" the utterance thus composed, and finally, if he was drilled in "delivery" (in voice production and in facial and bodily gesture), he could expect the rhetorically incompetent to pay him some attention—even if it were the attention of the unconvinced, who, as Peter France says, "step back mentally and admire the orator instead of really absorbing his message."[43]

Nothing the rhetorically trained speaker can do, however, can move all potential hearers of a public address, or can prevent some of them from taking this mental step back, or (if some members of the audience are determined enemies of the collective action his words are intended to promote) can absolutely prevent them from interrupting his rhetorical performance with objections, with simple jeering, or even with bullets. Just as scientific language fails with all but a tiny percentage of a randomly assembled audience, so rhetoric fails with all but a relatively larger percentage—sometimes even a majority—of such an audience. Many listeners to Martin Luther King, Jr. could understand the logic of his words, could appreciate his classic rhetorical cadences, and could still respond only to his inborn and earliest learned violations of the Western culture of deference—to the blackness of his dialect and skin.

[43] France, p. 147.

Even in America, dialect counts. There are the dialectal jokes, in the exchange of which one may claim recognition as a member of the dialectal "in-group." White American listeners often find themselves bewildered in the presence of black Africans or West Indians educated in England—black speakers whose logical and scientific capacities, rhetorical skills, and dialects strongly signal the appropriateness of deference, while their skins signal that to defer would be to patronize or to surrender. Native black Americans who speak the General American dialect may provoke a similar confusion, though one suspects that they would be taken less seriously than foreign blacks. The phenomenon of rhetorical and dialectal hypercorrection, noticed by William Labov in New York City, especially among such status-conscious groups as lower-middle class women, generally provokes not the Establishment's deference, but its mirth, as in the classic case of Mrs. Malaprop, from the Enlightened English stage, and of "the Kingfish," from the once-popular American radio and television comedy, *Amos 'n' Andy*. Early in the sixteenth century, Baldesar Castiglione warned against hypercorrection in *The Book of the Courtier*.

> Our Courtier will be judged excellent, and will show grace in all things and particularly in his speech, if he avoids affectation: which error is incurred by many and sometimes, more than others, by our Lombards who, if they have been away from home for a year, come back and start right off speaking Roman, or Spanish, or French, and God knows how!

On the island of Martha's Vineyard, more than four centuries later, Labov found a direct correlation between an islander's dialect and his intent to make a life on Martha's Vineyard or, like Castiglione's roaming Lombard, his intent to leave, to get an education, and to make his way in one of the mainland's centers of culture, wealth and power.[44]

Already, in touching upon the involvement of rhetoric and dialect in racism, I have found it necessary to recognize that a speaker has a face and a body (with an age, a sex, and a race) as well as a mind and a voice. He has, in other words, what is often called a "bearing," or "presence," and this, too, will affect his participation in the culture of deference, for as Ray Birdwhistell has put it, "men have not communicated with each other by spoken language alone any more than they have lived by metabolism." He says that "communication, upon investigation, appears to be a system which makes use of the channels of all of the sensory modalities...the audio-acoustic..., the kinesthetic-visual..., the odor-producing-olfactory..., [and] the tactile." Moreover, these channels work together, producing "redundancy." New York's legendary Mayor LaGuardia, Birdwhistell reports, could speak Italian, Yiddish, and American English, and persons familiar with those three cultures, watching newsreels of LaGuardia speaking,

---

[44] Labov, pp. 30-39, 122-42; Baldesar Castiglione, *The Book of the Courtier*, trans. Charles S. Singleton (Garden City, New York: Anchor Books, 1959), p. 47.

but with no soundtrack, could still tell which tongue he was using, apparently because "(at least for Western European languages), a set of necessary and formal body motion behaviors...are tied directly to linguistic structure." One can quarrel, however, from the viewpoint of this paper, with Professor Birdwhistell's Johnsonian assertion that "multichannel reinforcement is positively adaptive [because it] makes it possible for a far wider range within the population to become part of and to contribute to the conventional understandings of the community than if we were a species with only a single-channel lexical storehouse."[45] Clearly, as the cases of racism and sexism suggest, the multichannel redundancy of the culture of deference not only admits but also excludes individuals from public recognition.

The matter of facial and bodily bearing is only beginning to be scientifically investigated within and across cultures. But insofar as the West is concerned, a noble bearing is clearly one which is alert and active, but which avoids any hint of involvement with exhausting, frustrating, laborious activity. *The Book of the Courtier* is again a *locus classicus* for this awareness in preindustrial literature. In it, Castiglione coins the term *sprezzatura* to express the basic character of a noble bearing. He puts the idea in the mouth of Count Lodovico da Canossa, one of a number of gentlefolk we are to imagine conversing about the behavior proper to a courtier:

> I have found quite a universal rule which in this matter seems to me valid above all others, and in all human affairs whether in word or deed: and that is to avoid affectation in every way and (to pronounce a new word perhaps) to practice in all things a certain *sprezzatura* [nonchalance], so as to conceal all art and make whatever is done or said appear to be without effort and almost without any thought about it. And I believe much grace comes of this: because everyone knows the difficulty of things that are rare and well done; wherefore facility in such things causes the greatest wonder; whereas, on the other hand, to labor and, as we say, drag forth by the hair of the head, shows an extreme want of grace, and causes everything, no matter how great it may be, to be held in little account.[46]

Just as Puttenham was to say that rhetoric consists of means by which the nobleman could distinguish his speech from that of "the vulgar," and so dazzle them into laboring in the nonhuman sphere of action, so Castiglione here says that the noble body must distinguish its bearing from that of laboring bodies; for the hatred of difficulty and the contempt for people laboring at difficulties begins with laborers themselves. Hence, to avoid the contempt and win the deference of labor, one must do what labor knows all too well is difficult and make it look easy. *Sprezzatura,* in short, is a kind of conspicuous stoicism.

[45] Ray L. Birdwhistell, *Kinesics and Context: Essays on Body Motion Communication* (Philadelphia: University of Pennsylvania Press, 1970), pp. 70, 85-91, 102-3, 107-8, 127.

[46] Castiglione, p. 43.

Another participant in Castiglione's dialogue interrupts to ask Count Lodovico if his *sprezzatura* is anything more than the very affectation which he claims to despise. Is it not precisely such pretended nonchalance which characterizes a dancer who, "to make it quite plain that he is giving no thought to what he is doing, ... lets his clothes fall from his back and his slippers from his feet, and goes right on dancing without picking them up"? Count Lodovico answers that such a dancer shows affectation, not *sprezzatura,* "because we clearly see him making every effort to show that he takes no thought of what he is about, which means taking too much thought."[47]

A noble bearing, then, is one which shows itself capable of difficult physical activity, analogous to labor, but clearly distinguishable from it. The male body best suited to bearing itself nobly should "be neither extremely small nor big; because men who are so huge of body are often not only obtuse of spirit, but are also unfit for every agile exercise, which is something I very much desire in the Courtier. And hence I would have him well built and shapely of limb, and would have him show strength and lightness and suppleness, and know all the bodily exercises that befit a warrior." What is noteworthy, here, is that the noble body is fit for armed combat but does not give the impression of being fit for more plodding, laborious kinds of athleticism, such as lifting weights, or hand-to-hand, unarmed combat, where size and competence tend to go together. Later, another of Castiglione's experts on noble bearing warns against liberal and friendly wrestling with peasants—unless the courtier is "well-nigh sure of winning." One must look as if one could dominate even the greatest hulk of an unarmed peasant physically, with arms, in other words, and one must not foolishly jeopardize that impression. When young or old, moreover, the courtier should try to bear himself like a man in middle life.[48]

It is significant that classical ballet seems to have emerged as an abstraction of the courtly, non-laborious, difficult, but graceful bearing of which Castiglione had written. According to John Martin, "Both ecstasy and mimesis are ruled out of [ballet's] principle and its historic practice. In its beginnings it was evolved quite coldly, albeit from living sources, by experts who were seeking elegance of carriage, graciousness of gesture, and a general refining of movement away from crude, everyday utilitarianism. Ecstasy is patently out of place in such a program, and mimicry focuses on the realistic instead of on the ideal. Such was the basis of the court dance...." Again and again, Martin returns to laboriousness, realism, and practicality as terms antithetical to the aesthetic use of the body, and before he has finished his illuminating essay, he is drawing upon the clearly social implications of action which avoids looking like hard, inevitable work: "Heaviness, effort, the overdramatization of difficulties conquered, are essen-

---

[47] Castiglione, p. 44.
[48] Castiglione, pp. 36-37, 101, 107-9.

tially vulgar and mark the parvenu in [classical ballet]." The good dancer, in short, is all *sprezzatura*. It is in the play of the arms about "the central straightness and rigor of the body," Martin writes, "that the aristocracy of the ballet reveals itself." Unless the dancer is truly noble, his arms will be "two rather superfluous appendages whose uselessness is obvious except in a world of eating and drinking and practical accomplishment." Moreover, "the parvenu will expose himself most likely in the use of the torso [by allowing] it to become a heavy and solid mass carried about with no little effort by the legs." And as for the noble dancer's face, "certainly it will not reveal the effort or the physical strain that a mere human undergoes in creating this exalted abstraction of himself, but neither will it wear the hideous mask of a fixed smile."[49]

"Verticality," according to Martin, "is the keynote of the entire procedure."[50] There are no fat dancers, and obesity detracts from anyone's participation in the Western culture of deference. Presumably the hypercorrect sort of body produced by today's weight-lifting body-builders would not be a clear asset either in Castiglione's eyes or in Martin's.

It is, of course, significant that women figure little in this sketchy treatment of bearing. Both Castiglione's courtier and Martin's dancer are males, and although both bear themselves in a manner suggesting the feminine, neither does any more than to suggest it. The difficulty women experience in gaining access to the culture of deference is clear. Folklore has it that they talk more than men do, but the fact is that in mixed company they talk a good deal less. They are constantly patronized, and when they become coolly assertive, rather than shrewish, they are resented and even feared.

Like bearing, costume is a huge subject. It is the first category of deference sign on our continuum which the determined speaker does not have born in him or does not need to learn, as best he can. With costume, we become aware that one may buy signs predisposing others to take one seriously—signs which have nothing to do with native or learned competences. Clothes are a way of making an impression without running the risk of making one's audience tired and contemptuous of one's little repertoire of verbal and bodily competences. Like modern sociologists such as Goffman and Klapp, Federico Fregoso, another of Castiglione's experts on nobility, warns the prospective courtier against overexposure.[51] "I should be very glad," says Federico, "to have him shun the

---

[49] John Martin, "The Ideal of Ballet Aesthetics," in *The Dance Anthology*, ed. Cobbett Steinberg (New York: New American Library, 1980), pp. 301, 307, 308-9.

[50] Martin, p. 307.

[51] Erving Goffman, *The Presentation of Self in Everyday Life* (Garden City, New York: Anchor Books, 1959), pp. 218-28. See also Orrin E. Klapp, *Symbolic Leaders: Public Dramas and Public Men* (Chicago: Aldin, 1964), p. 224. Klapp remarks that "mystery ... is an important source of color. It does not always pay to thrust one's self upon the public. There is not only the risk of 'saturating' the audience with one's image but there are also

vulgar herd or at most put in a rare appearance with them, because there is nothing in the world so excellent that the ignorant will not grow tired of it and esteem it little, from seeing it often." Hence, Federico advises "neat and dainty" attire with "a certain modest elegance"—clothes which project "what manner of man [the courtier] wishes to be taken for ... even by those who do not hear him speak or see him do anything whatsoever."[52] This is tantamount to saying that logical, scientific, rhetorical, and kinesthetic competences quickly lose their appeal in the fallen, preindustrial world; and that when these competences fail, the human sphere of action must be controlled by the sumptuous, backed by the threat of armed violence. Again, we have been returned to Pascal's notion that hatred can only be managed through concupiscence and force, and Pascal explicitly draws the connection between the fundamental incompetence of the *ancien régime* and the reliance on sumptuous costume in the culture of deference by which it neutralized hatred.

> Our magistrates have shown themselves well aware of this mystery. Their red robes, the ermine in which they swaddle themselves like furry cats, the law-courts where they sit in judgment, the fleurs de lys, all this august panoply was very necessary. If physicians did not have long gowns and mules, if learned doctors did not wear square caps and robes four times too large, they would never have deceived the world, which finds such an authentic display irresistible. If they possessed true justice, and if physicians possessed the true art of healing, they would not need square caps; the majesty of such sciences would command respect in itself. But, as they only possess imaginary science, they have to resort to these vain devices in order to strike the imagination, which is their real concern, and this, in fact, is how they win respect.[53]

In vandalizing the *ancien régime,* the Enlightenment changed clothes. A taste for the country costume of the English gentleman came to France with the Enlightened taste for free, English empirical thinking. The embroidered male costume of Versailles, trimmed with lace, ceased to be emulated there, and, for a time, even woman's clothing underwent a radical simplification, as David's famous portrait of Madame Récamier reveals. "During the Terror," James Laver reports, "it was dangerous to wear fashionable clothes of any kind, but after the execution of Robespierre, those who had survived the guillotine began once more to dress as they pleased"—in the English hunting coats, boots, short waistcoats, and high collars and neckcloths of the wigless *Incroyables.* Ever since,

---

positive advantages in mystery. ... Napoleon preferred not to be seen too often in public. He often wore mufti, avoided parties, and drove out alone. When cheered at the theatre, he would draw back into his box, saying, 'If I am seen three or four times at the theater, people will cease to notice me.'"

[52] Castiglione, pp. 104, 122-23.

[53] Pascal, pp. 40-41.

Western males have been sansculottes—without the knee-breeches and white stockings of the final years of the old aristocracy. The relative proportion of the total output of goods and services that went into clothing the ruling class declined. Carlo Cipolla conjectures "that in the sixteenth and seventeenth centuries [expenditures on clothing and jewelry, a form of hoarding] absorbed, according to the situation, from 10 to 30 percent of consumption of the rich and the well to do," while "at the end of the fifteenth century, the expenditure of the king of France for jewelry and clothing amounted to no less than 5 to 10 percent of all the royal revenues."[54] Clearly, those days are now over, and it would appear that the Enlightened faith in human competence against the nonhuman as the only moral status symbol, as well as the industrialization of the textile industry, explains their disappearance—though court dress, based on the military uniform for males, remained sumptuous until the First World War.

The effect of the relative democratization of costume and of the communications revolutions that characterize the modern age is that the rulers of the postindustrial world, effectively, can hide from the masses. The American president's power is far greater than that of any "absolute" monarch of the seventeenth century, and his ideological purity would be compromised were he to insist very heavily on sartorial assertions of it—as in the case of President Nixon's abortive attempt to dress the White House police in uniforms reminiscent of *fin de siècle* Vienna. In 1651, after his defeat at the battle of Worcester, the future Charles II of England, well-known though he was, escaped back to safety in France despite the concentrated military and naval manhunt organized by the forces of Parliament. But during the Vietnam War, a single policeman, punching automobile license numbers into a computer terminal at the Canadian-American border, found and arrested the one draft-evader among the faceless thousands of motorists passing his post that day. If we feel that we are free because most of us can afford to dress much as our rulers do, we have surely fallen prey to a historical illusion. It is *they* who can now afford to dress as *we* do.

The constant impossibility of enforcing sumptuary laws specifying who could out-dress whom in preindustrial England suggests that costly as aristocratic costume was, it remained financially available to more people than those whose ranks and offices legally entitled them to wear it. But there were other classes of bought deference signs—those Erving Goffman calls "setting"—which were so staggeringly expensive that they vastly reduced the number of people who could afford them, and afford with them the fullest possible access to the social range of signs in the deference continuum. Goffman defines the setting as "involving furniture, decor, physical layout, and other background items which supply the

[54] James Laver, *The Concise History of Costume and Fashion* (New York: Scribners, 1969, pp. 148-53; Cipolla, pp. 35-36. See also Quentin Bell, *On Human Finery,* new edition (London: Hogarth, 1976), pp. 118-34.

scenery and stage-props for the spate of human action played out before, within, or upon it." These "other background items" may include retinues of people— servants (laboring and professional), family members, friends, and even lovers. Both William Wycherley and the Earl of Rochester, two court wits of the English Restoration, likened a lover or a mistress to sumptuous clothing, worn not primarily for physical gratification and comfort but for social display, as a deference sign. And the friend of another Restoration courtier, Francis North, Lord Guildford, suggested to him that he was ill thought of at court, despite his service, because he kept no mistress, and that he should take the trouble to find one.[55]

But the chief elements of setting for powerful speakers in the *ancien régime* were architecture, fine and decorative art, gardening, and access to media for transmitting a speaker's import beyond the temporal and spatial confines of the moment of utterance. It should be obvious, though in the modern humanities it is sometimes considered vulgar to point this out, that most of the efforts of preindustrial artists—of painters, print-makers, sculptors, architects, gardeners, musicians, actors, poets, and even scribes and printers—were devoted to making deference signs. That is, the liberal arts were devoted to providing nonverbal and verbal redundancies backing and transmitting the rhetoric of a nobly born body, nobly clothed. As César Graña has written, we all learn that art museums, "often ancestral places," are the repositories of "our cultural heritage."

> [But] the fact is, of course, that in spite of all the ... utterances about "our heritage,"
> in most cases that heritage is not really ours. When the present-day museum visitor,
> perhaps the child of a working class family, perhaps the descendant of an
> eighteenth-century yeoman, encounters Van Dyck's portrait of Charles I, with its air
> of indolent, inaccessible self-assurance and subtle disdain for the common world,
> does he look upon it as art, as history, as curiosity, as a vague manifestation of
> grandeur, as an object of awe and obeisance, of anger, moral suspicion, class
> antagonism, or amused incomprehension?

The portraits to which Graña refers, of course, had a practical purpose in the Stuart scheme of social management. They were not just objects of aesthetic contemplation. Charles I was England's first large-scale collector and patron of classical, Renaissance, and baroque art. Rubens, who both made and procured works of art for Charles, called him "the prince with the greatest love of art in the

---

[55] Frances Elizabeth Baldwin, *Sumptuary Legislation and Personal Regulation in England* (Baltimore: Johns Hopkins University Press, 1926), pp. 54-55, 70, 101, 107, 111, 117-18, 150, 167, 196, 238-40, 247-49; Goffman, pp. 22-23, 220-21; *The Complete Plays of William Wycherley*, ed. Gerald Weales (Garden City, New York, Anchor Books, 1966), p. 350; *The Complete Poems of John Wilmot, Earl of Rochester*, ed. David M. Vieth (New Haven: Yale University Press, 1968), p. 107; Keith Thomas, "The Double Standard," *JHI* 20 (April 1959): 195.

world," and ironically, it was under Rubens's painted apotheosis of Charles's father, on the ceiling of Inigo Jones's classical Banqueting House in Whitehall, that Charles walked to the window leading out to the scaffold where he was beheaded in 1649. His patronage of art was part of what cost him his life. It was part of his dynasty's attempt to centralize political power in as august a court, on the continental model, as the English country gentry, protecting its decentralized, local prerogatives in Parliament, could be made to pay for.[56] Charles I was by no means a modern aesthete.

Nor was Louis XIV of France. His great minister, Colbert, reminded him that even if he did not really take much pleasure in beautiful surroundings, "a great prince must pretend that he loves them, and cause all such works of art to be made." Probably apocryphally, but no less typically, Louis himself is reputed to have told his Academy of artists that "I entrust to you the most precious thing on earth—my fame." Particularly during the early part of Louis's reign, "Colbert used a system of pensions and gratifications to elicit from the poets selected by Chapelain a stream of panegyric for the King, when the Academy, now under Louis's direct protection, was seen by many of its members as an instrument for furthering the royal glory, and when architects, gardeners, painters, and sculptors were setting up in Versailles, the eternal monument of the Sun King." Significantly, the engraver Nanteuil persuaded Louis to issue the edict of Saint Jean-de-Luz, whereby engraving was elevated from the industrial arts to the rank and privilege of the liberal arts.[57]

In seventeenth-century England, too, there was aristocratic patronage for improvements in the quality of pictures that could be cheaply produced in great numbers. The dashing Prince Rupert of the Palatinate helped perfect the technique of the mezzotint, which he brought to the court of Charles II, where the painter Sir Godfrey Kneller used it to duplicate his pictures of the great. The interest of these princes in the mass-production of faithful portraits of themselves and of their chief servants, "in robes of office, treading on a baroque litter of professional paraphernalia," cannot be accounted for as an interest in bringing aesthetic pleasure, at popular prices, to the masses. It was an interest in transmitting the deference signs of the royal and courtly presence beyond that presence, and it seems to have worked well enough that in 1720, Adam Petrie, "the Scottish Chesterfield," in his *Rules of Good Deportment, or of Good*

[56] César Graña, *Fact and Symbol: Essays in the Sociology of Art and Literature* (New York: Oxford University Press, 1971), pp. 106-7; Michael Jaffe, "Rubens," Encyclopedia of World Art, 1966 edition; Perez Zagorin, *The Court and the Country: The Beginning of the English Revolution* (London: Routledge and Kegan Paul, 1969), p. 72.

[57] Francis Haskell, "Patronage," *Encyclopedia of World Art,* 1966 edition; France, p. 150; Arthur M. Hind, *A History of Engraving and Etching from the 15th Century to the Year 1914* (New York: Dover, 1963), p. 146.

*Breeding. For the Use of Youth,* felt the need to caution against the overrefinement of not sitting with one's back to a picture of the monarch.[58]

Architecture, of course, provided the actual stage for the royal presence itself, which pictorial and verbal media publicized. "What were country houses for?" asks Mark Girouard in beginning his social and architectural history of the great houses of England.

> They were not originally...just large houses in the country in which rich people lived. Essentially they were power houses—the houses of a ruling class....[For] basically people did not live in country houses unless they either possessed power, or, by setting up in a country house, were making a bid to possess it.
>
> This power was based on the ownership of land. But...the point of land was [not farming but] the tenants and rent that came with it....Anyone who had sufficient resources and followers, and displayed them with good enough prominence, was likely to be offered jobs and perquisites by the central government in return for his support. Acceptance produced money, which could be turned into more land, more power and more supporters....[Hence] land...was of little use without one or more country houses on it....[A country house] was a show-case, in which to exhibit and entertain supporters and good connections....It was an image-maker....Trophies in the hall, coats of arms over the chimney-pieces, books in the library and temples in the park could suggest that [the owner] was discriminating, intelligent, bred to rule and brave.[59]

To enter a great house and approach its lord was to be repeatedly instructed by its design and by the conduct of its human staff in the appropriateness of deference. Traditionally, in England, probably since before 1318, the king had withdrawn to his great chamber from eating at the high table of his hall in the presence of his entire household and guests, including servants. Lesser English lords followed this example, though dinners, in state, before at least the elite of the household, continued in the great chamber. In the great English houses of the sixteenth and seventeenth centuries, the great chambers were "usually the most richly decorated [rooms] in the house, and [were] often as large as the hall," which survived as a more public space to which the lord might descend on high ceremonial occasions to eat, as of yore, with all ranks of his dependents. Great chambers were usually reached, after entering the house by the hall or an adjacent gallery, by climbing sumptuous staircases, at first of stone, but in the early seventeenth century of carved and painted wood. Beyond the great chamber was

---

[58] A. Hyatt Mayor, *Prints and People: A Social History of Printed Pictures* (New York: Metropolitan Museum of Art, 1971), illustration no. 291; John E. Mason, *Gentlefolk in the Making: Studies in the History of English Courtesy Literature and Related Topics from 1531 to 1774* (1935; reprint, New York: Octagon Books, 1971), p. 269.

[59] Mark Girouard, *Life in the English Country House: A Social and Architectural History* (New Haven: Yale University Press, 1978), pp. 2-3.

a withdrawing chamber for business, and beyond that, one or more private rooms for sleeping, business, and prayer. Withdrawing chambers, at first, were occupied by servants to protect the lord at night, but gradually, during the sixteenth century, "became the private sitting, eating, and reception rooms" of the lord occupying them. In the greatest Jacobean houses, such as Hatfield, which Robert Cecil built with the idea of entertaining and cementing his connection with the sovereign and his queen, this sequence of hall, stairs, sumptuous semi-public great chamber, withdrawing room, bedchamber, and closet was repeated in each of two wings—one for the king's household, and one for the queen's. The plan was for the Cecil household to occupy the ground floor during royal visits, using the state rooms in the queen's wing when the royal households were absent.[60]

Analogous but somewhat less specialized arrangements had evolved in the great French houses of the seventeenth century, such as Vaux-le-Vicomte, the splendid residence of Nicholas Fouquet, the ill-fated finance minister of Louis XIV. There, the sequence (called an *appartement*) had three rooms: the *antechambre*, the *chambre*, and the *cabinet*. The English specialization into rooms "for state, and a relatively private chamber for living and sleeping," did not apply in France. There, the *antechambre* was essentially a waiting room in which the *appartement*'s great occupant could give brief audiences to persons not important enough to be admitted to the *chambre*. The latter was "a very grand bed-sitting room...used for the reception of visitors and for private meals as well as for sleeping." The king's state bed was separated from the rest of the *chambre* by a balustrade within which only ranking courtiers could enter. The truly private room was the *cabinet,* relatively small, but ornate, perhaps containing the great occupant's richest artifacts. "To get into the *cabinet* of a monarch or great man one had to be in the inner ring of power."[61]

In building Vaux-le-Vicomte, Fouquet made the same mistake that Cardinal Wolsey had earlier made in building Hampton Court. Its effectiveness as a deference sign threatened that of the monarch's own palaces and chateaux. In 1661, three weeks after Fouquet entertained the Sun King in his new house, he was arrested for embezzlement, and eventually, on false evidence and on the king's insistence, he was sentenced to spend his remaining years in prison. It was Louis, not Fouquet, who had access to the final, political signs in the culture of deference, even though (against Louis's will) Fouquet's life was spared. Colbert, who had helped to ruin Fouquet, paid the ultimate compliment to the fallen minister's taste in deference-promoting settings. He hired Fouquet's architect, his painter, and his gardener to build Versailles for the king.

---

[60] Girouard, pp. 46, 90-94, 114-16.
[61] Girouard, pp. 126-28.

## IV.

Any conclusion to be drawn from this interactionist sketch of Western cultural history must necessarily be tentative.[62] Generally speaking, however, the West apparently hates obligatory physical labor with a unique intensity, and hates, viscerally, the failure of language—when the benevolent listener cannot think how to go on trying to understand the incomprehensible speaker, and when the uncomprehended speaker cannot think how to go on benignly trying to talk the listener around to his own views and actions. One can see the physical discomfort of the failure of language—the glazings of eyes, the glancings away, the facial tics, and the fidgeting limbs, as speakers and listeners begin to doubt each other's competence, sanity, or good will, and when each begins to look for ways of saving his own self-esteem at the expense of the other's.

Western culture is rich in redundancies for avoiding most dangerous misunderstandings, and for ending the few that still happen, more or less quickly, more or less short of violence. Its constantly repeated message is this: "If you cannot understand or agree with the speaker redundantly marked by deference signs, stay out of his way; don't question him, and keep your hands off his resources." But the West is poor indeed in redundancies providing for the amicable and comfortable prolonging of misunderstandings until all parties to them have talked their way to the feeling that the misunderstanding has passed, or is no longer dangerous. Ours, in other words, is not what might be called a pedagogical culture. It does not suffer fools gladly. Our least pedagogical places, perhaps, are the lecture rooms of our most conspicuous universities, where "teaching" is the monologue of the substantive expert, largely protected from vulgar interruption, and where "learning" is showing that one can sit still for such monologues and later act content to imitate them on examinations and in theses.

In the name of sport, people reared in the rhetorical ethos of the West will voluntarily undertake laborious, painful, dirty, and even nauseating or dangerous periods of confrontation with the nonhuman. Many people regard the sensations felt in such encounters as enjoyable in themselves. Others see sport as exercise necessary to maintain the tone of a nobly born body, or, if tastefully publicized, as

---

[62] The sociological perspective of this essay is that of "symbolic interactionism," grounded in American pragmatism. It is frequently criticized for concentrating upon the minutiae of face-to-face human confrontations and thereby ignoring history, politics, and large "structural" matters dealt with in traditional sociology. These criticisms are not warranted, I think, once we recognize that economies produce and distribute not only goods and services, but also deference signs. See Jerome G. Manis and Bernard N. Meltzer, *Symbolic Interaction: A Reader in Social Psychology* (Boston: Allyn and Bacon, 1967); Bernard N. Meltzer, John W. Petras, and Larry T. Reynolds, *Symbolic Interactionism: Genesis, Varieties and Criticism* (London: Routledge and Kegan Paul, 1975).

an amateur demonstration of *sprezzatura* essential to the nobility of setting within which managerial work becomes possible. It would appear, therefore, that there is nothing inherently unpleasant even in strenuous entries into the nonhuman sphere of action—at least for the healthy, nourished, and rested body trained for a particular physical competence, warmed-up before fully exerting it, and able to work at a pace it can enjoy. Indeed, one can become addicted to such experiences of competence against the nonhuman. What hurts, perhaps, more than the task of exercise itself is the task's social setting—whether it is labor, damaging to one's participation in the culture of deference, or leisure, contributing to it. Just as friction upon the genitals, in itself, tends not to produce arousal and orgasm when it occurs in the social setting of being raped, exercise against identical nonhuman resistances may well feel different, depending upon whether it is self-initiated or is ordered by an interrupter conventionally defined as "better looking," speaking a "better" dialect, wearing "better" clothes, and backed by uniformed, weapons-bearing followers.

Can it be that it is not our animal condition, in which we each do our own labor, between brief, unarmed territorial squabbles, upon the extra-specific resource base we inhabit, that makes individual humans so potentially vicious? Can it be that, worse than facing the economic, animal condition of labor, we hate the human condition of having to try to understand fellow humans who intrude their strange words upon our private moments of attention to the realities to which we are trained—to our own interior monologues and to our private sensations of physical need and competence?

If this is the case—if being spoken to is apt to threaten the listener's sense of living meaningfully as to increase it, and if being incomprehensibly spoken to or uncomprehendingly heard feels as bad (or worse) than laboring nonverbally at a physical task for which one has not trained, then it may be a blessing that Western culture largely relieves us of the need to try teaching others and learning from them when language fails and the discomfort of its failure sets in. The substantive expert, blessed by the social and political ranges of deference signs displayed by him, or by others for him, may not have to fight for his truth against the massive commonness of common sense. But such blessings are always mixed. Any deference sign, it would appear, can excite hatred as well as admiration. Thus, against the handsome, well-born, well-dressed, famous, rhetorically accomplished, sincere fool, the equally sincere Western speaker, hell-bent upon a hearing for the lessons of his private experience, but not so richly blessed with the social range of deference signs, may be able to think of nothing but war. In this failure of imagination, apparently, lies what Morse Peckham has called "the stupidity of human history."

What other ways can there be of making language work?

HENRY H. H. REMAK

# European Romanticism and Contemporary American Counterculture

THE MOST SIGNIFICANT TASKS of scholarship may be the least accessible to nonspeculative approaches. It is in this spirit—the spirit of Morse Peckham—that this essay is written: "essay" in its derivations of *exagere*: to drive, lead, act, do; to attempt, attack, make an effort (i.e., to force); to try, test, weigh. The romantic dilemma, tension against synthesis, demands the form of the essay.[1]

## I.

One of the shocker-sleepers of cultural history is the apparently barren seed that turns out to be just dormant. Given the right conditions of nurturing, it sprouts into a lusty plant many years afterwards. The dormant seed here dealt

[1] In the spring semester of 1972 I had the rare privilege of teaching at Indiana University an advanced undergraduate honors seminar in Comparative Literature on "Romanticism and Twentieth-Century Culture." The students constituted one of the finest assemblies of undergraduates I have ever had in one course. I owe a great deal of stimulation to the ideas they expressed in papers and discussions. My thanks to Doris Bellamy, Eve Berry, Marie Carija, Lynn Dickey, Jonni Gonso, Steve Gudeman, Eva Lively, Max Miller, David Mohler, Marjorie Pannell, Marsha Siefert, Dennis Skinner, Jane Taube, and Jan Wieben.

The context of this essay makes it advisable to hold documentation to a bare minimum. Readers who would like to obtain a selected critical bibliography may secure it by writing to the author.

I also want to thank my editorial assistant, Eva Langfeldt-Hogan, who came to my rescue and typed the manuscript of this essay in record time.

with is European romanticism. Carried at the time by the winds of cultural cross-fertilization across the ocean to America, it appeared to have made little penetration into a prevalently hostile soil until, more than a century and a half later, blossoms (or poison ivy, depending upon one's preferences) familiar to the literary historian emerged all over American campuses and in city and country communes, filled the newspapers, lent spice to the morning and evening television news, and sustained the paperback industry.

Any cultural syntheses must be reductionist, and any large-scale juxtapositions, especially those across distant spaces and time periods, are relative. There is no generalization without qualification. Some such reservations about the American germination of European romanticism will be stated explicitly in this synthesis; many more will be implicit. But one can also hedge too much and be caught on a sterile academic teeter-totter. Relatedness, even when conjectural and problematic, is more productive than nonrelatedness. Relatedness does not necessarily imply direct influence, a cause-and-effect syndrome. One hundred and seventy-to-eighty years elapsed between the beginnings of European romanticism and the nascence and flowering of the American counterculture. The roots of the 1960s and early 1970s are not the roots of European romanticism reappearing as such. Rather, to the extent that the two cultural and historical environments are analogous, they have evoked related responses. Our soil is, after all, composed of debris from the past.

It is my premise, which will emerge in detail, that European romanticism found its main expression in literature and the arts, whereas the counterculture was geared more toward general lifestyle. My comparisons will therefore be drawn chiefly between these categories.

## II.

Nowhere in the world is the Enlightenment as centrally linked with political institutions, traditions, goals, and personal convictions as in Anglo-American culture. According to the Enlightenment, every human being is endowed with reason. It is up to society, through social, political, economic, and educational institutions, to develop this reason—a mission which transfers the role of arbiter from the chosen or self-chosen few, especially the king, to every citizen. There is no limit to man's progress provided he sticks to reason. Not only *may* he, he *must* analyze rationally and objectively. He must see clear. Life is a constant process of enlightenment of self and of others. Rational analyses provide the basis for actions based on common sense. Words are no good unless they lead to action that improves the lot of man. If we are created in the image of the Maker, then God is in this world and we represent Him. Man must accept the responsibility for his well-being on earth to the largest extent possible and practical. We must observe and learn from this world, God's creation: not to do so is a repudiation of

God. Since we are not in the other world, speculation is suitable for its exploration, but this world we can and must *know*. Among the inalienable rights with which we are endowed by our Creator is the exercise of reason. Though "reason" is not explicitly cited in the Declaration of Independence, the entire document is a prime example of the exercise of analytical reason in explaining, point by point, specifically and empirically, why the colonies were forced to take this extreme action. Other men will judge them rationally, therefore "a decent respect to the opinions of mankind requires that they [i.e., the people] should declare the causes which impel them to the separation."

The manifestations of nature in the untamed New World seemed savage, destructive, irrational, and anti-humanistic. Those men closest to nature on the American continent constituted the enemy, "the merciless Indian savages, whose known rule of warfare is an undistinguished destruction of all ages, sexes, and conditions." "The Laws of Nature and of Nature's God" approvingly cited in the Declaration refer to the natural endowments and rights of man as sanctioned by God rather than to external nature. Tom Paine reinforces the synonymity of the "divine principle of the equal rights of man (for it has its origin from the Maker of man)" with the concepts of "equal natural right": "His natural rights are the foundation of all his civil rights." Since the gift of reason is not a privilege limited by the Creator to a chosen few but given to all men created in His image, regardless of social status or geography, the Enlightenment is universal, international, cosmopolitan. Opposition to groups (e.g., to Indians) cannot be justified by their innate inferiority but only by their incomplete progress on the road to reason.

The Enlightenment recognizes more than the individual's right to reason, it insists upon the obligation of the individual to reason and to act in the light of this reasoning. It also holds that the analogous rights and obligations of the community can only be viable on the basis of a consensus or a majority of freely reasoning people.

The cardinal tenets of European romanticism must or would have struck citizens of the new American nation, a bastion of Enlightenment, as regressive or irrelevant. The cult of the past, the nurturing of tradition, the stress on continuity, the resurrection or invention of myth had little appeal to those deliberately or forcibly leaving the Old World and embarking on the dangerous passage to the New World where creation could begin again. Fantasy, delving into the subconscious, psychological finesse, catering to internal complexities, assertion of the private sphere, anti-materialism, romanticizing the wild and the exotic, pristine nature and pristine savages (à la Chateaubriand or à la Seume), a return to hierarchical thinking and modes, the cult of the arts and of the artist, of the beautiful, of the lyrical, escape from external reality, sophisticated intellectualism, pessimism and self-pity, faddishness, anti-bourgeois proclivities—all of these romantic values must have seemed im-pertinent, in both senses of the word, to the American immigrants who faced the awful task of recreating a new

world on a continent presenting immense opportunities but also immense risks and demanding all the ingenuity, fortitude, and stamina of man and woman to survive and to succeed.

Filling this continent with immigrants was a process that accelerated in the 1840s and 1850s, continued with relatively brief interruptions due to the Civil War, the two world wars, recessions, depressions, and immigration restrictions through the 1950s—that is, through most of our history—and it is not ended yet: witness the most recent wave of immigrants from Vietnam, Cuba, and Haiti. Vast stretches of our continent are still underpopulated, by European standards. They could nourish many more people if necessary. Expansion is far from over. Each new wave of immigrants pushed up the preceding one. With the notable exception of blacks there was a perpetual motion leaving little time, incentive, or echo for self-reflection, for looking back, for self-analysis.

At the conclusion of the Eisenhower years (1960), America had reached a level of relative stability and affluence. With the economic miracle in Western Europe, immigration had slowed. The veterans returning from a war that had more than fulfilled their yen for adventurousness and collective concern had concluded their studies, obtained jobs, and established families. Simultaneously, the Supreme Court civil rights decision of 1954, declaring that "separate" was no longer "equal," established, at long last, a principle that required internal implementation—a change of personal attitudes, self-reflection as a concomitant to action. A new, economically secure generation, less conditioned than its fathers to the traditional American credo of economic expansionism and personal expansiveness, inspired by the Camelot-Kennedy years, and flooding the colleges (which constituted oases in American society for reflection, analysis, social criticism, and personal development), began to assert itself ideologically. It is not by chance that the Port Huron statement of the Students for a Democratic Society (SDS), the manifesto of the political arm of the American youth movement, was formulated in 1962.

## III.

This is the point where an attempt must be made to define what I mean by "American counterculture," or why I do not use such terms as "student movement," "student unrest," "protest movement," or "youth movement." Although the college and university campuses of America were the spearheads of what is sometimes called "the movement," it was not limited to them, extending to high school populations, city and country communes, minorities, and the thinking and life-styles of older groups. "Unrest" and "protest" give the phenomenon too negative, extrovert, ephemeral, and media-like a flavor, whereas "movement" may exaggerate the concerted and organized aspects of the trends. "Counterculture" seems best because it emphasizes the more pervasive,

more lasting ingredients of the changes, which were not only reactive to what was perceived as the majority culture but which also offered, or purported to offer, an alternative.

I do not claim that European romanticism was, knowingly or unknowingly, the chief guide to the total forces of change in American after 1960—rather than Marx, Mao-tse-Tung, Che Guevara, Trotsky, Frantz Fanon, sundry gurus, the Beatles, or Bob Dylan. By and large, I distinguish between two main components of recent change advocacy: an activist one, often programmatic, heavily ideological and rhetorical, aggressive, collectivist, usually Marxist-oriented but with an unorthodox flavor; and an individualistic component, contemplative, private, cultish, neo-romantic, nature-oriented.[2] It is the latter, highly personalized advocacy of change which I designate, in terms of this essay, as "the counterculture," without denying that it has certain links with the activist sector. I agree with D. W. Keim, one of the few scholars who has tried to define the counterculture, who calls it "the radical critique of technological society that rejects structural explanations and solutions and instead identifies society's problems and their resolution in terms of self, consciousness, and culture or world-view."[3] Although I eschew the term "hippies" because it is too casual, too simplistic, I realize that what I am talking about is often designated as such.

# IV.

Even at the time when European romanticism flourished and the rational, explicit bases for the "American way of life" were already deeply anchored in American mentality, certain features of European romanticism, itself a complex phenomenon, were not entirely absent from this continent. The term "The American Dream" is, to be sure, perhaps no more than a romanticized way of referring to the desire of immigrants to establish in the New World a more equitable, more egalitarian, more accessible, and more widely prosperous kind of society than the one they left behind in the old one. Nevertheless, "the American Dream" is also related to the utopias of Saint-Simon, Fourier, Bazard, and Enfantin that sprang up in the wake of French romanticism and soon spread to

---

[2] Henry H. H. Remak, "The Socialization of the Student Movement in the United States: The Late 1960s and Early 1970s Revisited," in *Russland Deutschland Amerika: Festschrift für Fritz T. Epstein,* Frankfurter Historische Abhandlungen, no. 8 (Wiesbaden: Steiner, 1978), p. 371. For supplementary retrospective observations on college unrest, see also my "Sweet and Sour: The Student Movement in Bloomington Revisited," *Indiana Alumni Magazine* (April 1980): 10-11.

[3] Donald W. Keim, "'To Make All Things New'—The Counterculture Vision of Man and Politics," in *Human Nature in Politics,* ed. J. Roland Pennock and John W. Chapman, Nomos: Yearbook of the American Society for Political and Legal Philosophy, no. 17 (New York: New York University Press, 1977), 200.

America. They were attempts to restore a paradise lost, but also to adapt it to more modern conditions. In contrast to England, neither the European continent nor the United States had, in the 1840s, made the grim industrial and technological progress that might have eliminated the romantic potential of utopianism. Ingenious adaptations of European utopian-romantic thought took place on the American continent.

Transcendentalism, which attracted some of the best minds of America in the generation of Emerson and Thoreau, combined the pantheism of German romantic philosophy and of English romanticism as well as orientalism with the assertion of the individual, the questioning of established authority, and the self-confident outdoor vitality of America. There was an explosion of American communes in the 1840s which hoped to put Saint-Simonism, Fourierism, or transcendentalism into practice. Hopedale (1841-1856), Brook Farm (1841-1847), and the Northampton Association (1842-1846), all in Massachusetts; the North American Phalanx in Red Bank, New Jersey (1843-1855); and the Wisconsin Phalanx of Fond du Lac (1844-1850) lasted from a few to fifteen years only, but these were significant years. And Mark Holloway reminds us that some religious communes founded in nineteenth-century America were often more durable. The Rappite Community lasted for almost a hundred years; the Zoarites (Ohio, 1819-1898) for almost eighty; the German-inspired societies of Bethel (Missouri, 1844-1880) for nearly forty; and Aurora (Oregon, 1856-1881) as well as the Oneida Community of John Humphrey Noyes in New York (1848-1881) for more than two or three decades. The Swedish Colony at Bishop Hill, Illinois, endured for a decade and a half (1846-1861). The Shakers, though almost extinct, still exist, and the Amana Community, first established near Buffalo, New York, in 1842, moved to Iowa in 1855, and is still functioning. There have been at least eighteen Utopian communities in Indiana alone from Father Rapp's New Harmony of 1814 to Daniel Wright's thriving Padanaram in 1981. All of these were or are "religious groups for whom communism was not an end in itself, but a means of perpetuating a religious way of life."[4] It may be a long way from Noyes to Marcuse, but they do have common elements. Both aim, as did early European romanticism, at the liberation of the individual from nonvoluntary social repression.

The emigration of Europeans to the United States, inasmuch as it was voluntary, meant a rejection of the past, of tradition, of continuity, elements usually associated with romanticism, but one may well ask how voluntary most of the departures were. Economic necessity was an essential factor in the decisions of many to leave, but economic circumstance has no romantic implications. Many religious sects, however, had to flee to the New World against their wills

[4] Mark Holloway, *Heavens on Earth: Utopian Communities in America, 1680 to 1880*, 2d ed. (New York: Dover, 1966), p. 222.

precisely because their heterodox, minority visions of salvation were being repressed. Sects are structured collective expressions of religious individualism, a combination of elements in tension characteristic of early romantic religiosity (Novalis and Chateaubriand). In the isolation of the New World, the Shakers could not only pursue their particular visions through appropriate structures but express them physically in the emotional liberation to which the name of their denomination refers. This structured outlet for each individual's religious frenzy in an otherwise highly organized and disciplined religious community, preserved until our own day by religious fundamentalism in America, by evangelical and pentecostal sects, represents a characteristically American compromise, a union or perhaps only a cohabitation of elements not compatible, it would appear, by rational standards, but fulfilling the complex compensatory needs of human nature. Any viable culture is built on the law of compensation. No matter how strict, extreme, and absolute a culture seems to be, it will provide for compensations that will allow human nature to exist under it, or human nature will create such compensations in defiance, subversion, or mitigation of the dominating elements of the official culture. This holds true for rational outlets for individuals in romantic or utopian cultures as well as for romantic outlets in primarily rational cultures such as the British or American ones.

We can go a step further: even those groups of immigrants which rejected segments of the old culture could not, whatever their original intentions, dismiss it outright as soon as they set foot in America. You have to remain something before and until you become something else. Spatial isolation in the countryside caused by its very vastness and inhospitality,[5] spatial isolation also in the city caused by social and economic restrictions, and the recognition that political weight was dependent on the vote-delivering cohesion of ethnic blocks forced immigrants to prolong their origins, their traditions. Centripetal forces offset, for a while, the centrifugal temptations and insecurities of this endless and unstructured continent. Anthropology, cultural history, folklore, and language students are well aware that older traditions, customs, mentalities, and linguistic forms are sometimes preserved in encapsuled American ethnic groups (Pennsylvania Dutch, Dakota Norwegians, Minnesota Finns, Michigan Dutch, Quebec or Louisiana French) longer than in the old country. The conflict between adaptation to a new, pragmatically demanding environment and the clinging to old habits and beliefs created a tension akin to that of romanticism.

---

[5] An ingenious though debatable thesis of "the tendency of certain American writers to dilate into space around them" (p. 166), contrary to European poets who face "everywhere the trace of men" (see William Cullen Bryant's poem quoted below), is proposed by Tony Tanner, "Notes for a Comparison between American and European Romanticism," in *Diverging Parallels: A Comparison of American and European Thought and Action* (Leiden: Brill, 1971), pp. 144-68.

There was so much—too much—nature in the infinite stretches of this new world, the settling down was so ferocious a struggle against the encroachments of nature, against the violent elements in a climate with extreme contrasts that a pantheistic nature worship, the need for romantic relief from crowds and civilization, was inappropriate through much of the nineteenth century. Yet Thoreau and Whitman did not fall from heaven. Ornamental as William Cullen Bryant's style was, he coined some firm, lean lines of American romanticism such as those in which he admonishes his friend, the painter Thomas Cole departing for Europe (1829-1830) to "keep that earlier, wilder image bright," the "lone lakes," the "savannas where the bison roves," the rocks, the "skies, where the desert eagle wheels and screams." The recurrence of "wild" is practically a code word for American romanticism, whether in the verse of Bryant, Longfellow, and Emerson, or as a theme in the paintings of the Hudson River school. The dramatic, elemental power of plains, prairies, deserts, and mountains, of huge, decayed and dead trees, of forest jungles, forbidding rocks, untamed rivers, waterfalls, the vast, only partly prettified vistas convey a sense of cosmic dynamics, of a quasi-religious infiniteness, a total environmentalism: "Over me soared the eternal sky, . . . I yielded myself to the perfect whole" (Emerson, "Each and All"). Directly influenced by the poetry and concepts of German pre-romantic nature verse is a poem like "Waldeinsamkeit," but even there Emerson's American accents are unmistakable:

> The black ducks mounting from the lake,
> The pigeon in the pines,
> The bittern's boom, a desert make
> Which no false art refines.

There is a taxonomic precision in this American version of romanticism, a conscious effort to show that this is "the real thing." Much more *raffiné*, effect-conscious, dazzlingly technique-oriented is the calculated morbidity of Edgar Allan Poe, a sort of American Musset and pre-Baudelaire.

All this is only to say, through a few examples, that cultural earthquakes or volcanic eruptions, though a hundred years and more may lie between the events, are often preceded by tremors. If the constellations were uniquely right for an American brand of cultural romanticism in the 1960s, there had to be a historical hinterland for it, if subdued and counterpoint: a potential, not a norm. The impact of Rousseau's pedagogical, civic, natural growth concepts on Thoreau and subsequently on American educational theory and practice in the twentieth century is also a major factor in the preparation of a nutrient soil in which the counterculture could grow, given irrigation at the right moment.

## V.

I shall now try to trace the principal configurations of European romanticism and then see to what extent there are corresponding features in the American counterculture of the late 1960s and early 1970s. To safeguard the integrity of such a comparison, I will follow the framework of my graphic representation of European romanticism as proposed in 1961, at a time when I did not have the slightest inkling of such phenomena as a student movement or the counter-culture.[6]

## 1) Cohesiveness

The first category of comparison is *chronological cohesiveness*. West European romanticism saw its heyday in England and Germany between the 1790s and 1830, in France between 1800 and the early 1840s, in Italy between 1816 and the 1850s, in Spain between 1830 and 1845. The span of the contemporary American counterculture was much shorter: from the middle 1960s to the early 1970s. It is likely that the tremendous acceleration of the communications industry and its frantic exploitation of trendy currents in the second half of the twentieth century makes the flux of cultural forces much swifter and exhausts them much sooner. But there are also other, inherent characteristics of the counterculture that make it, to be sure, a very interesting offshoot of romanticism comparable to it in themes, trends, and diffusion, but in no way up to it in depth, and therefore unlikely to generate equivalent duration.

A second part of cohesiveness is *self-consciousness*. Self-consciousness is sometimes mistaken, in the case of romanticism, for the self-labeling as "romantics." While the appearance and success, even among romantics, of the term "romantic" varied widely across Europe, there was in Germany, France, Italy, and Spain, to a lesser degree in England, a marked self-consciousness as adherents (whether individual or as a group) to beliefs, ideas, and artistic directions which we associate with romanticism. The same sort of self-conscious cohesiveness held for the counterculture: while highly individualistic and

[6] Henry H. H. Remak, "West European Romanticism: Definition and Scope," in *Comparative Literature: Method and Perspective,* ed. Newton P. Stallknecht and Horst Frenz (Carbondale: Southern Illinois University Press, 1961), pp. 223-59, particularly 238-45. The corresponding section in the second, revised edition (1971), pp. 275-311, particularly pp. 292-99, differs only occasionally from the earlier version. My first attempt in print to connect the counterculture and European romanticism may be found in "Trends of Recent Research on West European Romanticism," in *"Romantic" and Its Cognates: The European History of a Word,* ed. Hans Eichner (Toronto: University of Toronto Press, 1972), pp. 475-500, particularly pp. 478-80.

privately oriented, the counterculture opposed a set of spiritual and social credos to the values held by the American establishment. Basically, as Keim has pointed out, they rejected imposed structure, the cult of technology, materialism, systems in general, and they embraced private sensitivity, love of man, animals, plants, meditation: a humanistic creed. Communal living, often satisfied with the bare necessities, based on voluntarism without formal ties or commitments, constantly realigning relationships replaced fixed social and economic obligations explicit or implicit in bourgeois society. Free association with the other sex, though with a sense of responsibility, was also a tenet practiced in the famous Oneida Community (New York, 1848-1881) of John Humphrey Noyes. It has been revived in many of the more secular and ephemeral present-day communes, in contrast to the return to traditional values in others. In this connection, we may remind ourselves that the rotation of partners on either side had been a significant feature of English, German, and French romanticism. The well-known male examples of Shelley, Byron, and Musset are fully matched on the female side by Dorothea Veit Schlegel, Karoline Schlegel Schelling, Sophie Mereau Brentano, Wilhelmine Schröder Devrient, Germaine de Staël, and George Sand.

Communes were, as I have noted, among the most characteristic socioeconomic manifestations of romantic-utopian thought in the United States. They made a particular impact on nineteenth-century America, especially at Brook Farm due to its association with Hawthorne, Emerson, and Margaret Fuller. Even though few of them survived a generation, their nineteenth-century cohesiveness ensured, relatively speaking, a longer life span for them than the much more casual country and especially city communes generally enjoyed in the 1960s and early 1970s. The many differences between and among nineteenth- and twentieth-century communes and the fact that they represented confluences in which romanticism was only one component are not to be gainsaid here: what matters is to point to the birth of a type of romantic commune in both periods founded as an attempt to combine spiritual individualism and communism, Christianity and Socialism, idealism and the demands of material support, in a mini-community that represented a social utopia, the modern equivalent of what prior to romanticism would likely have been wholly religious communities affiliated with and ultimately subject to structured church authority, not personal conscience.

A third determinant of cohesiveness in the case of romanticism is the *existence of a body of doctrine.* In 1961, I gave a negative reply to the question: does European romanticism come up with a coherent body of similar metaphysics, theory, or criticism? Ten years later, I thought it was a toss-up. In Germany, the combined weight of Kant, Schelling, G. H. Schubert, Schleiermacher, Schopenhauer, Schiller ("Über naïve and sentimentalische Dichtung"), the Schlegel brothers, Novalis, Kleist ("Über das Marionettentheater"), Hegel,

and Heine almost requires an affirmative answer; in France, while metaphysics played a small role, manifestoes of literary romanticism (Madame de Staël, Stendhal, Hugo) enunciated clear alternatives to classicism; in relativistic England, despite the efforts of Wordsworth, Coleridge, and Shelley, the formulation of doctrine is subdued; in Italy and in Spain, there is little or none.[7]

If romanticism, intellectually far more sophisticated than the counterculture, had difficulty coming up with coherent theory (probably *because* of its sophistication), how much greater were the difficulties of the American counterculture of the 1960s to rally around some kind of bible! If anything, the opening pages of the Port Huron Statement of SDS, which reached a third printing of 60,000 copies within four years of its publication, filled that need. The activist socio/political/economic program, which dominates most of the Port Huron Statement, and the subsequent radicalization of SDS have obscured the introductory sections ("Agenda for a Generation," "Values," pp. 3-8) which present an eloquent case for a socialist neo-romanticism. They attack the distaste of the times for idealism, utopias, crusades, visions, "oppose depersonalization," extol man's "unrealized potential for self-cultivation, self-direction, self-understanding, and creativity," his potential to find "a meaning in life that is personally authentic," "a quality of mind [that]...has full, spontaneous access to present and past experiences," "one with an intuitive awareness of possibilities," which "would replace power rooted in possession...by power and uniqueness rooted in love, reflectiveness,...and creativity" as well as in reason. One of their "root principles" of "Participatory democracy"—"that decision-making of basic social consequence be carried on by public groupings"—has probably come closer to being implemented in the nineteenth-century communes than in any other American context.

My last criterion for cohesiveness is the *pervasiveness* of the romantic movement in various national settings. I concluded in 1961 that romanticism has been the strongest single influence on German culture in the last century and a half when one adds up its impact on literature, art, music, religion, philosophy, historical scholarship, political thinking, and science. French romanticism also went considerably beyond literature: Berlioz in music, Delacroix and Géricault in painting, Michelet in historiography, Cousin in philosophy and education, Cuvier in science, but its latter-day influence in France has been less penetrating than in Germany. The radius of romanticism in English culture has been more circumscribed yet (Turner, Carlyle), and in Italy and Spain romanticism seems largely restricted to literature and politics. Still, despite marked national differences, European romanticism is expansive by nature.

---

[7] I would have to revise this verdict somewhat today. There is some consistency to the limited, sensible, and practical characterization of Italian romanticism by Berchet and Manzoni.

We are too close to the American counterculture to be able to assess the pervasiveness of its impact on our total culture. But it has certainly permeated our life-styles far more than is generally recognized. The declining number of available jobs has brought back the traditional competitiveness, vocationalism, and materialism to our youth, but when one talks to them individually one perceives that the counterculture has left its traces. Success and comfort at any price hold less appeal to them than to preceding generations. Unconventional life-styles are not only practiced more widely than fifteen years ago but are accepted or tolerated, even when not personally favored, by what seems to be a majority (or at least a considerable portion) of college students and by a substantially greater segment of the total population than was the case fifteen years ago. Cohabitation before marriage is more frequent: it is deliberately practiced—wisely or unwisely but not just casually or hedonistically—as a commitment, if temporary, of two people to each other, as a life-style alternative, not necessarily as a rebellion against the majority life-style but as a complement. Sex is no longer seen as an official taboo permitted only under certain conditions prescribed by religion or society, isolated out of context by the media (glossy magazines, Madison Avenue, pornography, film, television, literature) but as a matter of personal decision involved in a larger option for a life-style emphasizing feeling, reciprocal sensitivity, respect for the individual, for "otherness." Note, for example, the frequency with which personal commitments and qualifications, not to speak of folk or folk-like music, have been introduced by bridegroom and bride into traditional marriage ceremonies. The ceremony is, increasingly, an official confirmation of a life already shared together for months or years preceding the wedding. Encounters, vibration sessions, sensitivity training, stripping protective covers from inner emotions and resentments, while they have declined in their more radical and trendy form, have resulted in what every sensitive teacher of college youth knows is a greater awareness of, willingness to admit, and ability to express inner feelings; e.g., in the diaries now part of undergraduate work in some courses. Homosexuality and lesbianism are still minority life-styles but are practiced more openly, tolerated more widely, and in some towns even protected by ordinances and official provisions. Concern for the underdog (which may be taken literally: recall the cult of stray dogs in the counterculture) has been a leitmotif throughout the counterculture: the black, the Indian, the Latino, the woman, the homosexual, the child, the handicapped, old age, the environment, the consumer. Man's and woman's counterculture dress habits, with flowing hair, simple, rustic, even tattered clothing, sandals or barefootedness for both sexes, plus flourishing, untrimmed beards for the male, look, in many cases, like portraits of earlier eras, including those of romantics. The luxuriant hair culture, "feminine" clothing and accessories (e.g., colorful, ruffled shirts, open jewelry, handbags, all for *men*) have undoubtedly receded from their peak in the early 1970s but nevertheless remain, albeit often in fashionable guise, part of the life-style landscape.

To the extent one can draw a comparison at so early a stage, the counterculture cannot, far from it, measure up to the total intellectual, artistic, religious, scholarly, political, and scientific contribution of romanticism to our culture. In all of these areas, the quality, not the quantity of the latter-day romanticism of the counterculture seems distinctly inferior. Charles Reich's *The Greening of America* (1970), hailed as "a first-rate piece of creative thinking" by none other than Supreme Court Justice William O. Douglas, serialized by so hyper-sophisticated a medium as *The New Yorker,* or even the far more substantive books by Theodore Roszak can certainly stand no comparison with the critical prose of Schiller, the Schlegel brothers, Novalis, Kleist, Heine, Wordsworth, Coleridge, Shelley, Carlyle, Mme. de Staël, Chateaubriand, Hugo, Musset, Manzoni, Stendhal, or Larra, and neither can any of the other fast-written, media-oriented products of the counterculture. Allen Ginsberg, while no mean talent, has howled too long and too loud. Woody Guthrie's "This land is your land, this land is my land, from California to the New York Island" may have been the harbinger of the revolution for Reich, who presents it as such, but whatever its noble sentiments it must belong to the most impoverished octaves of good literature. Andy Warhol's Pop Art will never be considered by future generations in the same category as Caspar David Friedrich, Philipp Otto Runge, Delacroix, Géricault, or Turner, nor will rock 'n roll be placed in the same league as Beethoven, Weber, Schubert, Schumann, Mendelssohn, and Berlioz.

To some extent, however, the counterculture's relative lack of artistic and intellectual excellence is beside the point when talking of life-styles rather than of high culture. Counterculture music not only liberated, for better or worse, the irrational potential, the primitive frenzy of youth frowned on by rational society, but also a kind of lyric and compassionate sensitivity previously inhibited by our "don'ts."

In the common attitudes, in the daily mentality of millions of people, the counterculture has made a difference that may be covered up for a time or pruned, but not obliterated. The world can never be the same again as it was before 1967, all wishful thinking notwithstanding. The democratization and individualization of the counterculture, stripped of its too time- and fashion-bound excrescences, will be with us for a long time, affecting many more people in their daily lives than romanticism managed to touch in its day.

## 2) Attitude toward the Past

The second category in my 1961-1971 survey of romanticism is the *attitude toward the past*. English, French, and German pre-romanticism and romanticism displayed a strong interest in nonclassical (Nordic, Celtic, Scottish) mythology: Schütze, Mallet, Ossian, Percy, Gray, Warton, Herder, Scott, Coleridge, Fouqué, Oehlenschläger, Goldschmidt, and Hugo represent this

current, which reaches its peak in none other than Richard Wagner. The only contemporary equivalent of which I am aware is the tremendous popularity of J. R. R. Tolkien's *Lord of the Rings* trilogy in the 1960s and 1970s. How closely, if at all, it can be linked to the counterculture I am not prepared to say. It may reflect a more generalized yearning in a confused, hyperrelativized age for romance, for heroic myths, for clear distinctions between good and evil.[8]

The major difference between European romanticism and the American counterculture in regard to their senses of the past is that French, Italian, and, to a lesser extent, English, German, and Spanish romanticism were reacting against the cultural hegemony of Greece and Rome by either rejecting it or by romanticizing the classical heritage, whereas to the counterculture classical models meant next to nothing.

The next characteristic of European romanticism's attitude toward the past, its affinity for *folklore, primitivism,* and the entire concept of *childhood,* or *childlikeness,* is most strongly shared by the counterculture. Collecting folksongs, folk ballads, and folktales was one of the central aims of romantics in Germany and Scandinavia. England had gotten an early start with Percy's *Reliques of Ancient English Poetry* in the 1760s and sustained it with Scott. High culture in France was taken with the idea of primitivism (Rousseau), but showed little interest in the folklore of France's various regions. Spain, much less centralized and Europeanized than France, had preserved a much stronger tradition of regional culture, of folk adages, than her neighbor to the north. Italy, always strongly classicistic, evinced little concern with her folklore.

The causes of this descent to the folk are linked to eighteenth-century ideas of the relativity of cultural values: the uniqueness of each people and its culture, the revitalization of literature through the unspoiledness of a sane and hearty population layer still closer to nature than their rulers and unaffected by centuries of increased artificiality and privilege, the discovery of a secularized religion rooted in the origin of people, in their original equality, and a populism with wide literary, musical, philosophical, anthropological, social, and political implications. All this is equally relevant to the cult of the folk in the counterculture, down to dressing like the folk, a strained endeavor not devoid of artificiality itself: the cult of dungarees,[9] of sandals or bare feet, of flowing hair, of

---

[8] Tolkien-type literature has flourished and continues to do so: see, for example, the *Earth Sea* trilogy by Ursula K. LeGuin, Fritz Lieber's *The Swords of Lankhmar,* Anne McCaffrey's *Dragonquest.*

[9] The longevity and intensity of the craving for "Levis" not only throughout the West but even in the Communist countries is one of the most telling, if diluted, phenomena of the counterculture. Starting mainly as a semi-political opposition gesture, it has been co-opted, like so many ideas of the counterculture, by the manufacturing Establishment in the western hemisphere and even by the powers-that-be in the eastern orbit, though there it retains some opposition flavor.

raggedness or worse, of a kind of "naive" language. Working on the soil, if haphazardly, communion with nature, limited material wants, opposition to the intrusion of technology on simple needs, mistrust of the Establishment: the counterculture had all of these romantic affinities with the folk. The return to a deliberately chosen old-fashioned primitivism devoid of the corrupting blandishments of modern technology and advertising, opposed to mass production of objects as much as to the standardization of people permeated the counterculture. Undoing the evils of civilization, starting all over again with God's or nature's creature links the two movements. The pristineness of the child, an unspoiled work of nature, corresponds to the childhood of man, whose primitive occupations of woodcutting or pottery-making or ornament-carving or metal-hammering or plant-growing the counterculture tried to restore.

There is a connection between the flower children of the counterculture and the Wertherian themes of biblical primitivism and veneration of Homer, Werther's reciprocated love of children and of the common folk, and how he nurses his heart "like a child"—themes interwoven in letters written within four days of each other (12-15 May, 1771). The canine proclivities of the counterculture are but a visible illustration of this love of the primitive creature. There is undoubtedly a difference in the viability of these primitivistic aspirations now and a century and a half ago: in romanticism, which occurred before technology and urbanization had progressed very far, what was sought was a change of personal consciousness to less rational, less materialistic, less worldly values. The environment was hardly in the danger in which it finds itself toward the end of the twentieth century. The polluted Establishment against which the romantics reacted was in the mind more than in the backyard. "Turning back the clock" in the 1820s seemed much more feasible than it did in the 1970s. The odds against the environment are far greater now than they were 150 years ago. Runaway industrialization and urbanization may lend urgency to the cry of the counterculture for a vaguely Rousseauistic "return to nature" (that includes the origins or at least the earlier stages of *human* nature), but the undeniable comforts of modern middle-class living make such a reversal unlikely.[10]

Another significant difference is the link that exists in romanticism (but not in the counterculture) between folklore/primitivism/cult of childhood and the assertion of *national identity*. In countries such as Norway, in what is now Yugoslavia, Czechoslovakia, Poland, Hungary, Rumania, and Bulgaria, dominated by alien powers, or in lands such as eighteenth-century Germany and Spain greatly swayed by foreign cultures, notably French, the folk seemed to represent the last hope of preserving ethnic or national identity. Nationalism, with its early-twentieth century flavor of aggression, is, however, completely alien to the

---

[10] For an amplification of the complex connections between primitivism, folklore, medievalism, and the cult of childhood, see my "A Key to West European Romanticism?", *Colloquia Germanica* 1/2 (1968): 41-43.

American counterculture. But there is a desire to perpetuate a down-to-earth American past patterned after the eighteenth and early nineteenth century and now in danger of being swallowed up by Madison Avenue, Wall Street, and Washington. In addition to linking up again with mainstream Americanism of the past (Reich's Consciousness I), the counterculture is sympathetic to ethnic revival, to a nonmilitary form of self-preservation of collective minority identity.

*Medievalism* is the third item of consequence in romanticism's attitude toward the past. Given the post-medieval origins of the United States, it is out of place in the counterculture. Still, the growing popularity of Renaissance fairs in this country reflects something of a nostalgia for costuming, for the colorful, differentiated past of America's mother continent, Europe, a protest against the functional, prefabricated, standardized cement block aspects of our culture.

## 3) General Attitudes

Passing to my third category, *general attitudes,* the first element that will rank high in any definition of romanticism is *imaginativeness.* The counterculture is, almost by definition, imaginative in proposing new options in American lifestyles: inner satisfaction rather than success, companionship rather than competition, love rather than struggle and tension, relaxation rather than effort, inner evolution rather than achievement, dreams rather than prosaic reality, highs rather than lows, flux rather than channels. Imagination, dreams and nightmares, unreality as the ultimate reality—a very romantic tenet—are stimulated by the use of drugs as they were in the days of romanticism and post-romanticism: Coleridge and De Quincey were addicts; Keats, Poe, and Baudelaire partook of drugs; Nerval and Rimbaud probably did, possibly even Mérimée; Scott used them occasionally. E. T. A. Hoffmann and Verlaine stayed, more conventionally, with alcoholic drugs. "Spaciness"—drug-induced or not—is part of the counterculture as it is part of romanticism (Blake, Novalis, Coleridge, and Nerval). The inventiveness of the counterculture tends toward the improvised, the situational, the reactive, the ephemeral; toward pantomime, masks, dances; toward fanciful clothing, rather than toward the permanent works of art and the monumental milestones of romanticism.

The *cult of strong emotions and sensualism* is a marked feature of romantic works and, in some cases, lives: Coleridge, Byron, Shelley, Scott, Poe, Blicher, Oehlenschläger, Goldschmidt, Novalis, Friedrich Schlegel, Tieck, Kleist, Hugo and Stendhal. The privileged status of emotions is also a major distinguishing mark of the counterculture. So are its fewer inhibitions in showing and implementing sensual attraction. But eroticism and sex in the counterculture are not like romantic sensuality. They are intimately tied up not with passion, but with the diffused cult of sensitivity, of vibrations; counterculture eroticism is too passive, too derivative to be a passionate movement like romanticism. The

dynamics of counterculture sensuality are dispersed and do not seem to find expression in strong lives or works.[11] Furthermore, the counterculture's distrust of intellectual modes (its typical "I [we] *feel* that..." rather than "I [we] *think* that...") does not correspond to the profound originality of much romantic thinking.

*Restlessness* and *boundlessness*, however, are traits that join the counterculture with romanticism.[12] "Finding oneself" was one of the favorite preoccupations of the counterculture. This restless fixation on growing toward ever-receding personal bounds reminds one of the absorption in adolescence and youth, in biological, generational confrontation inherent in the German romantic tradition all the way up to Hesse, who probably constitutes the single most influential literary source of the American counterculture.[13] The prolongation of adolescence in the counterculture is a protest in the romantic manner against structured society, whether capitalistic or socialistic, fascist or communist, that wants to make every citizen a productive part of the system as soon as possible. The cult of adolescence in the counterculture also has hedonistic motivations not on a par with less "instant-gratification" oriented romantic endeavor. Aversion to assuming responsibility, catering to one's own psychological comfort, fear of maturity, and confidence that ultimately compassionate bourgeois society will support its deviants anyway: these belong to the less admirable traits of the counterculture.

A beautiful contemporary example of the romantic combination in the counterculture of aggressive and passive, militant and contemplative, "progressive" and hedonistic ideology, of Marx, Schopenhauer, and Freud is the work of Herbert Marcuse, one of the prophets of the movement. Marcuse's semi-utopian visions of a post-industrial, humanistic, more "pleasure-and-fulfillment" oriented society have been dealt a blow, however, by the industrial slump of the 1970s.

[11] See Theodore Roszak's criticism of the psychedelic self-indulgence of the counterculture, which he otherwise favors, in "The Counterfeit Infinity: The Use and Abuse of Psychedelic Experience," *The Making of a Counter Culture: Reflections on the Technocratic Society and Its Youthful Opposition* (Garden City, New York: Doubleday, 1969), pp. 155-77.

[12] On romantic restlessness and other themes touched on in this essay, see my "Exoticism in Romanticism," *Comparative Literature Studies* 15 (March 1978): 53-65.

[13] On the impact of German adolescent motifs on the contemporary American youth movement, see James P. O'Donnell, "Behind the Revolt of the Young: From *Wandervogel* to SDS," *American-German Review* 35 (Spring 1969): 6-10; Walter Laqueur, "Reflections on Youth Movements," *Commentary* 47 (June 1969): 33-41; Jeffrey Sammons, "Notes on the Germanization of American Youth," *The Yale Review* 49 (March 1970): 342-56 (Hesse and Marcuse); and Egon Schwarz, "Hermann Hesse, the American Youth Movement, and Problems of Literary Evaluation," *PMLA* 85 (October 1970): 977-87.

*Individualism, subjectivism, introversion,* and the *cult of uniqueness* are further hallmarks of the romantic genius. The strength and continuity of this theme go back all the way to Rousseau and Diderot, to English pre-romanticism, to *Sturm und Drang,* and via romanticism proper, with authors and works too numerous to mention, to Baudelaire, symbolism, neo-romanticism, Hesse, Proust, and Thomas Mann. Psychological introversion may be considered the foremost single feature of twentieth-century fiction and lyrics. All four characteristics mentioned are practically synonymous with the counterculture. To discover and preserve the real self behind and under social and economic shibboleths imposed and perpetuated by the majority culture, to cater to the "vibes" of one's feelings (see again Charles Reich's *The Greening of America*) and to pick up those of others "encountered," the precedence to be granted to gut feelings over rationality, the adoption of Rousseau's tenet that the heart has its own reason, all these represent a departure from American norms which have emphasized social, rational, pragmatic, consensus controls of emotions. Individualism, a cherished traditional value of American life, has had to be corroborated by social and economic responsibility. Subjective opinions, likewise accorded considerable tolerance and even encouragement in this country, respond to a kind of unspoken control that prevents them from becoming too personal, too embarrassing. Personal discussions, in-depth, even between two friends (let alone among groups of them) are not "the thing to do." Introversion, an excessive concern with the self, is commonly frowned on in America as some kind of abnormality, since social cooperation, doing good (or, more commonly, doing well) constitute the horizon of expectation. Originality in America is therefore subject to consensus controls. Inventiveness and enterprise are highly esteemed; but most highly prized—not just pragmatically but morally—is the kind of originality that results in social and economic progress, in a "better life" not only for oneself but for others. Originality to fulfill oneself, originality in ideas that may run counter to America's rationalism in matters social, political, and economic is not eligible for a very high rating in our national creed, except in matters religious where a tremendous diversity reigns, perhaps another example of cultural compensation. At any rate, the counterculture strove mightily—and quite successfully—to expand the air and the space granted to subjective values, to uniqueness, in American society.

The eighteenth century, particularly Rousseau and Goethe, had conditioned men and women to gain an *empathy for nature* that went beyond the decorative stage. Romanticism intensified the Enlightenment's deism and pantheism by probing the depths of the links between nature and man's nature, and in some cases went so far as to assign nature a role in man's existence separate and even independent from God and running the gamut from closest intertwining with man to the kind of neutrality or indifference starkly described by Vigny, Leopardi, and Heine. The counterculture's affinity for nature (country com-

munes, simple non-chemical farming, vegetarianism, natural foods, plant remedies, love of animals, farm-like clothing) is not cast in the theological, philosophical, or otherwise intellectual mold of romanticism but rather in the less demanding shape of an intensely personal, sentimental desire to seek refuge in rural nature from the urban complexities of contemporary technology and big organizations.[14] Here, however, a rare tripartite coalition, environmentalism, has been forged between the more individualistic, more passive segments of the counterculture, its more public, more aggressive activists, and the general public. What was originally a private sentiment of revulsion against the pollution of nature, against its surrender to material progress has struck roots in the existential anxieties of so many "normal" citizens that the ecology has become one of the strongest political forces in American life, well organized, well financed, and assured of continuity even now that it has suffered some setbacks at a time of equal concern with inflation and recession. The main reasons why the romantic care about nature, in the garb of ecological responsibility, has been able to achieve this leverage is that it appeals to the rational daily concerns and desires of the average citizen, to his fear of catastrophe. (Without the anti-nuclear movement environmentalism might not be as strong, just as the student movement of the 1960s and early 1970s needed Vietnam as a pacemaker.) But environmentalism has also brought about a definite change of consciousness, an adjustment of values, both romantic and countercultural, that emphasizes the quality of life as against the quantity of commodities. (One recalls Rousseau's protest against the comfort and luxury prized by such representatives of eighteenth-century Enlightenment as Voltaire).

A *rediscovery of the potential of religion* is another of the dominating lineaments of romanticism. It is related to the rehabilitation of feeling and its unfettered expression (including torrents of tears) by the eighteenth century. That epoch, with all its secularization and skepticism, cultivated a vigorous, highly individualized religious spirit, far more personal than organizational, particularly in the Protestant countries where sects combined individual yearnings with collective needs. Romanticism went one step further: it reintegrated transcendental religion into man's daily existence as a vital force and reestablished it as one of the fountains of human consciousness in mythology and history. Romantic medievalism leaned, of course, heavily on religion. There was a marked Catholic trend in religious romanticism even when the poets remained Protestant like Novalis, not to speak of conversions or reconversions: Friedrich Schlegel, Brentano, Zacharias Werner, Görres, Adam Heinrich Müller, Manzoni, Chateaubriand. This return to the collective security of Catholicism

[14] See, for instance, Zbigniew Brzezinski, who speaks of an anti-technological romanticism supported mainly by the "soft" sciences and the humanities in his *Between Two Ages: America's Role in the Technectronic Era* (New York: Viking, 1971).

was, in part, a reaction to the sullied ideals of the French Revolution which resulted in a period of conservatism and reaction between 1815 and 1848 that kept the lid on the continually sprouting liberalism. Even among writers less marked by personal religious crises religion reasserted itself as a powerful motif: Kleist, Eichendorff, Mme. de Staël, Lamartine, Vigny, Hugo.

In the counterculture, there is also a dimension of religious revival. Because, probably, of the apparent quasi-monopoly of rational, practical, consensus thinking in America, and because the counterculture was largely limited to adolescence, the "movement's" reassertion of sentiment during the 1960s and early 1970s took on decidedly anti-rationalistic, nonlogical, even anti-intellectual tones that made it the despair of well-meaning observers struggling to do justice to it. The religious side of the counterculture has had, unlike romanticism, little to show in the way of intellectual advance. Charisma and personal example rather than theological insights or beliefs explain why the Jesus cult has retained a strong hold on many American youth to this day. The worship of Jesus and of John Lennon have much in common. As in the aftermath of the French Revolution and later on of Napoleon, when disappointment with mundane leaders led to the resurrection of spiritual leaders, young America's disenchantment with Presidents Johnson and Nixon and frustration over the assassination of such worldly best hopes as President Kennedy, Senator Robert Kennedy, and Martin Luther King provided the counterculture with fertile soil in which born-again Christian and non-western spiritual movements could germinate. Much of religious countercultural activity has been an adaptation of Oriental religion to American life, ranging from visual and olfactory Oriental paraphernalia and drugs, from contemplative habits of relaxation and abstinence to worship of a mystically endowed sage as guru or shaman. Collective discipline and semi-indoctrination seem to have prevailed in these transcendental denominations. These sects seem to have declined, but they are far from out of the picture. Here religion is clearly intended to fill the vacuum felt by a generation of youths no longer held or beholden to a normative morality in society. There is a fascination with primitive, non-establishment religions. A feminist variety of this cult has resulted in the rehabilitation of witches, acclaimed as suppressed females.

Counterculture religiosity is a difficult area to assess, particularly in its intellectual quality, which seems low, whereas its personal significance has been considerable and remains so. The force of the religious revival among American youth is certainly fed by the perennial vitality of religion in America, which is far greater than its strength in Western Europe, an observation that is perhaps the most striking insight gained by a West European who compares the two cultures. Much of this aliveness of American religion is due to the uniquely successful Puritan mixture of ethics and economics, which is one of the foundations of this nation. It is also due to the lucky fact (for religion) that it is strictly separate from the state, not only in theory but in practice. Hence American churches have

provided independent forces in but not necessarily for the Establishment, relying completely on volunteers and thus ensuring the spontaneity and vigor of religious critiques of social, economic, and political power in America. The religious sensitivities of the counterculture, though going into mystical directions at odds with majority religion in the United States, thus feed on the indirect support of a cultural system to which they appear antagonistic—a system which fosters discipline in politics (only two major parties), but anarchy in religion.

Saint-Preux, Werther, René, Obermann, Adolphe, works of Coleridge, Lamartine, Byron, Vigny, Musset, Larra, Espronceda, and Leopardi, even, on occasion, Wordsworth ("The World is too much with us") are variations on one of the most sustained themes of pre-romanticism and romanticism: *Weltschmerz, le mal du siècle.* The theme of being "turned off" by a world that is no habitat for sensitive souls, inadequate at best, sordid at worst, is also echoed in the counterculture and its music. This penchant might be attributable to what struck the counterculture as a deeply engrained fixation on material comfort in American bourgeois society, a kind of hopelessness about competing with the technological thrills of the society that dutifully punches the time-clock from 8 a.m. to 5 p.m. and pushes television entertainment buttons from 8 p.m. to the late show. Both romantic *Weltschmerz* and counterculture repugnance for middle-class priorities enjoyed a privileged sanctuary. In the eighteenth and nineteenth centuries, *Weltschmerz* could be considered an appanage of the aristocracy; in the twentieth century, American universities provided the equivalent of the aristocratic setting in which *le mal du siècle* was endemic. On sheltered campuses, students or former students could find a constant supply of recruits; here they could count on tolerance and even some sympathy not extended to them in the marketplaces of the land. Instead of aristocratic parents, friends, or patrons, they could bank, if the chips were really down, on the financial support of their ever patient and hopeful mother and, perhaps less frequently, father, and on help in some form or other from the university community. What distinguished the counterculture's *mal du siècle à l'américaine* from its romantic predecessors was a willingness and perhaps even eagerness, very much in the mainstream American tradition, to resort to manual labor as a way out of or at least as a temporary relief from the marketplace, whereas this was hardly suitable to the pre-romantic and romantic *enfants du siècle.*

One of the most complex aspects of European romanticism is its seemingly contradictory *mixture of liberalism, cosmopolitanism, and nationalism,* depending markedly on the stage of political evolution reached by the particular culture. Equally intricate and much less explored seem to be the political sympathies of the more privately oriented American youth culture of the 1960s and early 1970s, particularly its mixture of strong personal liberalism with aversion to big organizations, including liberal governments and liberal universities. They disliked system, *any* system. There is, however, one striking analogy. Romanti-

cism, with the impetus coming principally from the ideas of Locke, Montesquieu, Vico, Rousseau, and Herder, combined belief in the uniqueness of the individual with belief in the uniqueness and relative equality of specific cultures and thus gave rise not only to romantic individualism but also to romantic collectivism: the uniqueness and inviolability of ethnic or national cultures. As has been noted above, nationalism was alien to the counterculture, but respect for ethnic diversity was strong. It was fed, to some extent, by opposition to what was seen as military interference in the ethnic integrity of Vietnamese culture, which, it was held, American intervention was unhealthily westernizing, modernizing, and commercializing. It was also fed by sympathy for racial and ethnic groups in America (blacks, Latinos, Indians, etc.) that, so it was claimed, had been repressed by the WASP majority and its sympathizers. Ethnic revival and, more than that, revival of indigenous American traditions, local or regional, the cult of our roots and their protection against technological encroachments has spread, interestingly enough, from minority to majority culture and has proved to be one of the most enduring contributions of the youth movement to America.

## 4) Works

My 1961 survey of European romanticism lists as the first item under the category of "works" the *supremacy of lyrical moods and forms*. This would certainly apply to the counterculture, too. Introversion, individualism, and subjectivism lend themselves best to the lyrical mode. The looseness of contemporary fiction is a suitable receptacle for the counterculture, but the structured, disciplined, dialogue-oriented dramatic form is not, except as dialectical-ideological exercises or in its improvised, spontaneous forms like street or guerilla theater, masks, theatrical interruptions of Establishment meetings, etc.

*Exoticism,* a marked propensity of romantic works and their authors,[15] is likewise a highly profiled trait of the counterculture. But whereas romantic exoticism was comprehensive, encompassing North and South, East and West, the counterculture's exoticism is much more eclectic and mainly Oriental. It has co-opted the non-materialistic serenity of Oriental religions and beliefs, whether rooted in the traditions of India, China, Korea, or Japan, achieved by complete relaxation, and focused on meditation or intuitive consciousness.

The counterculture's rejection of worldly ambition and competition and the liberation of consciousness from self-imposed and other-imposed restrictions, from the frantic pressures of "the world" are akin to romantic exoticism and remind one of the teachings of the great post-romantic philosopher Schopenhauer, but there is no evidence that the counterculture knew his work.

---

[15] See my "Exoticism in Romanticism" essay, above.

Finally, *occultism* is a prominent feature of romanticism as well as of the counterculture. It is responsible not only for a revival of witches and demons in countercultural theatrical masquerades but has led to increased materials of this sort in successful fiction and on television (exorcism!).

While the counterculture has not done very well by traditionally central genres, it has revived and strengthened certain arts (folklore, poetic song, pantomime, poster art) and crafts (buckles, belts, jewelry). It has elevated the song into an effective mixture of psychic, folkloristic, social, and even political elements that, carried by the music and performed by singers of tremendous popularity, has caught on with audiences far beyond those directly affiliated with the counterculture. Unlike romantic lyrics and *Lieder,* the songs are not likely to survive long as great works of art, but in this regard the anti consumer-society oriented counterculture is itself subject to consumer demand for its own products which is so great and so constant that it must be fed by constantly new repertoire. Ironically, the counterculture is Big Business. Anti-Establishment modes have become grist for the insatiable media mill of the Establishment in a way unimaginable for the early nineteenth century.

This would have been a great surprise for Hermann Hesse, perhaps the single most important literary guru for the younger elements (high school and early college) of the counterculture. The Hesse cult, previously outlined, is in itself a striking example of the sudden, completely unexpected popularity of a writer who appeared to be thoroughly alien to America. Through the 1950s, even though Hesse had been singled out by a Nobel prize in 1946, he had been written off by the critics' Establishment as an epigone of German romanticism, of interest perhaps to a naive, unworldly, retarded generation of German post-World I youth with their particular hang-ups but not to the up-to-date, sophisticated, and much more realistic reading audience in the United States. But when the time was ripe for Hesse, American youth went aflame for him and his distinctly romantic themes and notions. They were attracted by his openness to and sympathy with the adolescent psyche. They responded to his themes of generational conflict, of repression of sensitive, idealistic youth by an uncomprehending, threatening, middle-class, value-oriented society, by teachers, or by young bullies. They felt the wheels of society and its pedagogical armature rolling over the adolescent (*Unterm Rad—Beneath the Wheel*). They went for the author of the *Steppenwolf* which seemed to imprint a modernist focus, the shifting of consciousnesses complete with drugs, jazz, masks, and a "magic theater" on Hesse's traditional romantic preoccupations. The Oriental gurusim of the counterculture derived happy confirmation from Hesse's *Siddharta.* Even Hesse's refusal to get into any collective endeavors of social activism or political activities of the day while waging an unrelenting fight against technology and its worst product, modern war, was exactly tailored to the point of view of the counterculture.

## VI.

To sum it up, there are striking analogies, qualified similarities, and significant differences between European romanticism and the American counterculture. They have in common chronological cohesiveness and self-consciousness as agents of cultural change. They are anti-rationalistic, stressing sympathy, sensitivity, the raising of consciousness, imaginativeness, psychic experience, sometimes facilitated by drugs. In collective terms, cultism, utopianism, and communes intended to implement these beliefs flourished—and perished. In literature, the lyrical mood and talent prevails. Music is a major allied force. In both, an anti-prescriptive, anti-repressive, anti-institutional individualism asserts itself in all aspects of living, including clothing, drugs, and sexual activity. The "outsider" syndrome is cultivated. The emphasis is on becoming rather than being (in the wake of Rousseau and Hesse). Process, flux, "finding oneself," and adolescence become prime virtues. Restlessness, nostalgia, and exoticism (especially Orientalism) are dominant in both. Religion and transcendentalism are reintegrated into life. Empathy with nature as a mystical force goes, beyond rustic revival, to a cherished discovery of the wild, unprogrammed, chaotic elements of the natural environment. Primitivism is extended, collectively, to the childhood of man, and to the base of society, the people. Popular culture and various ethnic revivals reflect the assertion of the inherent worth of collective individuality.

Qualified similarities include a nostalgia for the past that means, for the counterculture, a return to populism rather than to medieval splendor and religiosity, though with a foible for vaguely historical costuming. The specific mythology of the counterculture, however, is not historical but contemporary: rock 'n' roll. The collective yearnings of romanticism end up in macro-communities: nations and nationalism; those of the counterculture in micro-communities: communes. The *Weltschmerz, le mal du siècle* of the counter-culture seems more transient than that of romanticism. Decisive as the impact of music is on the counterculture, and, through it, on the life-style of the young, it is a much more ephemeral art product than the musical creations of romanticism.

Finally, the differences between romanticism and the counterculture may not be numerous, but they are profound. Even though only ten to fifteen years have elapsed since the counterculture came into its own, it seems likely that its duration and its subsequent impact will not compare with romanticism either in continuity or in depth. The intellectual and artistic substance of the products of the counterculture (not its basic concerns) is not only distinctly but sometimes shockingly inferior to the substance of romanticism. The pictorial arts, with the exception of posters and perhaps film, of the counterculture have yielded little that emulates romanticism. The desperate, tenacious, and, even when unsuc-cessful, admirable struggle of romanticism for synthesis and wholeness is little more than embryonic in the counterculture. Hedonism subverted the apparently

romantic idealism of the counterculture more than one might have hoped. The passion of the counterculture translated into trendy language rather than into sustained, searching emotion. On the other hand, the counterculture eschewed the nationalism into which romanticism eventually fell after its rebound from individualism. And, up against post-industrial technology, a far more formidable foe than early romanticism could dream of, the counterculture fed into environmentalism, one of the great forces of the last three decades of our century.

It would be inappropriate to end this essay with a decisive flourish. I am concerned not with the identification of the American counterculture as neo-romanticism, but with the survival and vitality of romantic notions across time and space under conditions both analogous to and different from those that prevailed at the turn of the eighteenth to the nineteenth centuries.[16] Ideas are forces, and romanticism engendered a force with a staying power equaled only by its protean dynamics.

[16] I do not want to garb this essay in the pretentious raiments of theory, but it could be considered as a particular application to literary and cultural history of stadialism, the theory of literary and cultural analogy developed by the Russian scholar Alexander Nikolayevich Veselovsky (1838-1906) and his adapters, among them Victor Zhirmunsky. See Gleb Struve, "Comparative Literature in the Soviet Union, Today and Yesterday," *Yearbook of Comparative and General Literature* 4 (1955): 1-20; 6 (1957): 7-10; 8 (1959): 13-18.

JOHN H. GAGNON

# Success = Failure/Failure = Success

BY THE END OF THE NINETEENTH CENTURY the behavioral responses which had comprised the program of cultural innovation which resulted from romantic individualism were in the late stages of assimilation by segments of the dominant culture.[1] The key innovation of the romantic program, the existence of a self that could be differentiated "from culture, or society, or values, or beliefs, in short from... the other"[2] was itself fundamentally dependent on a shifting complex of behaviors, the utility of which was their inaccessibility and unacceptability to the other. The capacity of conventional culture in the nineteenth century, a capacity which grew throughout its course, to turn the unacceptable into the acceptable, to co-opt, either piecemeal or *in toto* the various elements of the romantic program, was responsible for both the accelerated rates of change in these elements and

[1] My use of the term "program" follows that of the historian of science Imre Lakatos. See Imre Lakatos and Alan Musgrave, *Criticism and the Growth of Knowledge* (Cambridge: Cambridge University Press, 1970). He uses the word to refer to a core theory that cannot be falsified, surrounded by a set of auxiliary theories which can be tested and refuted by experiment. I would add to this that there is also in the empirical sciences a penumbra of experiments which is tied to the research program. That is, certain experiments are also part of the protective belt surrounding the core theory. From this base the scientist can make risky assertions which can be justified by reference to the core theory. I take it that the belief in the existence of the self is the core belief of the romantic program, a belief that is surrounded by peripheral beliefs or explanations (e.g., the significance of the imagination in creativity) and various experiments to test the auxiliary beliefs (travel, drug taking, etc.). The core belief remains in place once the program has evolved while the auxiliary theories and the body of experiments change over time.

[2] Morse Peckham, "Reflections on Historical Modes in the Nineteenth Century," in *Romanticism and Behavior: Collected Essays, II* (Columbia: University of South Carolina Press, 1976), 40-66.

the final collapse of the program itself. No prior innovative movement had demonstrated such stylistic dynamism within a comparable period, in part because of the internal pressures created by the fragility of the primary goal of its members, but more importantly because of the rising cultural acceptance of their goal (the self as the primary judge of value) as well as the cultural products and performances and activities that made up the program itself.

The innovative cultural products of romantics, whether in establishing a particular personal style and/or in the making of cultural products, involved a systematic process of rule violation, of offending certain accepted and sometimes cherished values and models. It is the systematic character of romantic deviation that distinguishes it from the majority of social rule breaking.[3] The innovative behavior of most deviants is a function of mislearning, error, or drift; and, as a consequence, it is largely self- or other-corrected. Further, the goal of romantic deviation was to maintain the split between the self and the culture, while the majority of non-programmatic deviants either long for a return to the culture, to possess its products, or to merge their selves into life-simplifying social movements. Romanticism became a cultural program and the source of cumulative cultural change because it rested upon a shared belief in a new term for action, the "self," and upon the relation of that term to the culture. Romanticism was a political movement in that it offered an alternative final term to justify behavior (in contrast to "God," "History," "the Folk," "Nature") as well as alternative explanations for action that were competitive with those offered by the dominant culture.

In the last decades of the eighteenth century the "self" had emerged, at least for a narrow cultural elite, as the term that could justify the creation of innovative cultural products. However, the simple assertion by an individual that he or she possessed a unique self and that this self was sufficient justification for cultural deviance was not immediately persuasive either to the individual or to an audience in the climate of the early nineteenth century. The assumption that all individuals possess by nature (or equally magically, by socialization) a unique self—an assumption which has been a core belief of cultural elites during the latter half of the twentieth century in advanced industrial societies—is a consequence, not an antecedent, of the century and a half existence of the romantic program.

[3] The majority of deviant acts are committed by those defined as conventional social actors, who at no point conceive of their actions as a reflection of who they really are. Thus those who buy stolen goods, purchase the services of prostitutes, or drive through red lights all have legitimating justifications for these violations. Some persons who have stable occupational roles in supplying such services have *some* of their conduct defined by roles the contents of which are anti-conventional. Romanticism posed much more far-reaching questions.

The original demonstration that a self had an existential reality and that it was a sufficiently powerful ground for innovation/deviance required more than its verbal assertion. The self had as problematic a status for the romantic as salvation and membership in the elect had for a Calvinist in the early days of the Reformation.[4] Persuasive evidence that an individual Calvinist had an ultimately unprovable membership in an otherworldly congregation required a family of behavioral responses in this world. Thus, plain speech and plain dress, saving and toiling were behavioral responses which offered some form of temporal reassurance that they were saved to individual Calvinists and to the audiences for their conduct. Similarly, a wide range of behavioral responses, a family with historically changing elements, became to romantics the external reassurance that a self existed and that it was uniquely differentiated from the other.

The family of responses that characterized the conduct of innovative romantics of the nineteenth century included physically leaving their received culture; abandoning their own social origins within the society; reinterpreting the history of their culture or themselves (the historicizing impulse); the creation of anti-roles; experimentation with extreme forms of mind-altering experiences (either chemical or erotic); and, in some cases, the expression of these experiences in their cultural products. This congeries of self-affirming responses was aimed at the maintenance of alienation. That is, the activities themselves were the external correlates of the felt state of estrangement from the culture as it existed. The existence of self was a resultant of the program of activities in the world and at the same time served as the justification for them.

The central purpose of romantic physical and social journeys was the removal of the self from the presence of the other. Consider the role of geographical wandering which was a particularly important component in the early family of responses. Physical displacement from the culture of origin offered a critical opportunity for isolating the self from cultural demand. Either an alien physical environment or an alien culture (or their combination) offered a break from cultural demands in terms of expected roles in which conventional feelings, perceptions, and thought are embedded. In the absence of the demands for regularized responses, occasions for novel, extreme, and unshared, perhaps ineffable, experiences and emotions were of increased likelihood. In the romantic wanderer's new, partially inchoate circumstances, the self is painfully free to search for new meaning.

The mountains, the deserts, the sea, the tropical islands were places in which one could free oneself from the other. If such journeys involved profound cultural disorientation so much the better, since the powers of the self, indeed its very

[4] See Max Weber, *The Protestant Ethic and the Spirit of Capitalism* (1904-1905; reprint New York: Scribners, 1950); and R. H. Tawney, *Religion and the Rise of Capitalism* (1922; reprint, New York: Harcourt Brace, 1926).

existence, could be found in its ability to survive dislocation. The innovative cultural products that were constructed from experiences of isolation were themselves another form of evidence for the primacy of the self. The romantic self even in its return from the journey could continue to resist the demands of the other by creating cultural products that invited rejection.

The goal of the physical journey outside was to create the framework for the psychological journey, but this latter journey was also possible without undertaking the former. Wanderings into the past, either of the culture or of the individual, decisions to reanalyze the origins of the collectivity or the personality were also occasions for a break with conventional culture. Gathering new facts, reinterpreting old facts, and providing new explanations for the past were part of the revisionist component of the romantic program. Old sacreds were replaced by new; the new became old and was replaced, in turn, until the existence of any sacred except the self was denied.

The analytic historian or autobiographer who revised the past with new fact and explanation was the positivist parallel to the romantic novelist and poet whose journeys into the self characterized the later phases of the innovative period of the romantic program. Such antiquarian journeys did not require physical movement (even though they might depict alien environments); they could be conducted in the library, the study, the country house, even in the presence of family and friends. The discipline required to maintain selective alienation in the presence of the other, to innovate without a physical departure, to cut the ties of common speech, of the news, of the post, and of physical convenience, as well as cutting the bonds of affection, suggests the possibilities of the privacy afforded to certain romantic figures in the nineteenth century. The romantic journey inward, without benefit of externally provided opportunities of physical detachment, may be one of the great seminal lessons for innovators in the twentieth century.

Regardless of the type of journey taken by the romantics, it often involved moments of extreme psychological difficulty. Even the simple journey abroad of the early romantics must be judged against the historical and cultural context as must be the more extreme drug/eroticism induced journeys of the last half of the century. There were no tour guides or gurus, indeed the territory being mapped was not being discovered, it was being invented by the explorers. The self as now experienced was then in the process of formation.

Travelers of this kind often assumed (and may have desired) few or no followers. The original journey often involved conditions of extreme anxiety, associated with states of radical indecisiveness, that resulted from an entirely novel experience of freedom from social constraint. The existence, character, and value of the self was found in the level of anguish experienced in innovation and in the decisions that finally afforded relief from the anxiety of creation. The post-innovative calm was in part associated with the relief from the anxiety associated with the apparently unsocialized decision making.

The attempt to reduce the frequency of instruction from the culture (the other) and to increase the proportion of "uninstructed," self-based decisions by romantic innovators radically increased the psychological costs they paid for innovation. By expanding the range and number of choices to be made in each act of innovation, the first romantics made innovation more difficult from inception to completion. And the effect of the earliest romantic innovations was cumulatively to increase the burden of innovation on subsequent practitioners of romanticism. The number of decisions to be made and instability of the final decision-maker, the self, made the romantic program particularly exhausting for its participants under the best of circumstances.

Nevertheless, the overwhelming problem for the romantic program as a whole was not primarily the psychological crises of individuals induced by the conditions of solitary innovation, but the rapid and interactive changes in the character of the other which were provoked by romantic innovation. By the middle of the nineteenth century the vast increase in literacy created an audience for romanticism, particularly among the upper middle class, but also among other social formations—an audience not only for the cultural products, but also for the performances and for the family of behavioral responses that were integral to the romantic program. No other program of cultural production had defined the role of its dominant surrounding culture as negative—a negativity that not only looked upon the products of the dominant culture as instructions about what romanticism was not to produce, but a negativity which also assumed that its own producers would be negated in their turn. The eventual acceptance of various elements of the romantic program by that which was ostensibly the other was a major source of the pressures toward innovation felt by successive generations of romantic artists. To the degree that the other, as manifested in various concrete audiences, came to share in the evaluation of the program and its products, including the self—to that degree, the estrangement of self and other necessary to romanticism was being continuously overcome. The accessibility of the entire romantic program (including the belief in the unique self) to imitation and co-optation by those defined as the other meant that its representatives had to add more and more extreme elements to their repertoire of behavioral responses as well as to their products or performances. The anxiety of innovation which was associated with the pursuit of continuous alienation was in this climate an invitation to personal collapse on the part of the artist. The rising hysteria and agitation notable in the late romantics is perhaps the best evidence of a rising cultural pressure and demand for innovation.

The acceptance of romantic works into an established canon began early in the century. The audience for new works, often of a difficult and sensational character, expanded from the thousands to the tens of thousands by the middle of the century. Romantic modes of thinking, feeling, and evaluating became accessible in only slightly modified forms for the education and entertainment of general audiences. In addition, behaviors that were associated with normative

violations (particularly sexual violations on the Continent) became part of the usual content of romantic literature. Representations of romantic journeys (sorts of Baedekers), physical and psychological, became part of poetry, the plastic arts, and music. There was resistance in the provinces, but by the end of the nineteenth century nearly every major romantic work in music, painting, and literature had an audience.

This process of cultural co-optation of the romantic program can be specifically observed in the ways in which behavioral elements in the program were appropriated by the audience. For instance, the journey into strange territories and cultures (which had been a key technique for creating romantic isolation from cultural demands to begin with) was eventually beset not only by the genuine traveler, but also by mere tourists.

The appeal of the mountains as a place for extreme physical and psychological experiences for the early romantics was quickly disseminated to a far wider audience in the newly leisured middle class. The Alpinism of the 1840s was shortly followed in the 1850s and 1860s by walking tours of the Alps and their views conducted for ladies of adventurous spirit. Travel to Africa, to the Near East, and to the Far East became available to a few—and then to the many. The use of travel to meet the needs for social isolation by romantic figures required more and more extreme efforts. In the 1890s and early 1900s, going "outside" was only useful if it also involved going native as well.

A further complication was that many of those who followed the romantics' leads were concerned solely with transitory isolation from cultural demands and, in addition, were experiencing that transitory isolation for purposes of eventual affiliation with conventional goals and purposes. The adventurous journalist or scientist might undertake a journey of extreme physical danger and isolation, but for the purpose of merging himself or herself with the collective. The journey outside was taken in order to bring back a record which indicated the value of the self, but a self that existed in agreement with social demand. By 1912 it was possible for the explorer-scientist R. F. Scott to report that the death of his party on the return from the South Pole should be an example to the English race of the courage and fortitude of its individual members.[5] The failure of Axel Heyst, the hero of Conrad's novel *Victory,* to achieve his goal of permanent isolation from the other may represent the obituary of the journey outside for persons most sensitive to the collapse of this element in the romantic family of responses.[6] For Conrad, who is a bridging figure between the late romantics and the early moderns, there is more than a suspicion that the self cannot escape the other.

The journey outside steadily loses its ability to differentiate the self from the other over the course of the nineteenth century. No longer can this journey, at

[5] R. F. Scott, *Scott's Last Expedition,* 2 vols. (New York: Dodd, Mead, 1913), 1: 411-17.
[6] Joseph Conrad, *Victory* (1915; reprint, New York: Anchor Books, 1957).

least for those at the edge of innovative cultural production, serve its original purpose by providing social isolation and unique experience. This does not mean that such romantic journeys outside have not been undertaken well into the present. Such journeys to alien places and cultures have continued to be the mark of the period of proliferation and dissemination of elements of the romantic program to mass audiences, particularly among former colonial populations. The problem is that during this period of "consumer romanticism" (from 1900 to the near present) the utility of the journey as an occasion for high cultural innovation was severely eroded.

These same forces can be observed eroding other aspects of the romantic program as well. Access to the family of behavior responses or to the romantic anti-roles or to the romantic art-product has created a large number of persons who are seeking the romantic goal, the possession of a unique self somehow differentiated from others. The alienation sought by most of them, however, is neither permanent nor directed at innovative cultural products. The new consumer romantic's purpose in appropriating a specific element from the romantic program is more imitative than innovative. Thus, for example, the tourist is seeking an experience or an adventure in foreign travel. In this journey, the tourist replicates the original romantic's exploit and exhausts its potential for uniqueness and self-affirmation.

The success of the romantic program may, by now, be measured in the generalized popular belief promulgated by the social sciences in the twentieth century that everyone has a unique self. As a result, the relationship between the behavioral elements of the romantic program and the individual has changed radically since its inception. The earliest romantics engaged in the program to demonstrate the existence of their own selves. For them, the possession and uniqueness of an entity called the self was in doubt. The self as a cultural construct and as a personal possession was still in the process of creation. At the present time, however, the self is assumed to exist as the natural outcome of growth and development. Everyone is presumed to possess a self somewhat in the same way that one possesses citizenship. The vulgate self now exists, therefore, *before* the individual begins to experiment with the behavioral components of the romantic program. As a sort of birthright, then, it requires only transient affirmations of its existence and affirmations that are generally available. Thus, even the more extreme experiments with anti-roles and violative chemical and sexual conduct are fairly routinely available to high school students (the bohemian-cum-hippy marijuana user) or to adults (the orgies at swing clubs). That these elements are appropriated for the quite modern purpose of affirming the self before an audience of assumed other selves, that the temporal relation between the emergence of the self and the acquisition of the behavioral repertoire has now shifted, and that the elements themselves are now generally available must make the romantic program, except for the culturally innocent, of limited utility in differentiating the self from the other.

As the journey outside has weakened in its utility for attaining cultural detachment, the journey within has assumed a more salient role in the romantic repertoire, a journey that in itself needed to be associated with other rule violations. This point presumes some temporal order in the history of the romantic program, with more weight given to journeys within, even though historical and personal analysis based on historicizing explanations existed early in the romantic period. The issue is that one member of the family of responses became less useful and left a greater burden for the others. The journey within became the more dominant strategy toward the end of the nineteenth century, and its products were more complex and symbolically idiosyncratic. Its very idiosyncrasy made each new journey inward a far more difficult path for others to follow, for its products could be attributed to special biographical experiences or to actions of an imagination provoked by drugs or eroticism.

However, even the late nineteenth-century journey into the self, with its more threatening anti-roles and its cultural products of decreasing accessibility (even to specialists), only slowed the processes of cultural co-optation and assimilation whereby the success of the romantic program was becoming its failure. The anti-roles themselves attracted a fairly large number of those rejecting—and rejected by—the conventional culture. Communities of bohemians, students, artists, and intellectuals sprang up in metropolitan centers to share in the life-style elements of the romantic program. More and more often they were characterized by persons who wanted to be artists, but who found the demands for the creation of highly novel cultural products beyond their emotional or technical ability. By the end of the century the drive for the new had come to dominate the art scene, a drive that could be located in the original demands of the romantic program for differentation of the self from the others in art, past and present. As larger and larger numbers of potential adherents were recruited to the program from the less affluent segments of the society, such sites as Greenwich Village and the Left Bank became parts of the cultural outside. The length of romantic journeys to such artists' colonies, however, may have been limited by the ease of the return from them to conventionality. The frightened self could always retrieve the safer other in Brooklyn or in Passy, a subway stop or two away.

A more important threat to the journey within, whether it involved self-analysis or self-change, was the rise of the historicizing therapies, particularly psychoanalysis, at the end of the nineteenth century. Such therapies did even greater damage to the romantics than did the spread of travel and tourism, for they assumed the existence of the self in the person (even as they might be in the process of persuading the patient of its existence during therapy) and that the self evolved in antagonism to culture. Further, these therapies were based on the elements in the romantic program that were invented to maintain alienation, but were used by analysts to subvert romanticism's goals of permanent estrangement.

Freud's views on human development and the forces involved in character formation are an assembly of early to late romantic models; however, these models are embodied in a strategy of cure which inverts the original intentions of their creators. The result is an extraordinary and complex irony. Some cultural innovators working in extensions of the romantic program in the twentieth century used analytic ideas to justify further innovations (commonly sexual) that emphasized the interests of the self as against the interests of the culture. However, the major thrust of psychoanalysis was to create a bureaucracy offering ever-larger audiences routine access to the romantic journey into the self. For the romantic term "imagination" one needs only to substitute Freud's "unconscious."

The body of theory and therapy that has dominated psychotherapeutic interventions since the turn of the century (except for behavior modification) has been based on a conglomerate of romantic explanation and its supporting family of responses. It is assumed that the self or character develops in a wilderness of sexual deviation where pleasure is in constant contest with reality. The struggle between biology and culture, child and parent,[7] self interests and collective interests from which therapists believe the self emerged could not help but attract the interest of innovative figures in the arts. The romantic artist's struggle to create the self was a universal human struggle for selfhood, identity, or personality. Still, orthodox Freudians (and other cultural conservatives) saw a necessary, if somewhat tragic, resolution of the struggle, in which culture and reality gain the upper hand over pleasure and individuality. Thus did analytic theory and therapy reject the romantic aspiration for the triumph of the self over culture.

The anti-romantic character of psychoanalysis (more narrowly) and psychotherapy (more generally) is most strongly stated in its appropriation of the very family of behavioral responses of romanticism for the purposes of cultural domination. The healing techniques of psychoanalysis replicate the responses used to affirm alienation in romanticism. The patient is isolated in the analyst's room, separated from sources of cultural demand, with minimal instructions about what to talk about, searching sometimes wildly and anxiously through the rubbish heaps of childhood memories. The goal of these romantic journeys is to produce a self-renovation, a fictionalized history of the self that will heal the alienation of self from role, present from past, individual from culture. The psychoanalytic journey was to be a temporary passage that had at its end a remerging of self and other, a time in the desert that preceded reintegration into the congregation of mental health.

---

[7] The identification of the family as the primordial other, the fundamental non-self, is particularly visible among the children of Jewish immigrants to the United States. Their subsequent attraction to psychoanalysis and to redemptive political movements may be a reaction to this narrowing of the romantic program to a family drama.

The history of psychoanalysis, particularly in the United States, is representative of the large dissemination and dilution of the entire romantic program. The set of romantic ideas and practices that are at the core of psychoanalysis made it attractive to many marginal and innovative figures who continued to work in the romantic tradition after the First World War. Thus, novels were written, subject matters for paintings chosen, and personal and intellectual histories revised in accordance with the vandalizing elements of psychoanalytic theory. The resistance of the other (by now the bourgeoisie) to analytic ideas made psychoanalysis more attractive to its supporters and patients by creating the illusion that they were culturally advanced. However, the actual goal of psychoanalysis was to reduce vandalizing responses to social demand, to assuage the pain of alienation, to build a connection between true self and social roles. In this guise, psychoanalysis has been (in the cultural colonies of Europe) a major source and support of the development of democratic and consumer romanticism.[8]

Even as the romantic program was verging on explanatory collapse at its European center, its export downward in the class system and outward to the former colonies assured the vitality of its products, of its family of responses, and of its primary source of valuation (the self) for the ensuing years of the twentieth century. The dominance of the nineteenth century over the twentieth has been, in part, ensured by romanticism's inclusion in the curriculum of the schools. Nineteenth-century English literature is taught in the high schools; nineteenth-century European literature is introduced in the universities. The lingering of romanticism is further promoted by the widespread taste for painting in the late nineteenth- and early twentieth-century French traditions, and by the well-known preference of musical audiences for the nineteenth-century repertory in opera houses and concert halls. At the same time, most successful artists and writers of the twentieth century follow nineteenth-century forms closely. Most of our artists still imitate the artistic postures of romanticism and are sure that the objects they are creating are properly attributed to their own true selves.

The central category of value which was to be forged in the romantic journey was the self. The journey, the product, the performance (including the anti-roles) were devoted to creating and maintaining the self. A major source of evidence for the existence of the self resided in the special character of its experiences and the resistance of the culture to its innovations. From its beginnings, however, the romantic program of innovation has been under the most subtle form of attack—that of acceptance by the other. Each of the elements of the romantic program has become an acceptable form of activity—at first for an avant-garde, and then

---

[8] The success of psychoanalysis as a radical movement in the United States may be in part attributed to the culturally retarded character of the society at the beginning of the twentieth century.

for the mass. Romantic journeys have turned into the travel industry, into the routines of the mental health industry, and into the human potential movement. Wordsworthian social isolation has given place to the sensory deprivation tanks of the radical therapists, while drugs and eroticism now constitute the leisure-time activities of the entire culture. No anti-role can now be invented that cannot find a guru and followers.

The self is everywhere and in everyone. Its existence is now an assumption, and the value of its choices is democratically supported in the marketplace of ideas. An idea is good because its holder assures the audience that it is his or her true and authentic self that is speaking or writing or painting. The self is the fundamental entitlement of the twentieth century.

This aspect of the triumph of romanticism is critical to its collapse as a source of cultural innovation. The democratization of the self has resulted in its devaluation as a source for differentiating one person from the other. This problem was recognized by a number of major artistic figures in the modernist period who produced works of greater and greater difficulty which assured them of a suitably limited audience. Still, the growth of a body of learned interpreters (mostly critics and college professors) who now have to stand between the innovator and the audience has extended, but not seriously enlarged, the popularity of romantic art-products.

In goodly measure romantic works and the works of the post-modernists—because of their focus on the materials of the product (the words, the paint), because of the arbitrary and sometimes deliberately random character of innovative decision making, and because of the unreliability of the evaluative process—have begun to cast doubt upon the romantic conception of the self as a sufficient ground for justifying innovation. As this doubt about the validity of the self grows, so does an uneasiness about the existential reality of the self as a unique and private possession. Perhaps the self is simply one more construct among the many that justify action, a term that makes modes and styles of conduct legitimate in the same fashion that "God," "Art," and "Democracy" do. Perhaps the knowledge that one has about oneself does not have any priority over the knowledge that others have of the self. The self then becomes an object of negotiation, but a negotiation in which the internal processes of debate cannot be distinguished from the external. If the self exists solely in interaction, how are its decisions to be distinguished from the decisions of the other? The relation of the self to social roles then shifts, for it is no longer an entity nakedly surrounded by cultural demands, nor even an entity which mediates its relations to the culture via a shell of roles that are partly self and partly not-self. The self is thus one of many roles, another role created in interaction with the other. The "true self" would then share a status similar to such roles as banker, husband, midwife, pervert, or artist. And if the self does not have a special status, then it can have no special evaluative capacity which can justify innovative or conforming conduct.

The contemporary cultural crisis, which is characterized by a proliferation of non-styles in the world of the arts, is one that was long delayed in coming by the period of dominance of the romantic program in peripheral societies and cultures, primarily the United States. The self as a term for action is now in a state of collapse along with the rest of the romantic program. What lies beyond the self as a category through which cultural innovation can be justified remains as mysterious to us as romanticism's invention of the self was to still earlier minds acting on notions such as "God," or "Nature," or "Communism."

BARBARA HERRNSTEIN SMITH

# Towards the Practice of Theory

ALTHOUGH I MEAN TO ARGUE in behalf of the spirit, not the letter, of Jonathan Culler's observations, I should like to begin by suggesting that we avoid embroilment in false issues created by terminological slippage.[1] Two of our central terms here, *interpretation* and *criticism,* have had a long and complex history of usage, yielding a number of quite different senses, each of which has some claim to legitimacy but disparate implications for the topic at hand. Thus, if we take interpretation to mean the general activity of drawing inferences from and/or attributing meaning to events, it is clear that no one can go "beyond" it for, in that sense, interpretation is the very process by which we perceive and comprehend the universe—not only the speech, texts, and other objects and events produced by our fellow creatures, but everything that exists for us.

Clearly Culler does not mean us to take "interpretation" in that sense but rather as the narrower—and much more historically and culturally particular—

---

[1] An earlier version of this paper was presented to a special session of the annual Modern Language Association meeting in 1979. The session, sponsored by the Society for Critical Exchange and entitled "Beyond Interpretation," focused on the following three statements which appeared in an article also so entitled by Jonathan Culler. (*Comparative Literature* 28 [Summer 1976]: 244-56).

1. "...the most important and insidious legacy of the New Criticism is the widespread and unquestioning acceptance of the notion that the critic's job is to interpret literary works."
2. "...in fact the interpretation of individual works is only tangentially related to the understanding of literature."
3. "...if there is one thing we do not need it is more interpretations of literary works."

Proceedings of the entire session were printed in *SCE Reports,* 1979.

set of activities that have been regularly performed by numerous professors of literature and their students within the walls of academic institutions and upon the pages of associated professional journals for roughly the past forty years, especially in America, and especially—though not exclusively—exemplified in the work (studies, textbooks, classroom practices) of the New Critics.[2] It is evidently interpretation in this sense—that is, the production of publicly articulated "readings," explications, critical analyses, etc., of individual works of literature (in the sense of canonical texts)—that Culler sees as dominating and confining the present pursuit of literary studies and that he urges us to go beyond. Although I do not share exactly his view of the most interesting and fruitful direction to move toward, I think that the general shape of his argument is correct and that its implications are of central significance for our profession and discipline.

Profession and discipline: that conjunction brings us to a second terminological problem and also to the heart of the issue that concerns us here. The term "criticism," which appears in the subtitle of Culler's "Beyond Interpretation" ("Prospects for Contemporary Criticism"), is not only radically ambiguous but also currently compromised by repeated invocation, definition, and redefinition in polemical contexts. I prefer, therefore, to use the more neutral phrase, "literary studies," which, while less battered by the hazards of debate, still conveys an important doubleness that I should like to examine. I refer to the fact that while all of us would presumably describe ourselves as engaged in the profession—or is it discipline?—of literary studies, the phrase (as that alternate designation itself suggests) may be seen to encompass two quite different kinds of pursuit: different in their origins and allegiances, and different in their objectives and justifications.

Thus, to begin with, literary study may be conceived of primarily as a humanistic profession, consisting of all those more or less custodial, priestly, and pedagogic activities that serve or center on the establishment and preservation of the canonical texts of the community and also the elucidation, articulation, and transmission of the cultural beliefs and values which those texts have been—or could be—seen to embody or imply. Literary works need not, I think, function solely or most significantly, for either the community or the individual, as the transmitters of specific traditional beliefs or values—but that is another issue. I would agree that, as professors of literature, our minimal social obligation is to

---

[2] I discuss the distinction between these (and a number of other) concepts of interpretation in *On the Margins of Discourse: The Relation of Literature to Language* (Chicago: University of Chicago Press, 1978), pp. 32-40, 73-75, 137-54. For an exceptionally useful analysis of interpretation in the first, broader sense, see Morse Peckham, *Explanation and Power: The Control of Human Behavior* (New York: Seabury, 1979), pp. 135-38. Peckham provides his own extension of this analysis to "critical" interpretation in "The Infinity of Pluralisms," *Critical Inquiry* 3 (Summer 1977): 803-16.

help create and maintain a community of readers for whom the experience of literary works—whatever that experience may be—is both possible and desirable. It would follow from this conception of literary studies that we should seek to develop methods for meeting that obligation most effectively. It might be claimed, moreover, that interpretation in some version of the narrower sense outlined above (e.g., what is commonly referred to as "practical criticism") has figured and must continue to figure among those methods. All that may be granted. But, it may be added, that is not all there is and certainly not all there could be. It is with this import—that is, as urging the recognition of the legitimacy, necessity, and centrality of another mission for literary studies beyond practical criticism—that I understand and endorse Culler's observations.

Accordingly, I would observe that literary study could be regarded not primarily as a humanistic profession, but, rather, as an intellectual—and, in the broadest sense, scientific—discipline, specifically as that discipline for which literature, in *its* broadest sense, is the central subject of inquiry. It has been so regarded at other times and is now so regarded in other places, for example in Athens two thousand years ago and for the past fifty years in Europe—in both cases under the name of "poetics," though, more in accord with American usage, I am content to call it "literary theory."[3] Literary study so conceived is not essentially humanistic—pedagogic or acculturative—in its operations, mission, or justification. Its fundamental mode of study is, rather, systematic inquiry and its defining objective is to make literature—in its entirety—intelligible; that is, to describe and account for all the phenomena, activities, and institutions of which literature may be seen to consist, all of their forms, aspects, functions, and effects, all of their relations to each other—*and* their relation to whatever else we know about human behavior, history, culture, and, ultimately, about everything else in the universe.

This is, to be sure, an ambitious enterprise, but also a modest one, the key word being *inquiry*: an intellectual activity, not an intellectual boast or territorial claim. There is, however, another key word, namely *systematic*, by which I do not mean

---

[3] Other recent proposals to conceive of the study of literature primarily as literary theory (or "poetics") include John M. Ellis, *The Theory of Literary Criticism: A Logical Analysis* (Berkeley: University of California Press, 1974); Jonathan Culler, *Structuralist Poetics: Structuralism, Linguistics and the Study of Literature* (Ithaca, New York: Cornell University Press, 1975); and Benjamin Hrushovski, "Poetics, Criticism, Science: Remarks on the Field and Responsibilities of the Study of Literature," *PTL: Poetics and Theory of Literature* 1 (January 1976): iii-xxxv. A comparable discussion of the relation between criticism and theory in the study of music may be found in Leonard B. Meyer's "On the Nature and Limits of Critical Analysis" in his *Explaining Music: Essays and Explorations* (Berkeley: University of California Press, 1973). For an interesting consideration of literary theory in relation to the view(s) of theory in contemporary philosophy of science, see J. J. A. Mooij, "The Nature and Function of Literary Theories," *Poetics Today* 1 (1979): 111-35.

schematic but, rather, rigorous, comprehensive, and, above all, connectable. What would distinguish literary theory as a discipline from those casual generalizations, individual insights, and ad hoc speculations in which we all engage in the course of reading or discussing literature is, precisely, that it would *not* be casual, individual, and ad hoc, but, rather, would be continuous, communal, and interactive.

An example will be useful. Pursued in connection with the sort of systematic inquiry described here, the study of, say, poetic meter would not consist simply of the stockpiling of innumerable inert articles on such scattered topics as the frequency of enjambment in Chaucer's later poetry or the influence of the Bible on Whitman's free verse—the sort of topics that now tend to be studied in isolation from each other and justified rather limply as "contributions to the scholarship" on a particular poet's work and thus as somehow contributing to our "understanding" or "appreciation" of that work. It would, rather, have a more comprehensive set of objectives, the pursuit of which would not only elicit interrelated research on such individual topics but, even more significantly, with respect to which that research would be justified and evaluated. Thus, the pursuit of a genuine theory of meter would undertake to explore the nature and functions of rhythm in all forms of verbal art, in oral as well as written poetry, in communal African chants and the counting-rhymes of children, as well as in Renaissance lyrics and contemporary free verse. It would seek to account for the perception as well as the production of meter, and the relation of both to the fundamental sound-structure of language(s). It would attempt to describe how conventional metrical forms originate, how they are learned and transmitted within and between literary cultures, and the extent to which they depend on such matters as traditions and conventions of performance. The theories we developed in connection with such questions would be expected to help us assess the general significance of meter in the value and experience of literary works. They would also be expected to indicate and explain what relation there may be between temporal patterning in poetry and comparable rhythmic features of other art forms, such as music and dance, and other activities and experiences, such as ritual and play. Finally, the terms and concepts of our descriptions and accounts would be translatable into the terms and concepts of such related disciplines as acoustics, musicology, and anthropology, and would not only draw from but also contribute to those disciplines. It is in reference to goals of this order that we should, I think, cheer and check our individual efforts. And it is, I would suggest, for lack of goals of this order that so much of our current research is trivial, repetitive, and incoherent. Some further observations are, however, necessary here.

First, it must be acknowledged that the sort of inquiry outlined above is likely to appear too technical, abstract, cerebral, or otherwise alien to many members of our profession. Indeed, it may be the case that there are now very few among us

who are, by virtue of temperament or training, interested in or capable of engaging in research of that kind. The issue, however, is not whether any of us could or would want to do it personally but whether the profession as a whole recognizes that it is what should be done. A vague wave of the arm, moreover, toward another quarter of the campus—"let *them,* over *there,* do it"—will not resolve the issue. For there is no one else to do it: no one, that is, other than some of us who are drawn and presumably devoted to literary studies—and those of our students whom we invite to follow us in that devotion.

Second, it must be emphasized not only that we are nowhere near any theory of the kind described above for meter or anything else, but also that we can never arrive at that destination: not because the goals are so ambitious but because it is in the nature of genuine intellectual inquiry never to be complete. As we continue to learn more about literature and everything to which it is related, we will be obliged to expand, refine, and adjust our theories to accommodate that knowledge. Theories are not permanent achievements; they are, rather, arrangements of knowledge, ways of putting things, containers continuously reshaped by their own ever-changing contents. It follows, however, that they should be assessed by how well they do organize our knowledge, account for the phenomena within their domain, and lend themselves to expansion, refinement, and adjustment, not by their immediate "practical applicability" or how readily they supply new critical approaches or new analytic methodologies.

To be sure, theories in any field are likely to arise not from out of the blue but in response to specific problems of current interest, often practical or technological problems; and literary theories, too, may be expected to be responsive to the practical problems of the profession. That responsiveness need not, however, be tied exclusively to providing material or methods for practical criticism, either in the daily conduct of literature courses or in the discussion of individual works in the professional journals. It may also be evoked by other aspects of literary scholarship; for example, literary history, biography, editing, and translation, as well as by other theoretical studies in the field and by studies in other disciplines. Indeed, because we cannot determine in advance all the implications of a theory, it will often be the case that theories developed precisely in this way—that is, without reference to particular practical problems—will ultimately prove most fruitful in solving these problems. Thus, we may expect a more subtle and comprehensive understanding of such matters as the sources of literary innovation, the acquisition of literary competence, and the social and psychological functions of verbal artworks to have not merely fruitful but quite radical implications for the conduct of literary education.

For these reasons, such familiar observations as "the trouble with all these fashionable theories is that you can't apply them to the actual teaching of literature" or "the only real test of a literary theory is how well it illuminates the individual work" are irrelevant. Indeed, such observations, familiar as they are,

reflect what I think are pernicious as well as false conceptions of both the nature and goals of any theory and the proper relation between theory and practice in literary studies. Two of them are especially common. One is the misinterpretation of the alternate objectives of literary theory as a denial or betrayal of the traditional humanistic goals of the profession, as when any interest in noncanonical forms of literature is derided either as evidence of insensitivity to the values of the canon or as a cynical capitulation to philistinism. The other is the misunderstanding of the generality and comprehensiveness for which literary theory must, by definition, strive as evidence of intellectual imperialism or as alien to the basic nature of literature. The latter misunderstanding is, I believe, responsible for the following complaint, which manages in the space of three sentences to conflate literary criticism, literary theory, literary experience, and literary education:

> ... many of our most influential modes of criticism, from formalism to structuralism and semiotics, have in common the assumption that what we ought to do is extract some kind of changeless universal pattern from the particularities and contingencies of the literary work. But surely we don't need Blake or Arnold to tell us that it is the concreteness of literature which is its characteristic strength. The engagement of the individual's mind, senses, and feelings, not with a universal model which the teacher or student has brought along, but with the stubborn resistance of the particularities of the other, or, to use Arnold's terms, of the "not-ourselves," exercises the imagination, and is thus the main source of the educational value of reading in literature.[4]

It must be added that comparable, if converse, misunderstandings are reflected in the invocation of a tattered version of scientific ideology precisely where it is least appropriate in literary studies, as when we claim to have constructed a rigorous method or devised an objective technique for determining the real meanings or establishing the true value of individual literary works.[5] As Culler suggests, the tenacity of such conceptions is evidence of a more fundamental disorder in our profession and discipline. I should like, however, to amend his remarks concerning the sources and scope of that disorder.

Like Culler, I think that the study of literature in America is at a singularly poor pass. I do not, however, think that we can attribute this situation to the legacy of the New Criticism or to any other single cause, whether it be rampant scientism, moral degeneracy, or the growth of the French menace (to mention some other frequently cited ones). Our debility and demoralization are, rather, the complex

---

[4] Ian Watt, "On Not Attempting to be a Piano," originally read at the 1977 annual meeting of the Association of Departments of Literature and reprinted in *Profession 78* (New York: Modern Language Association, 1978), pp 13-15.

[5] The dubious grounds of such claims are discussed at length in *On the Margins of Discourse*, pp. 157-201, and in my "Fixed Marks and Variable Constancies: A Parable of Literary Value," *Poetics Today* 1 (1979): 7-22.

products of a number of general conditions and specific afflictions, some of them wholesale and long-standing, endemic to the intellectual style and historical development of American institutions of education, some of them peculiar to literary studies, and all of them exacerbated by an economic situation which, as it tightens around us, increasingly controls the manner in which we conduct our professional lives and makes more visible and significant the various problems that have always been with us. Thus, while we continue to labor under a historical burden that leaves us fragmented in our endeavors and confused about our obligations, the need to justify our traditional institutions, practices, and assumptions grows sharper and, out of panic or complacency, we seem incapable of considering to what extent the sources of our distress may lie in those very institutions, practices, and assumptions. Instead, we look for scapegoats, decry our colleagues down the hall or up East, or transform the whole arena of debate into a theological battlefield, accusing each other of various forms of heresy and apostasy. In other words, in spite of whatever special wisdom we might expect of ourselves by virtue of our profession, we behave exactly as might be expected of any group that is buffeted and bruised by forces that it does not fully understand and cannot fully control.

There is, of course, no single corrective to this situation, either. It might help, however, if we at least try to separate the social, economic, and demographic forces that contribute to our demoralization as a profession from the sources of our intellectual debility as a discipline, if we acknowledge that many of us are confused about the proper and possible objectives of our teaching, research, and other professional activities—and, indeed, if we confronted the fact that many of us literally do not know what we are doing, or why. The increasing absorption of our energies in fevered polemics is only one sign of these confusions. The more important sign and consequence of them has been the focus of my observations here; that is, our continued subordination of all potential justifications for literary theory to the pedagogic needs and professional exigencies of the academy and, more generally, our holding the entire discipline of literary studies strictly captive and narrowly accountable to the traditional practices of literary acculturation. In short, we have boxed ourselves into the classroom and lost sight of any broader intellectual landscape. What I have been suggesting here is that one way out of these binds would be to recognize that literary theory is neither the enemy nor the servant of the profession but, on the contrary, the center of its intellectual justification and, as such, part of its strongest claim on the future.

GEORGE L. GECKLE

# Politics and Sexuality in Shakespeare's Second Tetralogy

IN THE FOLLOWING PAPER I would like to explore an area of Shakespeare's dramatic world that is seldom if ever dealt with in a satisfactory manner. It is Shakespeare's use of sexual material. The basic thesis that I propose to argue is that within some limitations of sources and genre Shakespeare frequently deals with sexuality in direct relation to politics. That is, where Shakespeare allows himself to concentrate on extra-historical matters, plays concerned with government are also concerned with sexual matters.

Although I intend to concentrate on Shakespeare's great history plays of the second tetralogy, a few observations drawn from other plays will establish my proposition. *Measure for Measure* is a good example. Generally considered to be Shakespeare's most sexual play, it opens with the Duke's comment: "Of government the properties to unfold, / Would seem in me t' affect speech and discourse."[1] Practically all of the rest of the play in some way or another deals with the relationship of government to the private and public sexual behavior of the characters. For Angelo and Isabella, attempts to ignore their sexuality prove, for different reasons, to be insufficient ways of coping with a complex society. At the other extreme, the sexual license of Lucio, Pompey, and Mistress Overdone is roundly condemned by both the law and sound reason. Claudio and Juliet, entrapped first by their sexual relationship and then by the law, stand to be

---

[1] All quotations from Shakespeare are taken from *The Complete Works of Shakespeare,* ed. Hardin Craig and David Bevington, rev. ed. (Glenview, Illinois: Scott, Foresman, 1973).

victimized by the higher principles by which Angelo and, indeed, the entire city of Vienna supposedly live. It is finally the Duke, who has essentially risen above sex, who is able by the play's end to control and put some order into both sex and politics.

Similarly, *Troilus and Cressida* is a very sexual play ("all the argument is a whore and a cuckold," argues Thersites), but is at the same time concerned with "degree, priority and place," "office and custom," as Ulysses tells us in his famous speech. Because of what Paris calls the "fair rape" of Helen, Troy is at war, and because Hector fails to adhere to those "moral laws / Of nature and of nations" which he expounds in Priam's palace, Troy falls. Troilus, who wins the great debate with his older brother, also wins Cressida, who unfortunately proves herself susceptible to the blandishments of Diomedes and becomes what Ulysses thought she was, one of the "daughters of the game." It is ultimately Ulysses, the wily politician who manipulates Ajax and Achilles and watches the disillusioned Troilus disintegrate before his eyes, who proves to be another of Shakespeare's heroes who has control over both his own sexual nature and the political lives of others.

A third play in which sex and politics are closely intertwined is *Hamlet*. If "As false as Cressid" rings the keynote of Troilus's sad affair, then "Frailty, thy name is woman!" echoes throughout the world of Elsinore as a refrain. Hamlet's relationship with Ophelia is tainted by the sexual behavior of his mother, and Gertrude herself is at the center of the corruption that emanates from "that incestuous, that adulterate beast," Claudius the King of Denmark. It can be plausibly argued, I think, that Hamlet's tragedy derives from his inability to come to terms with either sex or politics, each dependent as they are upon the other in the fallen world of Denmark. Similarly, if government is taken in its widest sense and can refer to both the individual and the state, then *Othello, King Lear, Antony and Cleopatra, Cymbeline,* and *The Winter's Tale* also fit the same pattern of sexual and political relationship.

What I have so far argued is that there is a larger Shakespearean pattern when it comes to sexual matters, and that pattern has not been adequately discussed by scholars and critics. A standard work in the area, of course, has been Eric Partridge's *Shakespeare's Bawdy*. Partridge's intention is to provide a lexicon, and his book is quite satisfactory in that respect and a welcome addition to the libraries of those who have to bear with the prudish reticence of most of Shakespeare's editors. Nonetheless, in the introductory essay to his book, Partridge makes some interesting observations that lead to questions that he does not consider answering. He points out, for example, that *Richard II* is "the cleanest play by Shakespeare and, by any standard whatsoever, a remarkably chaste one." On the other hand, *Henry V* is "in quality, the obscenest of the Histories." *1* and *2 Henry IV* are in between, but closer to *Henry V* than *Richard II*, with "Part I...much the 'milder'" and "Part II..., both in quality and in

quantity, the 'stronger'."[2] My question is, why? Falstaff's presence may well explain the bawdiness of *1* and *2 Henry IV,* but why should *Henry V* be "obscene" at all? Why is *Richard II* so "clean"? To my knowledge no one has ever raised such questions.

Even in a relatively recent study by E. A. M. Colman entitled *The Dramatic Use of Bawdy in Shakespeare* (1974) we do not find answers. Colman, for example, points out that twenty-one out of 2,993 lines in *1 Henry IV* are "demonstrably indecent" and that there are "seventy-four instances of bawdy" in 3,229 lines of *2 Henry IV,* but he does not do much with his statistics other than to note that Falstaff "has the lion's share of the bawdy lines."[3] Similarly, when Colman discusses *Henry V,* a play in which he thinks "bawdy plays a much less important role than in either part of *Henry IV*" and is "less firmly integrated thematically with the political material" (p. 104), he does little more than to explicate some of the relevant passages and then to conclude that in the *Henry IV* and *V* plays the bawdy conversations "help to root the political history in the soil of personal life" (p. 107).

What I propose to do here is to present a theory that may help to explain the relationship between politics and sexuality. The theory is not mine, but is that of my distinguished colleague, Professor Morse Peckham. In his book *Art and Pornography,* he makes the following observations: "Of the many forces... which can be metaphorically discerned to be at work in what we call 'society,' two of the most salient are social stability and innovation, and they are counter-forces which cannot be resolved; at best only an armed truce can be temporarily achieved. There are two things the human being cannot avoid doing: one is to make sense out of the world; the other is to innovate."[4] Making sense out of the world depends upon "a cognitive model, a system of expectancies," says Peckham, which an individual "applies *a priori* to a particular category of situation" (p. 67). Those of us who use "the same set of expectancies" are part of "the same belief system" or culture. Innovation, on the other hand, "is the disparity between any cognitive model and the actual situation it is applied to" (p. 68). Peckham goes on to argue that since "a belief system makes behavior predictable" (p. 68), those who have "social roles which exercise power" are mainly interested in "the management of these behavioral systems" (p. 69). When a social situation becomes unstable enough due to rapid innovation, revolution occurs. The revolutionaries, once they capture the power roles, then

---

[2] Eric Partridge, *Shakespeare's Bawdy,* rev. ed. (1947; rev. ed., London: Routledge and Kegan Paul Paperback, 1968), p. 45.

[3] E. A. M. Colman, *The Dramatic Use of Bawdy in Shakespeare* (London: Longman, 1974), p. 99.

[4] Morse Peckham, *Art and Pornography: An Experiment in Explanation* (New York: Basic Books, 1969), p. 67.

stabilize the social structure again. The area of sexuality enters into this pattern of stability and innovation because "power does not want to eliminate forbidden behavior. It needs a forbidden area in order to exercise unpredictably and arbitrarily its police function, the necessity for which is the irreconcilability of stability and innovation" (p. 74). The forbidden areas are what Peckham terms trivia—such things as "art" (p. 74), as well as "sex, pornography, eating, costume, theft, the rituals of religion and other relief institutions, drugs, death" (p. 252). He concludes that we police trivia because that "diverts attention from what is really important, the necessary inadequacy of the belief system in truly vital matters, economic production and the social structure which controls the distribution of goods and services, for it is obvious that the essential desideratum of human life, predictability, is of supremest importance in the area of economic expectancy" (p. 75).

Peckham's idea that sex is "trivial" may strike many readers of this as yet Freudian age as rather ridiculous, but his assertion does have sociological support. In a 1973 publication entitled *Sexual Conduct: The Social Sources of Human Sexuality,* John H. Gagnon and William Simon argue persuasively that sexual behavior is *learned* behavior. They repeatedly make the point that "women and men create or invent a capacity for sexual behavior, learning how to be aroused and learning how to be responsive."[5] Moreover, there is no factual evidence that sexual activity is the result of an innate "drive" (p. 181), or that "repression of drive" and "feelings of sexual deprivation" (p. 182) are particularly useful concepts for an understanding of the actual behavior of men and women. In short, conclude Gagnon and Simon, "all human sexual behavior is socially scripted behavior," and "the sources of the sexual scripts . . . find their origins not in biology or even training for sex itself, but in the application of social attributes to both the situation and the actors" (p. 262).

On the surface it may seem absurd to apply Peckham's (or Gagnon and Simon's) theories to Shakespeare's plays, for we are all quite aware that the so-called "Tudor myth" and "Elizabethan world picture" (with their own theories of divine kingship, relationship between microcosm, macrocosm, and body politic), as well as the "great chain of being," seemingly explain Shakespeare's social and political beliefs. But can we not argue that these are merely Renaissance metaphors used to support a belief system that was obviously less idealistic (or holy) than those who exercised power wished to admit?[6]

---

[5] John H. Gagnon and William Simon, *Sexual Conduct: The Social Sources of Human Sexuality* (Chicago: Aldine, 1973), p. 59. See also Gagnon's *Human Sexualities* (Glenview, Illinois: Scott, Foresman, 1977) for further discussion of sexuality in terms of social learning.

[6] See, for example, Harry Levin, "Shakespeare and 'The Revolution of the Times,'" (1971), in *Shakespeare and the Revolution of the Times: Perspectives and Commentaries* (New York: Oxford University Press, Galaxy Book Paperback, 1978), pp. 29-50; also

For example, sexual and political matter in the plays of Christopher Marlowe (*The Jew of Malta* or *Edward II*) or in the pervasively satiric drama of Ben Jonson (*Sejanus* or *Volpone*) and John Marston (*The Malcontent* or *The Dutch Courtesan*) or the cynical tragedies of John Webster (*The White Devil* or *The Duchess of Malfi*) and Thomas Middleton (*The Changeling* or *Women Beware Women*) should be proof enough that idealism was not all that pervasive in the Elizabethan and Jacobean drama. Moreover, there is even evidence that Peckham's assertion that sex is "trivial" and Gagnon and Simon's argument that all sexual behavior is "scripted" are not exclusively modern concepts without relevance to Shakespeare's time. Michel de Montaigne (1533-1592), for example, whose work Shakespeare knew (vide *King Lear* or *The Tempest*), has an interesting and amusing anecdote in his essay "Of the Force of Imagination" (book 1, chapter 20) relevant to the idea of "scripted behavior." During a general discussion of male impotence, Montaigne relates the story of a nobleman who on his wedding night "by reason of the bond wherewith the trouble of his imagination had tied him,...could not run on poste." Fearing that such an embarrassing situation might occur, the nobleman and Montaigne had by a prearranged signal agreed to meet outside the wedding chamber. The nobleman put on Montaigne's gown and took a charm—"a peece of golden plate..., wherein were ingraven certaine celestial figures, good against the Sunnebeames, and for the head-ach, being fitly laid upon the suture of the head"—held the charm by its ribbon and placed it "just upon his kidneyes" while uttering certain words "thrice over," and then tied the charm on himself so that "he should then boldly and confidently returne to his charge." "To conclude," relates Montaigne, "it is most certaine, my Characters proved more venerian than so-lare, more in action, than in prohibitiòn."[7] Here we have not a case of biological impotence but an example of the invention of "a capacity for sexual behavior" (to use Gagnon and Simon's phrase). As Montaigne elsewhere remarks, "I have not found *Venus* to be so imperious a Goddesse, as many, and more reformed than my selfe[,] witness her to be...."[8]

In short, Montaigne provides at least some contemporary evidence (John Donne provides more in his secular poems) that at least someone else in Shakespeare's age had what might be otherwise wrongly considered a uniquely modern view of sexual behavior. To return to my original thesis, I think that the action in Shakespeare's second tetralogy supports Peckham's theories, and the

---

Gordon Ross Smith, "Shakespeare's *Henry V*: Another Part of the Critical Forest," *Journal of the History of Ideas*, 37 (January 1976): 3-26.

[7] *Montaigne's Essays*, trans. John Florio (1603), introd. L. C. Harmer, Everyman's Library, 3 vols. (London: Dent; New York: Dutton, 1965), 1: 96-97.

[8] "Of Crueltie," *Montaigne's Essays*, 2:118. I am grateful to H.W. Matalene for these references to Montaigne.

theories in turn satisfactorily explain the action and behavior of the characters to an unusual degree.

*Richard II* can then, I think, be understood as a play about a revolution brought about by a king who was unable to perform his social role, that role being the exercise of power. That Richard is incapable of proper role-playing is seen from the very beginning of the drama when he first vacillates in dealing with Thomas Mowbray and Henry Bolingbroke and then later, incredibly, aborts the ritual trial by combat between the two men. Finally, after banishing both men, Richard revokes four years from Bolingbroke's sentence because John of Gaunt, his uncle and Bolingbroke's father, has a "sad aspect" (I.iii.209). Richard, in short, is an unpredictable ruler in political areas in which it is not wise to be unpredictable.

Richard's next unpredictable move is, of course, his most fatal because it directly involves economics. In order to finance a war against Irish rebels, Richard tells us, "We are inforc'd to farm our royal realm" (I.iv.45). John of Gaunt (who is presented unhistorically in terms of Shakespeare's sources) in his justly famous choric speech about England as "this other Eden, demi-paradise" (II.i.42) ends his great periodic sentence with the hard economic fact that "this dear dear land, / Dear for her reputation through the world, / Is now leas'd out, I die pronouncing it, / Like to a tenement or pelting farm" (II.i.57-60). His harshest criticism of Richard is, "Landlord of England art thou now, not king" (II.i.113). Richard, who does everything wrong, receives news of Gaunt's death by announcing that Lancaster's property will help to finance the Irish wars. The Duke of York, Richard's other uncle, is horrified that Henry Bolingbroke's inheritance is being arbitrarily taken away:

> Take Hereford's rights away, and take from Time
> His charters and his customary rights;
> Let not to-morrow then ensue to-day;
> Be not thyself; for how art thou a king
> But by fair sequence and succession? (II.i.195-99)

The economic realities of the political situation could not be clearer. As one of the great political realists, Machiavelli, points out, the astute ruler should "forbeare to lay his hands on other mens goods; for men forget sooner the death of their father, than the losse of their patrimony."[9] Richard is, of course, not a Machiavel, but neither, unfortunately, is he a political realist.

Richard's crucial political error leads, of course, to the return of Bolingbroke, whose justification for his behavior is quite simply economic:

---

[9] Machiavelli, *The Prince* (1532), trans. Edward Dacres (1640), in *Three Renaissance Classics,* introd. and notes by Burton A. Milligan (New York: Scribners, 1953), p. 63.

> As I was banish'd, I was banish'd Hereford;
> But as I come, I come for Lancaster.
> ....................................
> ...I am a subject,
> And I challenge law: attorneys are denied me;
> And therefore personally I lay my claim
> To my inheritance of free descent. (II.iii.113-14, 133-36)

Northumberland repeats Bolingbroke's assertions when he meets Richard before Flint castle in Wales: "His coming hither hath no further scope / Than for his lineal royalties and to beg / Enfranchisement immediate on his knees" (III.iii.112-14). And Bolingbroke repeats the same idea when he directly confronts Richard: "My gracious lord, I come but for mine own" (III.iii.196).

The fact that Bolingbroke ultimately gains the throne would seem to indicate that something other than economics motivates him. Shakespeare, however, keeps the whole issue vague (see also *2 Henry IV* IV.v.184-87), and we are led to believe that Bolingbroke backs into the kingship. There is no real contradiction anyway, since the kingship is the way in which political and economic predictability is maintained. This is, of course, why the powerful Percy family supports Bolingbroke and also why York (to the astonishment of many modern readers and playgoers) is willing to betray his son when Aumerle gets involved in a conspiracy against the new king. There is, in short, no room in England for a Richard who prefers the trivial roles of poet and tragedian (e.g., III.ii.4-62, 144-77; III.iii.143-83; IV.i.181-318), as well as Christ figure (IV.i.169-71, 239-42), to the crucial one of social and economic manager.

Richard's role-playing is one area in which we can readily see the way in which metaphors can be put to different uses. In a seminal study entitled *The King's Two Bodies: A Study in Mediaeval Political Theology*, Ernst H. Kantorowicz tells us that during the reign of Queen Elizabeth, a Middle Temple law apprentice named Edmund Plowden collected various "arguments and judgments made in the king's courts and epitomized [them] in his *Reports*."[10] In these *Reports* the king is described as having a dual nature; that is, two bodies, a body natural (or mortal) and a body politic (or immortal). Lawyers throughout the Elizabethan and Jacobean period described the concept of the Two Bodies in terms derived from theology, so that the doctrine "teaching that the Church, and Christian society in general, was a *'corpus mysticum* the head of which is Christ,' has been transferred by the jurists from the theological sphere to that of the state the head of which is the king" (p. 16).

This religio-political way of thinking and speaking is quite evident in Shakespeare's *Richard II*, as Kantorowicz makes clear in his second chapter (pp.

---

[10] Ernst H. Kantorowicz, *The King's Two Bodies: A Study in Mediaeval Political Theology* (Princeton: Princeton University Press, 1957), p. 7.

24-41). Thus, Richard evokes the image of the King's Two Bodies in the scene near Barkloughly castle on the coast of Wales when he says:

> Not all the water in the rough rude sea
> Can wash the balm off from an anointed king;
> The breath of worldly men cannot depose
> The deputy elected by the Lord. (III.ii.54-57)

When Richard receives news that Wiltshire, Bushy, Bagot, and Green have "made peace" (III.ii.127) with Henry Bolingbroke, he immediately calls them "three Judases" (III.ii.132), only to collapse to "sit upon the ground / And tell sad stories of the death of kings" (III.ii.155-56) when he hears that they have been executed. As Kantorowicz argues: "The king that 'never dies' here has been replaced by the king that always dies and suffers death more cruelly than other mortals. Gone is the oneness of the body natural with the immortal body politic..." (p. 30). Richard never regains this "oneness," and as Kantorowicz rightly concludes, the scene with the mirror (IV.i) "is the climax of that tragedy of dual personality" (p. 39) because the smashing of the looking glass "means, or is, the breaking apart of any possible duality. All those facets are reduced to one; to the banal face and insignificant *physis* of a miserable man, a *physis* now void of any metaphysis whatsoever" (p. 40).

Richard's failure as king can be seen, then, from a Renaissance point of view as a failure to manipulate the symbols of kingship. Rather than stressing the unity of his dual nature of king and man, he succumbs to the temptation to emphasize the body natural over the body politic. From a more modern point of view, he can be viewed as someone who was unable for reasons of temperament to keep the private man separate from the public man. Rather than submerging his private nature when in public situations, he allows it to destroy him by flaunting it in the most histrionic fashion at the worst possible times. Again, to use Peckham's terminology, Richard II is insufficient in "the management of...behavioral systems." In contrast, as we shall see, Henry V never allows his private life to become confused with his public life, and even when he feels a bit sorry for himself—

> ...O hard condition,
> Twin-born with greatness, subject to the breath
> Of every fool, whose sense no more can feel
> But his own wringing! What infinite heart's-ease
> Must kings neglect, that private men enjoy! (*HV* IV.i.250-54)—

he does it in soliloquy.

We can now, perhaps, understand why *Richard II* is, to quote Partridge, a "remarkably chaste" play. It deals with crucial economic and social issues during a

period of actual revolution. Dramatizing such a period in England, the time that led to the Wars of the Roses and vast social upheaval, Shakespeare was not interested in, nor did he probably feel that his audience would be interested in, such trivial matters as sex and bawdy dialogue. Those trivial things he saved for the ensuing plays in his tetralogy, plays that, it is true, dramatize an unstable political and economic situation in England, but at the same time focus on the emergence of Prince Hal as a shrewd and competent ruler.

The two parts of *Henry IV* are, to a large degree, about the growth and education of a prince. Prince Hal was legendary as a type of Prodigal Son, and Shakespeare has dramatized the young man as torn between various modes of behavior—unrestrained Falstaffian hedonism versus a rigid Hotspurian code of honor in *1 Henry IV* and more unrestrained Falstaffian hedonism versus the Lord Chief Justice's code of political responsibility in *2 Henry IV*. In short, it would seem that England's political and economic future was in grave peril because the worn-out King Henry IV—"So shaken as we are, so wan with care" (*1 HIV* I.i.1)—could not depend upon his son's proper attitude toward the role of kingship. Hence it is that Henry is forever comparing his son pejoratively with Hotspur, "A son who is the theme of honour's tongue" and "sweet Fortune's minion and her pride" (*1 HIV* I.i.81,83). Henry's belief that his son is a wastrel is relatively constant. He speaks of his "unthrifty son" in Act V of *Richard II* and berates Hal in person in III.ii of *1 Henry IV* because his son is acting in the very manner of Richard II, who "enfeoff'd himself to popularity" (III.ii.69).[11] When Henry says that Hotspur "hath more worthy interest to the state / Than thou the shadow of succession" (III.ii.98-99), Hal's response is interesting in its pragmatism:

> Percy is but my factor, good my lord,
> To engross up glorious deeds on my behalf;
> And I will call him to so strict account,
> That he shall render every glory up,
> Yea, even the slightest worship of his time,
> Or I will tear the reckoning from his heart. (III.ii.147-52)

---

[11] In a fascinating essay which explores the historico-social context of Shakespeare's plays, Maynard Mack comments on Henry Bolingbroke's concern over Hal's behavior in the following terms: "Like the society around it, the Elizabethan family depended for the attainment of its goals on a structure of strict obedience; and this presupposed, in turn, as Henry Bolingbroke knew so well, the maintenance of a certain ritual space around the patriarchal head, be he king or father, to preserve his person 'fresh and new', his presence 'like to a robe pontifical, Ne'er seen but wonder'd at', and his state 'Seldom, but sumptuous', like a feast (*1 Henry IV*, III.ii.55-9)" ("Rescuing Shakespeare," International Shakespeare Association Occasional Paper No. 1 [Oxford: University Press, 1979], p. 16). An informative essay on the subject of the "generation gap," cited by Mack, is Keith Thomas's "Age and Authority in Early Modern England," Raleigh Lecture on History, *Proceedings of the British Academy*, 52 (1976): 205-48.

Hal's economic metaphors reveal a young man who knows how to communicate with his very businesslike father. However, although the king gives his son the chance to prove himself at Shrewsbury, he seems surprised when Hal actually saves him from Douglas, and for dramatic purposes Shakespeare prolongs the generation gap into *2 Henry IV*, where the king continues to worry about his son's "headstrong riot" (IV.iv.62). On his very deathbed he castigates Hal: "When that my care could not withhold thy riots / What wilt thou do when riot is thy care?" (IV.v.135-36).

But, of course, "riot" is not Hal's forte. The audience has known that since the second scene of *1 Henry IV* when Hal informs us in soliloquy that Falstaff and his cohorts have no future in England: "I know you all, and will awhile uphold / The unyok'd humour of your idleness" (I.ii.218-19). This expository soliloquy bothers people because in it Hal sounds so calculating, just like his father, in fact. Moreover, the speech deprives Shakespeare of any dramatic suspense concerning Hal's "redemption." But Shakespeare was obviously concerned with other matters than suspense and did not want his audience, which knew the historical "facts" anyway, to get sidetracked, as does Hal's father.

What Shakespeare really wants us to concentrate on is Hal's education and maturation, that process by which he will become a great political leader, a leader able to understand aspects of English society that Henry IV can only grossly comprehend in terms of "honor" and "riot." Hence it is that Hal indulges the "unyok'd humour" of the Eastcheap denizens. He is learning some crucial things about an area his father knew nothing about, and having fun at the same time, as he tells Poins (and us) in the play-within-the-play scene: "I am now of all humors that have showed themselves humours since the old days of goodman Adam to the pupil age of this present twelve o'clock at midnight" (II.iv.104-07).

Unlike Hotspur, Hal rejects an oversimplified concept of the world: "I am not yet of Percy's mind, the Hotspur of the north; he that kills me some six or seven dozen of Scots at a breakfast, washes his hands, and says to his wife 'Fie upon this quite life! I want work'" (II.iv.114-18). The burlesque of Hotspur is brilliant, especially since we have seen the very situation in the preceding scene, a scene in which Hotspur ultimately rejects his wife's persistent questions with double entendres worthy of Falstaff: "I care not for thee, Kate: this is no world / To play with mammets [glossed as "dolls" by most editors, but, rightly I think, as "female breasts" by Partridge] and to tilt with lips" (II.iii.94-95). It has not, I think, been noted how overtly sexual Hotspur is in the two scenes (II.iii and III.i) with his wife. Moreover, his approach is quite aggressive; that is, his concern with military prowess and its concomitant, honor, carries over into the sexual area with his use of military idioms. His masculinity is thus validated by his manifest heterosexuality. Interestingly, his approach to sex is not entirely unlike that of Falstaff in *2 Henry IV* when he insults Doll Tearsheet:

*Fal.* You make fat rascals, Mistress Doll.
*Dol.* I make them! gluttony and diseases make them; I make them not.
*Fal.* If the cook help to make the gluttony, you help to make the diseases, Doll: we catch of you, Doll, we catch of you; grant that, my poor virtue, grant that.
*Dol.* Yea, joy, our chains and our jewels.
*Fal.* 'Your brooches, pearls, and ouches:' for to serve bravely is to come halting off, you know: to come off the breach with his pike bent bravely, and to surgery bravely; to venture upon the charg'd chambers bravely,—
*Dol.* Hang yourself, you muddy conger, hang yourself! (II.iv.45-59)

The obviously phallic allusions of both Falstaff and Hotspur do much to create an equation between jousting, warfare, and the sexual act that Shakespeare carries over into *Henry V*.

Hotspur, like Falstaff, has a narrow view of the world. Both men fail to see beyond their limited "cognitive models," to use Peckham's phrase. Hotspur thinks that only honor counts (see especially *1 HIV* I.iii.201-8,V.iv.77-80), whereas Falstaff thinks that honor is a mere word (*1 HIV* V.i.130-44). Hal, on the other hand, who eventually becomes the true supporter of social stability, is able to see beyond such trivialities as, to use Peckham's categories, sex, theft, and the rituals of religion to become an innovative ruler who will eventually confound and humble the French as easily as the Percy family. Hal's view of honor, for example, is clearly dramatized when he allows the outrageous Falstaff to claim credit for the death of Hotspur—"For my part, if a lie may do thee grace, / I'll gild it with the happiest terms I have" (V.iv.161-62)—and then lets his younger brother John of Lancaster gain esteem by delivering Douglas "ransom-less and free" (V.v.28). As for sex, Hal, unlike Falstaff, is always on the fringes but never in the petticoats, of such Eastcheap denizens as Mistress Quickly and Doll Tearsheet. Hal's adolescent relationships are essentially male—Falstaff, Bardolph, Peto, and especially Poins—but not, of course, homosexual. They demonstrate in such activities as drinking (although Hal never gets drunk), roistering (clever puns and wordplay prove Hal's intellectual superiority), and thieving (the Gadshill robbery) what Gagnon and Simon term "*homosociality,* that is, a period in life when valuation of the self is more keyed to those of like gender than it is to those of opposite gender" (p. 68). Shakespeare probably keeps Hal away from direct sexual involvement with prostitutes for the same reason he has him return the stolen Gadshill money—Hal is, after all, Prince of Wales, and by the opening scene of *Henry V* a budding expert in divinity (or what Peckham calls "the rituals of religion"). In other words, Hal's social class and its attendant roles preclude direct sexual activity with lower-class women (see Gagnon and Simon, pp. 67-71).

Once again, I think that Peckham's theory aptly describes Hal's behavior: "The individual ... must first enter fully into the trivial, experience it thoroughly, even

to the risk of addiction, in order to incorporate as richly as possible into his cognitive processes the conviction that it is trivial" (p. 253). Once one understands triviality one is able, argues Peckham, to "transcend" it (pp. 252-54). "Great innovators," concludes Peckham, "by which I mean simply those the culture has validated as great, are marked by the singular rationality of their lives, their extraordinary ability to abandon the trivial and to enter upon a course of sexual asceticism" (p. 255). Shakespeare's Hal, one of England's great rulers, who is *in*, but not *of*, the world of Eastcheap, falls into the category of both "singular rationality" ("calculating," if you will) and "sexual asceticism." This is why Hal is so much like the Duke in *Measure for Measure* and Ulysses in *Troilus and Cressida* and so unlike Hamlet. (One might also go further and point out that most of Shakespeare's *tragic* heroes have sexual problems and often more than a touch of irrationality.) A key scene in this respect is II.iv of *1 Henry IV*, the justly famous play-within-the-play: Falstaff and the other habitués of the Boar's-Head Tavern think that it is all a game, which in many respects it is, when Hal plays the king and banishes "that villanous abominable misleader of youth, Falstaff, that old white-bearded Satan" (II.iv.508-9). The audience knows, however, that the "play" is not merely mimesis but partly prolepsis. The point is reinforced at the same structural point in *2 Henry IV*, when Hal, again with Falstaff at the Boar's-Head Tavern, is informed that his sick father is faced with renewed civil war: "By heaven, Poins, I feel me much to blame, / So idly to profane the precious time, / ... / Give my my sword and cloak. Falstaff, good night" (II.iv.390-91, 395). The next meeting is between Falstaff and the newly crowned Henry V.

The two parts of *Henry IV* can be understood, then, as plays about a country in a state of seeming decay because of civil war (the Percy family expected Henry Bolingbroke to be their man, of course) and problems of succession to the throne. The decay is only temporary, however, because the heir apparent is rapidly maturing and, as history proved, becoming a great ruler. The two plays dramatize an increasing amount of sexual action and dialogue because the closer we get to Hal's reign the more obvious it becomes that the trivial must and will be transcended. If Hotspur can be seen as an "honor" addict and nutriment "for worms" (*1 HIV* V.iv.86-87), then Falstaff can be seen as a pleasure addict and similarly relegated to the graveyard:

> I know thee not, old man: fall to thy prayers;
> How ill white hairs become a fool and jester!
> . . . . . . . . . . . . . . . . . . . . . . . . . . . . . . . . . . .
>          ...know the grave doth gape
> For thee thrice wider than for other men. (*2 HIV* V.v.51-52,
> 57-58)

Hal's rationality may be harsh, but it is what comes of a man who has himself been publicly reborn in a scene of symbolic reconciliation with the Lord Chief Justice:

> My father is gone wild into his grave,
> For in his tomb lie my affections;
> . . . . . . . . . . . . . . . . . . . . . . . . . . . . . . . .
> . . . The tide of blood in me
> Hath proudly flow'd in vanity till now:
> Now doth it turn and ebb back to the sea,
> Where it shall mingle with the state of floods
> And flow henceforth in formal majesty. (*2 HIV* V.ii.123-24, 129-33)

Hal's speech is, on the surface, strange since we have not seen him "flowing in vanity" in *2 Henry IV,* his only contact with Falstaff being the short one in the fourth scene of the second act. Nevertheless, the speech is thematically relevant because of its allusions to the concept of spiritual rebirth (see John iii.4-5). Hal is publicly rebuilding a political and social image.

That Hal is quite adept at public relations when he wants to be is evident in *Henry V.* The Archbishop of Canterbury has been sold on Hal's seeming reformation: "The breath no sooner left his father's body / But that his wildness, mortified in him, / Seem'd to die too" (I.i.25-27). The Archbishop elaborates (I.i.27-37) with baptismal imagery and allusions to reformation and salvation. But we, of course, know that Hal has never needed to repent and reform. He has merely created a new public image, one of a statesman and warrior—hence the opening Chorus's reference to "the warlike Harry" (1.5) who will *"Assume* the port of Mars" (1.6, emphasis mine). No doubt keeping firmly in mind his father's advice "to busy giddy minds / With foreign quarrels" (*2 HIV* IV.v.214-15), Hal accepts the churchmen's interpretations of "the law Salique" (*HV* I.ii.11) and decides to conquer France, an innovative move that will serve to unify England once again and to solidify his own position of authority and power.

Having decided to dramatize Henry V's achievements, Shakespeare points out in both his opening and subsequent Choruses that the audience needs imagination: "For 'tis your thoughts that now must deck our kings, / Carry them here and there; jumping o'er times, / Turning th' accomplishment of many years / Into an hour-glass" (ll.28-31). I think that we may have here *one* of the reasons for what Partridge terms the "obscene" quality of *Henry V.* If the audience is going to have to engage in many difficult "suspensions of disbelief," to borrow Coleridge's terms, then it will also have to be shown many easily acceptable, amusing bawdy scenes (primarily involving Mistress Quickly, Pistol, Nym, and Bardolph) for a proper grounding in "real" life and subsequent maintenance of interest.

Moreover, if the audience is going to see a dramatization of its past military history, it will also like to see how its great king manages to separate his private and public roles. In short, Shakespeare was not about to turn Hal into a Richard II or a Hotspur. True, Hal transcends the trivial in *1* and *2 Henry IV,* but that does not mean that Henry V has to be without normal humanity. Hence, the apparently crude wooing scene with the French Princess Katherine in which the king sounds suspiciously like Hotspur: "If I could win a lady at leap-frog, or by vaulting into my saddle with my armour on my back, under the correction of bragging be it spoken, I should quickly leap into a wife" (V.ii.141-44). We once again get the military idiom in a sexual context, but unlike Hotspur, who never seems to be able to find time for a private life because of his constant need "to pluck bright honour from the pale-fac'd moon" (*1 HIV* I.iii.202), Henry V is given a long courtship scene at a crucial structural point, the last scene of the play. Here Henry is given time to validate both his love for Katherine and his own masculinity: "If thou canst love a fellow of this temper, Kate, whose face is not worth sunburning, that never looks in his glass for love of any thing he sees there, let thine eye be thy cook. I speak to thee plain soldier: if thou canst love me for this, take me; if not, to say to thee that I shall die, is true; but for thy love, by the Lord, no; yet I love thee too" (V.ii.153-59). The imagery recalls the mirror scene in *Richard II,* but Henry V is never self-indulgent and never confuses his role as honest English wooer with his role as mighty English king:

*K. Hen.* . . . If thou would have such a one, take me; and take me, take a soldier; take a soldier, take a king. And what sayest thou then to my love? Speak, my fair, and fairly, I pray thee.
*Kath.* Is it possible dat I sould love de enemy of France?
*K. Hen.* No; it is not possible you should love the enemy of France, Kate; but, in loving me, you should love the friend of France; for I love France so well that I will not part with a village of it; I will have it all mine; and, Kate, when France is mine and I am yours, then yours is France and you are mine. (V.i.174-85)

With Henry V we can see a truly integrated personality who can play any role the occasion demands (cf. also IV.i with Bates and Williams in which Henry defines the roles and responsibilities of both the king and his soldiers). Moreover, his role as king and wooer can be viewed as a microcosmic reflection of the macrocosmic conflict between the two nations of England and France with the English representing masculine aggressiveness and the French representing feminine passivity. So while Henry attacks Harfleur with the Falstaffian "once more unto the breach, dear friends, once more" (III.i.1; cf. *2 HIV* II.iv.53-59), the effeminate Dauphin later speaks of writing sonnets to his horse (III.vii). While Henry threatens Harfleur's maidens with "hot and forcing violation" (III.iii.21),

the maiden Princess Katherine has a bawdy English lesson about "de foot et de coun" (III.iv.54), proving that she too is a normal young woman in her private life and worthy of England's finest.

That such a sexual interpretation[12] is not wholly fanciful is substantiated by the exchange at the end of the play after Henry V has conquered France and is now formalizing his politically advantageous marriage with Katherine's father:

*K. Hen.* ... you may, some of you, thank love for my blindness, who cannot see many a fair French city for one fair French maid that stands in my way.
*Fr. King.* Yes, my lord, you see them perspectively, the cities turned into a maid; for they are all girdled with maiden walls that war hath never entered.
*K. Hen.* Shall Kate be my wife?
*Fr. King.* So please you. (V.ii.343-52)

The ever practical Prince Hal shows no less astuteness as King Henry V as he gains both wife and dowry and unites England and France, bringing political order out of disorder and sexual union out of an aggressive courtship.

That Shakespeare adhered to a vision of order and stability is obvious not only in the histories but also in the comedies and tragedies. For Shakespeare, at least in his plays, order is natural. Innovation is unnatural unless it occurs within established modes of behavior within the cultural belief system. Hence, Hal as prince and Henry V as king can do things forbidden to the Falstaffs of the world. On the other hand, Falstaff can, like most of the rest of us, indulge himself in the world of trivia. Therefore, the world of Eastcheap is a forbidden area of sexual license at the same time acceptable and unacceptable. When the time comes, those who exercise power arbitrarily wipe out Falstaff's world by carting Mistress Quickly and Doll Tearsheet off to jail (2 *HIV* V.iv), although the good Hostess is, we learn, quickly rehabilitated by marrying Ancient Pistol (*HV* II.i).

I would finally like to draw two conclusions: one is that Prince Hal/Henry V is one of Shakespeare's ideal heroes. He is the "courtier's, soldier's, scholar's, eye, tongue, sword" for the very reasons that Hamlet is not. That is to say, Hal is not bothered by ambiguous metaphysical and ethical problems nor any of the other trivia, such as sex and religious problems (especially those concerning revenge), that consume Hamlet's intellectual energy. Perhaps, too, Hal is much less interesting and less human in the long run. My final conclusion is that the second tetralogy can be viewed as Shakespeare's dramatic model of the complex process of what Peckham calls "cultural transcendence." Hence, within it we find the representatives of the old culture with their tribal loyalties, visions of personal honor, and irrational passions overcome by the new hero who creates, albeit only

---

[12] Such an interpretation was, in fact, first suggested to me by an undergraduate, Niki Alpert, at the University of Wisconsin several years ago.

for a time, an infinitely more rational civilization and, at least in the mind's eye, an "other Eden, demi-paradise":

> Small time, but in that small most greatly liv'd
> This star of England: Fortune made his sword;
> By which the world's best garden he achiev'd.... (*HV*
> Chorus,5-7)

G. ROSS ROY

# *Hardyknute*—Lady Wardlaw's Ballad?

BECAUSE OF THE CONTROVERSY which surrounded it the ballad *Hardyknute*, now generally accepted as the work of Lady Elizabeth Wardlaw (1677-1727), is one of the most interesting to be published in the eighteenth century. By following the poem from its first publication through Child's dismissal of it in 1886 as "tiresome and affected" and "of slight account"[1] we gain an insight into ballad editing customs over a century and a half.[2]

Contrary to what literary histories say, *Hardyknute* was not first published in 1719, but in an anonymous chapbook c. 1710, bearing the title *Hardyknute. A Fragment of an Old Heroick Ballad*.[3] The ephemeral quality of chapbooks doubtless accounts for its not having been previously noticed; the 1719 publication, containing twenty-nine stanzas (three more than in 1710), was an elegant folio printed by James Watson who had already shown his interest in early Scottish poetry by publishing *A Choice Collection of Comic and Serious Scots Poems both Ancient and Modern* (3 parts, Edinburgh, 1706-1711).

Allan Ramsay next picked up the poem and included it in the second volume of *The Ever Green, being a Collection of Scots Poems, Wrote by the Ingenious before 1600* (Edinburgh, 1724). Ramsay may either have written the additional

[1] Francis James Child, *The English and Scottish Popular Ballads,* 5 vols. (1882-1898; reprint ed. New York: Dover, 1965), in a note to *Fause Foodrage* (No. 89).

[2] See Sigurd Bernhard Hustvedt's *Ballad Criticism in Scandinavia and Great Britain during the Eighteenth Century* (New York: American-Scandinavian Foundation, 1916) where aspects of the *Hardyknute* controversy are examined within the context of general eighteenth-century editing.

[3] Thomas Percy suspected that this edition was the earliest, but although I listed it in *New CBEL* in 1971, such recent works as Maurice Lindsay's *History of Scottish Literature* (London: Robert Hale, 1977) still cling to the later date.

stanzas or he may have had access to a manuscript of the poem, or, again, perhaps he knew Lady Wardlaw; in any case the twenty-nine stanzas of 1719 became forty-two in *The Ever Green*. This is the number of stanzas in all subsequent reprintings. But that was not all. Ramsay's version used older forms of many of the words in the poem. This was apparently deliberate "antiquing" on his part, and was not confined to *Hardyknute*—Alexander Montgomerie's *The Cherry and the Slae* appears in Watson's *Choice Collection* in much more modern orthography than it does in Ramsay, as Alexander Campbell pointed out.[4]

With regard to *Hardyknute* this may have been an attempt to make what Ramsay knew was a recent production look old, but what is surprising is that he included the work in the second volume of *The Tea-Table Miscellany* (Edinburgh, 1726) in a much less "antique" form. Far more readers must have seen the poem in its more modern form which, however, still retained some of Ramsay's "antiquing," because *The Tea-Table Miscellany* became something of an eighteenth-century best seller, whereas *The Ever Green* was republished only once during the century.

The first edition to contain any critical commentary was published in 1740, the work of John Moncrief, although the editor remained anonymous. He unreservedly accepted the antiquity of the poem which he said contained "a Grandeur, a Majesty of Sentiment diffus'd through the Whole... which nothing can surpass."[5] The editor went on to state, "the Language ... is plain old *English,* such as the Poets here made use of in Queen *Elizabeth*'s Time."[6] He must have recognized that Ramsay's "antiqued" text in *The Ever Green,* which was the one he used we are told in a footnote, would present a difficulty to some readers, because he proposed to pull off "the Mask of Antiquity, which has hitherto concealed it," and thereby to "contribute not a little to the Pleasures of the Curious."[7] The changes he made, which were similar to those that Ramsay made in *The Tea-Table Miscellany,* were such things as *when* for *quhen, soft* for *saft, dear* for *deir,* as well as dropping the use of the *z* which Ramsay used in lieu of the yogh, thus the word ʒit became *yet.* The copious notes are explanatory and laudatory, sometimes appearing rather quaint to the modern reader. The importance of Moncrief's edition is twofold: the author's stated acceptance of the work as a fragment of a larger work of considerable age (although he did suspect it to be of more recent composition than the other poems in *The Ever Green*) must have established it in the public mind as genuine, and, secondly, its publication in London instead of Edinburgh assured it of a much wider audience.

[4] Alexander Campbell, *An Introduction to the History of Poetry in Scotland* (Edinburgh, 1798), p. 156.
[5] *Hardyknute: A Fragment* (London, 1740), p. 3.
[6] Ibid., p. 4
[7] Ibid., p 4.

The poem was published with the text only in Glasgow in 1745, and with *Chevy-Chase* in Aberdeen in 1754, with an abridgement of Moncrief's notes. We may also pass over two editions by the Foulis Press of Glasgow in 1745 and 1748, which were published without notes or commentary, the text apparently taken from *The Ever Green*.

In 1754 Thomas Warton inserted a paragraph on *Hardyknute* in his *Observations on the Fairy Queen*. Eight years later he repeated the passage almost as it was in the earlier edition: "I cannot omit this opportunity of expressing equal regret for the loss of great part of a noble old Scottish poem, entitled, *HARDYKNUTE;* which exhibits a striking representation of our ancient martial manners...."[8] At the same time he added a footnote to the passage indicating that he was aware of the claims for recent composition of the poem, although he still felt that the first stanza was old. Obviously his position as Professor of Poetry at Oxford made his a voice of authority and his retention of the comment even when he believed that little of the ballad was traditional must have given a boost to the poem's reputation among its admirers.

Thomas Gray, whose interest in the Ossian controversy is well known, held *Hardyknute* in high esteem but he did not accept the theory that it was of recent composition, as we see in a letter of his to Horace Walpole of c. April 1760:

> I have been often told that the poem called Hardicanute (which I always admired, and still admire) was the work of somebody that lived a few years ago. This I do not at all believe, though it has evidently been retouched in places by some modern hand....[9]

With the publication of Percy's *Reliques* in 1765, controversy began. The bishop published *Hardyknute. A Scottish Fragment* as the last poem in the first book of the second volume, where for the first time it is attributed to Lady Wardlaw; but with some reservation as to whether the poem is all hers. This is what Percy wrote:

> As this fine morsel of heroic poetry hath generally past for ancient, it is here thrown to the end of our earlier pieces; that such as doubt of its age may the better compare it with other pieces of genuine antiquity. For after all, there is more than reason to suspect, that most of its beauties are of modern date; and that these at least (if not its whole existence) have flowed from the pen of a lady, within this present century.[10]

---

[8] Thomas Warton, *Observations on the Fairy Queen,* 2d ed. (London, 1762), 1:156.

[9] *Correspondence of Thomas Gray,* ed. Paget Toynbee and Leonard Whibley, revised by H. W. Starr (Oxford: Clarendon Press, 1971), 2:665.

[10] Thomas Percy, *Reliques of Ancient English Poetry: Consisting of Old Heroic Ballads, Songs, and Other Pieces from our Earlier Poets* (London, 1765), 2:87.

After identifying the author merely as Mrs. Wardlaw, Percy recounted the story of how, when suspicion of the poem's origin pointed to her, she had added three more stanzas. He then referred, however, to "a gentleman of distinguished rank, learning, and genius" who believed that part of the ballad might be ancient, but "retouched and much enlarged."[11] The unnamed correspondent maintained that William Thomson, publisher of *Orpheus Caledonius,* claimed to have heard fragments of the ballad repeated during his infancy long before Lady Wardlaw's copy was known. Although Percy retained this note through the fourth edition (1794), the last with which he had any connection, it was not apparently taken seriously by most subsequent editors. In his second edition (1767) Percy added two pages of notes in which variant readings were given, as well as the text of two additional stanzas which belonged, it was asserted, between stanzas 36 and 37. He owed this additional information to Dr. John Clark's notes passed on by his son David, but Percy dismissed the alternative readings and additional stanzas as, probably, inferior early drafts and they were never incorporated in his text; in fact apparently only David Herd ever did so, and he printed the two added stanzas in italics.[12]

Sir David Dalrymple, Lord Hailes, in his reediting of the Bannatyne Manuscript in 1770, attacked Allan Ramsay for his "many and obvious inaccuracies"[13] in *The Ever Green* and dismissed *Hardyknute,* which he did not include, with the statement that it was "probably modern; certainly of no great antiquity."[14] While Ramsay had not mentioned *Hardyknute* as taken from the Bannatyne manuscript (in his preface to *The Ever Green* Ramsay claims that most of the poems were) it will be recalled that the subtitle of *The Ever Green* gives pre-1600 as the date of the poems included, thus inferring that *Hardyknute* was traditional.

Despite the information to be found in Percy's *Reliques,* John Pinkerton published the poem as traditional in his *Scottish Tragic Ballads* in 1781, where the poem was claimed to be "now first published complete," adding a second part consisting of fifty-five stanzas. In his prefatory dissertation "On the Tragic Ballad," dated 1776, he wrote:

> The mutilated Fragment of Hardyknute formerly in print, was admired and celebrated by the best critics. As it is now, I am inclined to think, given in it's [sic] original perfection, it is certainly the most noble production in this style that ever appeared in the world.[15]

[11] Ibid., 2:88

[12] [David Herd], *The Ancient Scots Songs, Heroic Ballads, &c.* (Edinburgh, 1769), pp. 217-27.

[13] [Sir David Dalrymple, Lord Hailes], *Ancient Scottish Poems. Published from the MS. of George Bannatyne, MDLXVIII* (Edinburgh, 1770), p. v.

[14] Ibid., p. vi.

[15] John Pinkerton, *Scottish Tragic Ballads* (London, 1781), p. xxxv.

Between stanzas 18 and 19 of the first part Pinkerton inserted an additional stanza, doubtless of his own writing, which serves to bridge the two parts of the poem. In his notes Pinkerton wrote, "This stanza is now first printed. It is surprising it's [sic] omission was nòt marked in the fragments formerly published, as without it the circumstance of the knight's complaint is altogether foreign and vague."[16]

In anticipation of those who would confront him with Percy's account of the ballad, Pinkerton said that doubtless Lady Wardlaw possessed a copy of the manuscript, adding:

> But that she was the author of this capital composition ... I will no more credit, than that the common people in Lanarkshire [where Pinkerton claimed to have recovered the additional stanzas], who can repeat scraps of both the parts, are the authors of the passages they rehearse. ... If conjecture may be allowed where proof must ever be wanting, I suspect, if we assign the end of the fifteenth century as the date of the antique parts of this noble production, we shall not greatly err; though at the same time the language must convince us, that many strokes have been bestowed by the modern hands.[17]

Of course there is no way of being certain, but it is quite possible that Pinkerton really did believe some of the first part to be traditional—after all Percy had suggested this possibility. Obviously the principal reason for the above passage was to gain acceptance of his second part.

Two years later, in 1783, Pinkerton published an enlargement of *Scottish Tragic Ballads* as the first volume of *Select Scotish Ballads* which reprinted the essay "On the Tragic Ballad" and both parts of *Hardyknute*, again claimed to be "Now first published complete." This was his mistake because Joseph Ritson attacked the edition under the pseudonym of "Anti-Scot" in *The Gentleman's Magazine*. Of the poem he wrote in part:

> This ballad has been substantially proved an artful and impudent forgery: but whether *Mrs. Wardlaw* were the *mother* or the *midwife,* is of very little consequence; the *bantling* is certainly *spurious.* There is not, I readily acknowledge, any great degree of criminality in reprinting a fine and popular ballad; even though ... you did not believe, or thought proper to deny, its true origin. But what excuse can you have for the publication of a *second part,* or continuation of this poetical fraud? Not ignorance surely? No; the composition must be altogether your own. ... The poetry is too artificial, too contemptible; the forger too evident.[18]

Pinkerton was caught out and in his *Ancient Scotish Poems, Never Before in Print* (1786) he admitted to having written the second part in 1776. Probably in an attempt to make it less obvious he buried his recantation under the heading

[16] Ibid., p. 94.
[17] Ibid., pp. 106-7.
[18] *Gentleman's Magazine* 54 (November 1784): 812.

"Sir John Bruce" in a sixty-eight-page chronological "List of all the Scotish Poets; with brief Remarks."[19] Pinkerton began by quoting extracts from the letter which he had also quoted in his 1783 volume. But whereas in 1783 Pinkerton used the passage to discredit the claim of Lady Wardlaw's authorship of the ballad, in 1786 he used it to bolster his conclusion that Sir John Bruce was the author of *Hardyknute*, attributing to him also *The Vision* and *The Eagle and the Red-breast* which Ramsay had published in his *Ever Green* where they were signed "AR. Scot," accepted by modern critics as standing for "Allan Ramsay, Scot."

In claiming the poems for Bruce, Pinkerton wrote incorrectly that the poems were signed "A Scot" which signified only the author's country. He went even further in his speculation stating that *The Vision* was "composed about 1715, to rouse the people in the Pretender's cause"[20] and suggesting that *Hardyknute* was written for a like reason. The date and purported purpose of *The Vision* Pinkerton had from James Beattie as we learn in a note to the poem.[21]

Pinkerton excused himself for not recognizing *Hardyknute* as modern:

> it is to be hoped he shall be pardoned for then [1776] taking the First Part of Hardyknute for ancient, as he really did, considering his small experience in such matters. But now that he has read almost the whole of ancient Scotish poetry ... he must say that he has no doubt but that Hardyknute is a poem of this century. It is easy to use ancient words; but to use ancient sentiments, idioms, transitions, &c. is most difficult.[22]

If he was indeed taken in he was neither the first nor the last to be thus mistaken.

Of his admission that he was the author of the second part nothing more need be said, except to note that both parts were republished as genuine in R. Morison's *Select Collection of Favourite Scotish Ballads* (4 vols., Perth, 1790), where it is the first ballad in the first volume; as late as the 1820s the *Paisley Repository* printed them. While he was at it Pinkerton admitted to being the author in whole or in part of several other poems in *Select Scotish Ballads*.

Several times the first part of the poem was reprinted in its forty-two stanza (*Ever Green*) version (usually with a disclaimer of its antiquity) in much the same way as Lady Nairne's *Bonny Charlie's Now Awa'*, along with other songs, is frequently published in Jacobite collections even though the baroness was unborn at the time of the '45. *Hardyknute* appeared without significant new editorial comment in such later eighteenth-century and early nineteenth-century collections as David Herd's *Ancient and Modern Scottish Songs, Heroic Ballads,*

[19] John Pinkerton, *Ancient Scotish Poems, Never Before in Print* (London, 1786), 1:cxxvi-cxxxi.

[20] Ibid., 1:cxxvii.

[21] John Pinkerton, *Select Scotish Ballads* (London, 1783), 2:179.

[22] *Ancient Scotish Poems,* 1:cxxviii.

*Etc.* (Edinburgh, 1769) and John Finlay's *Scottish Historical and Romantic Ballads; Chiefly Ancient* (Edinburgh, 1808). There was also an incomplete English version of the poem (203 lines) by Alexander Wilson published in his *Poems* (Paisley, 1790) which needs no comment.

Before the end of the century another significant development had occurred—the publication of James Johnson's *Scots Musical Museum* where the first sixty lines of the ballad were printed as number 280.[23] No authorship is given for music or words but the title reads *Hardyknute: Or, The Battle of Largs,* the first time that the site of the battle was identified in the title. When the *Musical Museum* was reissued in 1839 with notes by William Stenhouse and additional notes by David Laing (co-editor with C. K. Sharpe of the edition) Stenhouse identified the source of the tune as James Oswald's *Caledonian Pocket Companion*[24] where it is given in the Phrygian mode with B as the center tone. In harmonizing the tune for Johnson, Stephen Clarke transposed it to a minor retaining essentially the same note values, but including only the first half of it. In doing this, of course, the eight-line stanza had to be cut in two. As mentioned Johnson published only the first sixty lines of the ballad indicating the truncation by "&c." Stenhouse, after a six-page historical note on the Battle of Largs, repeated the claim that part of the ballad was traditional, stating that it was "improbable that so important a battle ... remained unnoticed and unsung by the Scottish bards of that æra."[25] He went on to recount the claim put forward already by Percy that William Thomson had heard stanzas of the ballad *sung* before its "first" appearance in print in 1719. Of Lady Wardlaw's part Stenhouse claimed that *Hardyknute* "was chiefly composed from some imperfect fragments of the old ballad."[26] After retelling Percy's story of how Lord President Forbes et al. accepted the entire poem as traditional, Stenhouse added, apparently for the first time, the statement, "The secret was at length divulged, and Lady Wardlaw favoured Allan Ramsay with a new and enlarged copy...."[27] If this statement was accurate it may have been Lady Wardlaw herself who "antiqued" the poem, although that appears improbable; it is possible that Ramsay was unaware at the time of printing the ballad that it was not traditional. This might explain why he later (1726) included it in *The Tea-Table Miscellany* even though he retained the subtitle *A Fragment of an Old Heroick Ballad.* In reply to Ritson's assertion about both parts of the ballad "there is not a single line which is not stolen from some old ballad, that has the most distant appearance of having existed before" Stenhouse wrote, "There are not only lines, but whole stanzas too, of undoubted

[23] James Johnson, *The Scots Musical Museum* (Edinburgh, [1787-1803]), vol. 3 [1790].

[24] James Oswald, *The Caledonian Pocket Companion* (London, [c. 1750-60]), 5:32.

[25] James Johnson, *The Scots Musical Museum,* ed. William Stenhouse, new ed. [ed. David Laing and C. K. Sharpe] (Edinburgh and London, 1853), 4:268.

[26] Ibid.

[27] Ibid., p. 269.

antiquity."[28] After pointing out the anachronisms in *Hardyknute* (including the title, for "hardy knycht") Stenhouse suggested these very mistakes as proof of the antiquity of parts of the poem, for, he wrote, "Lady Wardlaw was too elegant and accomplished a writer to have committed such blunders, had she been the author of the whole of this historical fragment, although several of the stanzas are undoubtedly hers."[29] Laing in his "Additional Notes and Illustrations" to Stenhouse added nothing new to the controversy but did mention that *Gilderoy* had been attributed to her, and added, "notwithstanding the great antiquity that has been claimed for 'Sir Patrick Spence,' one of the finest ballads in our language, very little evidence would be required to persuade me that we were also indebted for it to Lady Wardlaw."[30] Finally, while certainly not exonerating Pinkerton, and, quoting Sir Walter Scott on the mediocrity of his addition to *Hardyknute,* Laing felt that Ritson had gone too far in his condemnation of Pinkerton.

Considering his attacks on Pinkerton and earlier publishers of the ballad who accepted it as traditional, it seems strange that Joseph Ritson chose to include the work in his *Scotish Song.* He came down pretty hard on the misguided:

> That a composition abounding in evident imitations of, and direct allusions to modern and familiar poetry, in short, that a palpable and bungling forgery, without the slightest resemblance of any thing ancient or original, should have passed, either in England or Scotland, for a genuine relique of antiquity, would appear almost incredible and miraculous, if there were not subsequent instances of a similar delusion.[31]

Not content to leave the reference to Macpherson at this, Ritson quoted Johnson's phrase on the Ossian controversy, "a Scotchman must be a very sturdy moralist who does not love Scotland better than truth," and then went on to say that the forgeries of Buchanan, Sir John Bruce, Macpherson, Pinkerton, and others "stamp a disgrace upon the national character, which ages of exceptionless integrity will be required to remove."[32] As though determined to out-Johnson Johnson on the Scots[33] Ritson also roundly censured *The Ever Green* calling Ramsay "reprehensible" as an editor. And although he knew of the *Scots Musical Museum* he could still write, "The æra of Scotish music and Scotish song

[28] Ibid., p. 270.

[29] Ibid.

[30] Ibid., pp. 319*-20*.

[31] Joseph Ritson, *Scotish Song* (London, 1794), 1:lxii.

[32] Ibid., 1:lxiii.

[33] According to Boswell, Johnson only once mentioned *Hardyknute,* on 16 October 1769, when he had this to say: "The ballad of Hardyknute has no great merit, if it be really ancient." *Boswell's Life of Johnson,* ed. George Birkbeck Hill, revised by L. F. Powell (Oxford: Clarendon Press, 1934), 2:91.

is now passed."[34] In partial extenuation of Ritson it should be pointed out that the extent of Burns's connection with that publication was not made known until 1796. But with some of Burns's finest songs already published in the first four volumes of the *Museum* Ritson shows himself to be no judge of contemporary lyrics.

When Ritson published *Hardyknute* in his *Scotish Songs* he added a footnote "'A [pretended] fragment,' written in or about 1718."[35] The music which accompanied the ballad was the same as that in Oswald's *Caledonian Pocket Companion,* a work with which Ritson was familiar[36] and it is more than possible that this was the source of the tune as he printed it. On the whole Ritson did know ancient poetry as can be seen from his denunciation of *Bothwell Bank* as "a despicable forgery"[37] in reference to the ballad in the second part of Pinkerton's *Select Scotish Ballads,* and Pinkerton admits his authorship in his *Ancient Scotish Poems.*

So far as I have ascertained the last time *Hardyknute* was published with music[38] was in the *Paisly Repository* in the 1820s (none of the reference books assigns a precise date to this publication) in numbers 9-14. Both parts of the ballad were printed with notes taken largely from Pinkerton. A single leaf of music is bound in before number 9 containing the music to the first half of the air which is in b minor.[39] An early annotator has noted "R[obert] A[rchibald] Smith, Author of this Air" in the copy in the Mitchell Library, Glasgow, but as this version is essentially the same as that in Oswald, the statement cannot be correct. It is possible, of course, that Smith arranged the tune.

Walter Scott came upon *Hardyknute* in *The Ever Green* where he added a manuscript note: "Hardyknute was the first poem that I ever learnt—the last that I shall forget."[40] In his "Introductory Remarks on Popular Poetry" (first appended to the *Minstrelsy* in 1830) Scott accepted that there was a traditional source from which "a most spirited and beautiful imitation of the ancient ballad"[41] had been taken. On Pinkerton, Scott showed himself to be charitable and astute, characterizing him as "a man of considerable learning and some

[34] Ritson, *Scotish Song,* 1:cx.

[35] Ibid., 2:144.

[36] Ibid., 1:cviii.

[37] Ibid., 1:lvii.

[38] From the *British Union Catalogue of Early Music* I note the following entry: "*Hardyknute. A Scottish fragment, from...Percy's Reliques.* London: Printed for the author. [c. 1795]. Music by John Wall Callcott." The work has not been seen.

[39] I am indebted to Homer J. Walton of the University of South Carolina's Cooper Library for assisting me with the musical information in this article.

[40] *Minstrelsy of the Scottish Border,* ed. T. F. Henderson (Edinburgh and London: Oliver and Boyd, 1902), 4:10, n.1. Subsequent references will be to this edition.

[41] Ibid., 1:25.

severity as well as acuteness of disposition"[42] and suggested in an oblique condemnation of James Macpherson that the success of *Ossian* may have encouraged Pinkerton in his deception. Considering what Pinkerton had written about Macpherson this was an odd view for Scott to hold. Of the second part Scott wrote:

> It labours, however, under this great defect, that in order to append his own conclusion to the original tale, Mr. Pinkerton found himself under the necessity of altering the leading circumstance in the old ballad, which would have rendered his catastrophe inapplicable. With such licence, to write continuations and conclusions would be no difficult task.... The poetry smells of the lamp; and it may be truly said, that if ever a ballad had existed in such quaint language as the author employs, it could never have been so popular as to be preserved by oral tradition.[43]

However, in his "Essay on Imitations of the Ancient Ballad" (written in 1830 and meant as a continuation of "Remarks on Popular Poetry") Scott defended Lady Wardlaw thus: "If a young, perhaps a female, author chooses to circulate a beautiful poem—we will suppose that of Hardyknute under the disguise of antiquity, the public is surely more enriched by the contribution than injured by the deception."[44] Scott went on to point out how difficult it was to pass off a modern work for one of genuine antiquity. He recognized that it was unlikely to find someone who united "the power of poetical genius" with a "minute acquaintance with ancient customs, and with ancient history."[45] Only one person possessed all of these qualities in the early nineteenth century, Scott himself, and the passage reads like something of an apology for the inclusion of ballads admittedly of his own making in the third volume of *Minstrelsy of the Scottish Border*. And although Scott chose to ignore the history of how *Hardyknute* had been accepted by several well-informed people in the previous century, it is obvious that it was not easy either earlier or in Scott's own day to distinguish between the old and the new.

Writing in 1825 Allan Cunningham, the untrustworthy editor of Burns, accepted Lady Wardlaw as modernizer of the ballad but felt that it was "founded on the remains of some romantic ballad; and that into the story of the old minstrel, Lady Wardlaw poured a spirit and feeling of her own which communicated all the softer and more amiable qualities of the composition."[46] Like others before him he pointed out that many other ballads had been refurbished; *Gil Morrice* and *Tamlane* he wrote "owe no little of their present

[42] Ibid., 1:41.
[43] Ibid., 1:44.
[44] Ibid., 4:10.
[45] Ibid.
[46] Allan Cunningham, *The Songs of Scotland, Ancient and Modern* (London, 1825), 1:186.

beauty to such loving-kindness, and the variations of song and ballad conceal many affectionate touchings and infusions...."[47] Perhaps unwittingly Cunningham set the stage for attributing other ballads to the pen of Lady Wardlaw by regretting that no other works of hers were known; if he knew of Pinkerton's claim that *Hardyknute, The Vision* and *The Eagle* were by the same author he chose to ignore it.

Four years later Robert Chambers published a collection entitled *The Scottish Ballads* in which he included *Hardyknute*, attributed to Lady Wardlaw, under the heading "Imitations of the Ancient Ballads." Other than some footnotes, Chambers made no editorial comment on the poem. In the "Introductory" to this collection he wrote of historical ballads and those referring to real circumstances in private life that we must consider their antiquity, but in so doing he believed we are obliged to rely on conjecture not fact. "It is the belief," he continued, "of all previous enquirers into this subject—and common-sense countenances the theory most expressly—that, in almost every case, the ballads referring to real incidents were composed immediately after the transactions which called them forth."[48] Although he admitted to "slight reservations" Chambers stated that these two classes of ballads could be accepted "as in general forming authentic specimens of the popular poetry of their respective ages."[49] Like earlier editors he did not believe that the present form of a ballad represented anything more than "the last *shape* or *form* into which the stories which amused our earliest ancestors have been resolved."[50] He was to have a good deal more to say on the matter later.

In 1859 Chambers published a pamphlet entitled *The Romantic Scottish Ballads: Their Epoch and Authorship* (Edinburgh and London, 1859). Now Robert Chambers was no novice to Scottish literature—editor and partner with his brother William in the Edinburgh publishing firm W. & R. Chambers, he was certainly in a position to know the material he wrote about. What a surprise then to find that in this pamphlet he set forth the claim that Lady Wardlaw was the author not only of *Hardyknute* but of twenty-five other ballads including *Sir Patrick Spens, Gil Morrice* (or *Child Maurice*), *Edward, The Bonny Earl of Murray, Mary Hamilton, Clerk Saunders, The Douglas Tragedy* (or *Earl Brand*) and *Tamlane*!

He began his pamphlet by stating that after accepting them as ancient he had recently had his doubts. In fact Chambers had been working on this idea for several years—he had mentioned the idea that *Sir Patrick Spens* was from the pen of Lady Wardlaw in *Chambers's Edinburgh Journal* in 1843,[51] getting the

---

[47] Ibid., 186-87.

[48] Robert Chambers, *The Scottish Ballads* (Edinburgh, 1829), pp. 1-2.

[49] Ibid., p. 4.

[50] Ibid.

[51] This information is from Norval Clyne, *The Romantic Scottish Ballads and the Lady Wardlaw Heresy* (Aberdeen, 1859), p. 5. I was unable to find the article referred to.

144 ROMANTICISM AND CULTURE

idea perhaps from Stenhouse. In any case Chambers quoted Stenhouse to the effect that Lady Wardlaw's great-grandson wrote to Stenhouse that his forbear "was a woman of elegant accomplishments, *who wrote other poems....*"[52]

One of Chambers's principal objections to accepting the list of ballads as traditional was their diction—taking the group as a whole he writes of "their superiority in delicacy of feeling and in diction to all ordinary ballad poetry...."[53] Taking his argument a step further he claimed that the group had a common style which set them unmistakably apart from genuinely old English ballads, and he made the point that from the beginning of the seventeenth century all Scottish literature was "tinged by what had immediately before been in vogue in the south." Nowhere in Percy's *Reliques,* or Thomas Evans's *Old Ballads, Historical and Narrative* (London, 1784), or John Payne Collier's *Book of Roxburghe Ballads* (London, 1847) would the reader find "a trace of the style and manner of these Scottish romantic ballads."[54]

Chambers challenged the generally accepted opinion that oral transmission supposed alteration so that the oldest ballad might survive in quite modern dress. He wrote:

> Here I may...express my belief that the ballads in question are for the most part printed nearly, and in some instances, entirely, in the condition in which they were left by the author. In *Edward,* I question if a line has been corrupted, or a word altered. *Sir Patrick Spence* and *Gilderoy* are both so rounded and complete, so free, moreover, from all vulgar terms, that I feel nearly equally confident about them.[55]

The absence of early manuscripts or printed copies of these ballads from before the reign of George III and the fact that they escaped with one exception (actually two) the "collecting diligence" of Bannatyne, James Watson, Ramsay, and Herd was put forward by Chambers as an argument for rejecting them as traditional. But anyone familiar with Scott's assiduity in tracking down old ballads would not find it at all surprising that Sir Walter was able to collect such a large number of them. Communications were far better in his day; earlier editors probably relied far more on broadsides and chapbooks for the material they published, whereas Scott went to cottages and hamlets where the tradition had best survived.

Chambers concluded his pamphlet by pointing out that Caroline Baroness Nairne had kept the secret of her song writing so why should not Lady Wardlaw have been able to keep hers a century earlier? Finally he suggested that Sir Walter

[52] Robert Chambers, *The Romantic Scottish Ballads: Their Epoch and Authorship* (Norwood, Pa.: Norwood Editions, 1977), p. 10. This edition mistakenly has 1849 for 1859 on its facsimile titlepage.

[53] Ibid., p. 28.

[54] Ibid., p. 36.

[55] Ibid., p. 39.

Scott owed much of his inspiration to the author of *Hardyknute,* a lady who was "his literary foster-mother, and we probably owe the direction of his genius, and all its fascinating results, primarily to her."[56]

The counterblast was not long in coming. Norval Clyne answered with *The Romantic Scottish Ballads and the Lady Wardlaw Heresy* that same year, a pamphlet which demolished Chambers's theory point by point. Clyne seems to have overreacted somewhat for early in the pamphlet he wrote that *Hardyknute* contained "some good stanzas...but, on the whole, it is an indifferent composition...."[57] Such a comment might lead the reader to suspect that its author had prejudiced his case, but although Clyne selected those ballad passages which suited him to make his points (and which, of course, Chambers had done also) it must be admitted that he was fair in the rebuttals to Chambers's arguments.

Among his complaints Clyne pointed out that whereas Chambers blamed William Edmondstoune Aytoun for the liberties he had taken in his *Ballads of Scotland* (Edinburgh and London, 1858) in adjusting *Sir Patrick Spens* for historical accuracy, Chambers had himself been guilty of the same thing in his own collection.[58] Clyne attacked Chambers for seeing a common authorship in ballads in which similar expressions occurred. He also rejected Chambers's selection of certain words in the ballads in question as being of too modern use in Scotland since ballads went through a constant state of modernization. Some of the words Chambers had objected to as non-Scottish ("dale" for example) Clyne indicated were indeed to be found in Scotland (Teviotdale).

In reply to Chambers's assertion that the ballads in question "are wholly unlike any English ballads,"[59] Clyne replies that the ballads of both countries are very much alike. Today it is widely accepted that the Scottish ballads do in fact have characteristics of their own—Edwin Muir makes the point in a fine essay on the Scottish ballads in *Latitudes.*

Clyne ends his pamphlet by stressing the fact that the eighteenth-century ballad editors, who Chambers claims should have recovered more ballads if indeed they were traditional, had not collected in the same way as did the early nineteenth-century collectors:

> My belief is that, if any of the editors before Scott had done what he, Jamieson, Buchan, and others afterwards did, and had sought through the country for specimens of traditionary poetry, their success would have been the same or greater, and the earlier the period of making the search the richer would have been the treasure recovered.[60]

[56] Ibid., p. 46.
[57] Clyne, p. 7.
[58] Ibid., p. 18.
[59] Chambers, *The Romantic Scottish Ballads,* p. 36.
[60] Clyne, pp. 48-49.

Few readers would quarrel with that statement today.

Chambers must have recognized that he had been bested for he apparently abandoned any further attempt to have his exaggerated claims for Lady Wardlaw accepted. James Maidment referred to Chambers's pamphlet and Clyne's reply in his *Scottish Ballads and Songs, Historical and Traditionary* (Edinburgh, 1868) in which *Hardyknute* was given pride of place. It was published, also, with an introduction, in *The Ballad Minstrelsy of Scotland* (Glasgow, 1871, reprinted 1893) as well as in George Eyre-Todd's *Abbotsford Series of the Scottish Poets* in 1896. But Child's refusal (by omission) to admit that any part of the ballad was traditional probably ensured that it would be infrequently reprinted thereafter— I know of no twentieth-century edition of it and in fact several books about ballads do not even mention the work.

This is unfortunate because by any standard *Hardyknute* is a good poem. Just because it is not what it was once thought to be does not mean that it is without merit, and for this reason it is worthy of our attention as an example of what may be fragments of a much older poem made over by a modest poetess. Instances of reworking traditional material in the eighteenth and early nineteenth centuries abound and are often as shrouded in uncertainty as *Hardyknute*—for example *Auld Lang Syne*. Lady Wardlaw and her ballad are in good company. If it is her ballad.

CLYDE DE L. RYALS

# Irony in Browning's *Strafford*

AS WE NOW LOOK BACK over the career of Robert Browning it is increasingly difficult to account for his early poetry in terms of its relationship to Shelley, the poet from whom he is usually said to descend, or any of his romantic predecessors in England. However much Shelley's (or other romantics') influence may be reflected thematically in Browning's verse, there is still something about Browning's work, including his earliest, which seems totally different. Where Blake, Wordsworth, Shelley, even Byron seem allegorical, mythic, or visionary, Browning goes out of his way to disclaim all bardic notions of allegory, myth, and vision. Indeed, he frequently laughs at such bardic tendencies in himself as well as others. It is this very reflexive quality in his poetry—the ability to locate himself in his created world and simultaneously to detach himself from and observe himself in it—that sets Browning apart from the English romantics. It is the quality which we call irony.

Although it has been customary to regard Browning's earliest verse as confessional (hence "romantic"), recent criticism has called that opinion into question by focusing on the ironic structure of his first two works—*Pauline* (1833) and *Paracelsus* (1835).[1] The irony in these early poems is largely a matter of form—and elementary at that. The completion of *Paracelsus*, however, with its enunciation of the doctrine of becoming in the fifth part,[2] provided Browning

---

[1] See my essay "Browning's *Pauline*: The Question of Genre," *Genre* 9 (Fall 1976): 231-45; and F. E. L. Priestley, "The Ironic Pattern of Browning's *Paracelsus*," *University of Toronto Quarterly* 34 (October 1964): 68-81.

[2]     "things tend still upward—progress is
        The law of life—man is not Man as yet:...
        ...............................
        But in completed man begins anew
        A tendency to God." (V.741-42,771-72)

with a philosophical basis for his irony and permitted him to enlarge his conception of it to cosmic scope. *Strafford* (1837), the next work after *Paracelsus,* reflects Browning's growing sense of irony, and thus is an important document in a study of the poet's development.

Once Browning accepted the idea of progress with its attendant idea that being is also becoming—that *a* is both *a* and not *a*—then the way was opened to the kind of irony which is to be seen not so much as a form of irony but as a way of presenting it—what one theorist calls "really the dramatization of irony."[3] Many of the implications of such an ironic view were set down by Friedrich Schlegel, some of whose works Browning may have known directly or, more likely, as mediated through Carlyle.[4] It was, however, an Englishman who most probably delineated for the young Browning the dramatic possibilities of irony as a cosmic view. Writing on the irony of Sophocles in 1833, Connop Thirlwall observes that in *Antigone,* Sophocles impartially presents two equal and opposite points of view and, expanding on this, remarks that irony may reside in the attitude of an ironic observer or, more precisely, in the situation observed:

> There is always a slight cast of irony in the grave, calm, respectful attention impartially bestowed by an intelligent judge on two contending parties, who are pleading their causes before him with all the earnestness of deep conviction, and of excited feeling. What makes the contrast interesting is, that the right and the truth lie on neither side exclusively: that there is no fraudulent purpose, no gross imbecility of intellect, on either: but both have plausible claims and specious reasons to alledge, though each is too much blinded by prejudice or passion to do justice to the views of his adversary. For here the irony lies not in the demeanor of the judge, but is deeply seated in the case itself, which seems to favour each of the litigants, but really eludes them both.

---

This quotation and the subsequent quotations from *Strafford* (except as otherwise indicated) are from the London first editions (1835 and 1837). Line numbers have been added to correspond with the Camberwell Edition, *Complete Works of Robert Browning,* ed. Charlotte Porter and Helen A. Clarke, 12 vols. (New York: Thomas Y. Crowell, 1898).

[3] Eleanor N. Hutchens, "The Identification of Irony," *ELH* 27 (December 1960): 352-63. The most masterful study of irony, particularly as employed by nineteenth- and twentieth-century authors, is D. C. Muecke, *The Compass of Irony* (London: Methuen, 1969).

[4] Browning studied German at the University of London; his teacher, Ludwig von Mühlenfels, introduced the young poet to modern German writers, doubtlessly including the Schlegels. See John Maynard, *Browning's Youth* (Cambridge: Harvard University Press, 1977), pp. 274-77. Browning's admiration for Carlyle and the influence of the prose writer on the poet are well known. See especially Charles Richard Sanders, "The Carlyle-Browning Correspondence and Relationship," *Bulletin of the John Rylands University Library of Manchester* 57 (Autumn 1974-Spring 1975): 213-46, 430-62. For a study of Carlyle, Schlegel, and romantic irony see Janice L. Haney, "'Shadow-Hunting': Romantic Irony, *Sartor Resartus,* and Victorian Romanticism," *Studies in Romanticism* 17 (Summer 1978): 307-33.

The most interesting debates or conflicts are not, Thirlwall writes, those in which evil is pitted against good. For

> this case...seems to carry its own final decision in itself. But the liveliest interest arises when by inevitable circumstances, characters, motives, and principles are brought into hostile collision, in which good and evil are so inextricably blended on each side, that we are compelled to give an equal share of our sympathy to each, while we perceive that no earthly power can reconcile them; that the strife must last until it is extinguished with at least one of the parties, and yet that this cannot happen without the sacrifice of something which we should wish to preserve.[5]

It was with such ironic possibilities in mind, whether gained from Thirlwall or not, that Browning sat down to write *Strafford*—"to freshen a jaded mind by diverting it to the healthy natures of a grand epoch," as he says (ironically) in the preface to the play. Hence *Strafford* is important not only because it helps us chart Browning's development but also because it may well be the first play in English consciously designed as a dramatization of irony.[6]

Once we understand the ironic intent of the play, even surface ironies become almost immediately apparent. The characters are far from being "the healthy natures" of whom Browning speaks in the preface. At best Strafford and Pym are monomaniacs devoted, against all reason, to the furtherance of an idea—to the monarchical principle in the case of Strafford, to the parliamentary in the case of Pym. Yet if we investigate further, we find that what drives them, as well as Lady Carlisle, is not principle but love—in all three cases, love frustrated.

Postponing consideration of Carlisle for the moment, let us turn our attention to Strafford and Pym. In earlier life they had been friends and had shared a dedication to the rights of Parliament against monarchal repression; even now

---

[5] Connop Thirlwall, "On the Irony of Sophocles," *The Philological Museum* 2 (1833): 489-90. I can find no reference to Thirlwall's essay in Browning's published correspondence, but I believe it extremely likely that Browning was acquainted with this particular issue of *The Philological Museum* because it contains an imaginary conversation by Landor, the writer who had an enormous influence on the young poet ("Robert always said that he owed more as writer to Landor than to any contemporary," reported his wife [*The Letters of Elizabeth Barrett Browning*, ed. F. G. Kenyon (New York and London: Macmillan, 1897), 2:354]). The first volume of the *Museum* (1832) also contains one of Landor's imaginary conversations. Another popularizer of German ideas, Henry Crabb Robinson, borrowed heavily from Friedrich and his brother August Wilhelm Schlegel. His long essay on Goethe in the *Monthly Repository,* volumes six and seven (beginning in May 1832), bears indirectly on the kind of irony described by Thirlwall. Since the *Repository* was edited by Browning's friend W. J. Fox and since the young poet himself published in the journal, it is highly probable that Browning was familiar with Crabb Robinson's work.

[6] The only mention that I can discover of *Strafford* as an ironic drama is Arthur E. Dubois, "Robert Browning, Dramatist," *Studies in Philology* 33 (October 1936): 626-55, where the treatment of *Strafford* itself is slight. Other recent studies touching on *Strafford*

Strafford is susceptible to Pym's plea to return to his old friends. Yet somehow the king manages to captivate him, to seduce him away from his former friends. For even though he is fully cognizant of the king's waywardness and personal disloyalty, when Charles calls him "my Friend / of Friends" (I.ii.241-42) Strafford vows, more than once, "I am yours, / Yours ever... / To the death, yours" (II.ii.36-37). Hereafter, with the one brief exception in III.iii, in spite of every act of perfidy and disloyalty on Charles's part, Strafford remains utterly faithful to the king. Why? Because besottedly, like a romantic lover, he adores Charles, not the king but the man, has come, as he says, "to love the man and not the king—/ The man with the mild voice and mournful eyes" (III.ii.292-93). It is this love which results in his death.

In the case of Pym there is a contrary movement. Where Strafford casts off notions of office in manifesting his love for the person, Pym puts aside the notion of love and friendship to serve the office. In I.i, Pym declares his continuing love for Wentworth (the family name of the title character, created Earl of Strafford later in the first act), and expresses his hope that their former friendship might continue. In I.ii, he pleads with Wentworth to return to their old friendly ways and seems almost to succeed until the king appears and Wentworth lets Pym's hand drop. Though there is some expression of rekindled hope in II.i, Pym increasingly sees that Strafford (as Wentworth has now become) devotes himself exclusively to Charles. Hereafter Pym, like a scorned lover, becomes "the chosen man that should destroy / The traitor" (IV.ii.159-60), having seen himself as the embodiment of the will of England who seeks "England's great revenge" (III.i.29). Only at the last "meeting," about which they have frequently talked and where their paths irrevocably diverge, does Pym speak again of his love for the doomed man:

> I swore that Wentworth might leave us, but I
> Should never leave him: I do leave him now.
> I render up my charge (be witness, God!)
> To England who imposed it. I have done
> Her bidding....
>                     It is done.
> And this said, if I say...yes, I will say
> I never loved but one man—David not
> More Jonathan! Even thus, I love him now.... (V.ii.278-88)

---

and Browning's plays in general deal with political, philosophical, and historical themes: respectively, Lawrence Poston, III, "Browning's Political Skepticism: *Sordello* and the Plays," *PMLA* 88 (March 1973): 260-70; Mary Rose Sullivan, "Browning's Plays: Prologue to *Men and Women*," *Browning Institute Studies* 3 (1975): 17-39; Lawrence Poston, III, "Browning's Career to 1841: The Theme of Time and the Problem of Form," *Browning Institute Studies* 3 (1975): 79-100.

The dialectical movement of the antagonists shows that, in Thirlwall's words, "both have plausible claims and specious reasons to alledge, though each is too blinded by prejudice or passion to do justice to the views of his adversary." Both Strafford and Pym are led by belief in their causes to condone methods and actions of which they would otherwise disapprove. Strafford is loyal to a person whom he knows to be worthless and pursues a cause and courses of actions which he knows to be futile. Pym places his faith in Strafford despite his former friend's known opposition to the Parliamentary cause, and when it becomes plain that Strafford will support the king under all circumstances, he resorts to acts in total violation of Parliamentary principles, including connivance with the king and collusion with the king's party. This means that the audience is faced with the paradox that the better man represents the worse cause.

The degree to which cause (as opposed to man) is better is indicated by the behavior of the adherents to each side. The king is presented as a weakling controlled by his wife and courtiers. As Strafford says of him near the end: "And he's weak, / And loves the Queen, and..." (V.ii.316-17; ellipsis in the text). Yet Charles has wits enough to recognize that while all Strafford's plans on his behalf are the proper ones, he is unable to follow them. The queen and courtiers are presented as pursuing their own self-interests, with no regard for the country at all. The Parliamentarians, on the other hand, are shown in shifting attitudes. In the beginning they charge all the monarch's villianies to Strafford, although it is he who tries to mitigate the king's disgraceful actions with reference to Parliament. As Strafford knows, "this untoward step / Shall pass for mine; the world shall think it mine" (II.ii.37-38). Early in the play Vane, Rudyard, and Fiennes are the hotheads who wish to hound Wentworth from office, while Pym and Hampden advocate calm in consideration of a position to be taken with respect to Wentworth. In a reversal occurring in IV.ii, Vane, Rudyard, and Fiennes become the moderates insisting upon fair treatment of Strafford, as Pym and Rudyard, pressing for a bill of attainder, insist "We must make occasion serve" (l.173). The play leaves us in do doubt of the moral superiority of the Parliamentary faction, even though it has a demagogue for its leader.

The dialectical movement of the antagonists in addition provides an ironic structure for the play. This is a structure much like that of *Paracelsus,* in which true aspiration leading to false attainment is followed by the reverse pattern. From the second act on, it is inevitable that the diverging paths of Pym and Strafford must cross again. "Keep tryst! the old appointment's made anew," says Pym. "Forget not we shall meet again!" And Strafford replies, "Pym, we shall meet again!" (II.ii.154-55,166). In the third act, Strafford submits to his antagonist as the embodiment of the will of England: "England! I see thy arm in this and yield. / Pray you now—Pym awaits me" (III.iii.96-97). But this proves not the true meeting. For Strafford discovers that he was "fool enough / To see the will of England in Pym's will" (IV.ii.74-75). He impeaches Pym, and far from there being a meeting of the two, the occasion is one in which Pym shrinks from

and quails before Strafford (IV.ii.50, 59). To the Parliamentarians, who demand that Pym bear Parliament's pardon to Strafford, Pym says: "Meet him? Strafford? / Have we to meet once more then?" (IV.ii.186-87). And Strafford says in similar vein: "I would not look upon Pym's face again" (IV.ii.106).

Up to this point there has been an ironic reversal. Pym, the just man with a just cause, has grown in attitude and behavior to resemble the Royalists whose cause he detests and whose conduct he abominates—all because of his hatred for Strafford. He will stoop to any sort of baseness in his maniacal pursuit of Strafford's downfall. His compact with King Charles in regard to the bill of attainder marks Pym as a man who would scheme with Satan himself. Even the king recognizes Pym's motives: "You think / Because you hate the Earl... (turn not away, / We know you hate him)" (IV.iii.38-40). Strafford, on the other hand, grows in strength and dignity. Where in the first act he was a man willing to perform any kind of deed for the sake of the king, no matter how much it offended conscience or common sense, in the fourth act he marshals his energies for more apparently reasonable ends, even though on the king's behalf: "From this day begins / A new life, founded on a new belief / In Charles" (IV.ii.101-3). Strafford becomes in the eyes of the audience an increasingly sympathetic character in spite of the fact that his cause is shown to be less and less worthy and he himself a dupe. "We have all used the man," the king points out to Pym, "As though a drudge of ours, with not a source / Of happy thoughts except in us; and yet / Strafford has wife and children, household cares, / Just as if we have never been" (IV.iii.43-47). For the first time we learn that Strafford has a family while Pym is, as the king says, "a solitary man / Wed to your cause—to England if you will!" (IV.iii.48-49). The claims of "family" will assert themselves in the last act.

Strafford's new life falsely founded on a new belief in the king leads only to the Tower. It is no doubt an intended comment on the two antagonists that Strafford is shown with his son and daughter while Pym's "England" is depicted as "a green and putrefying charnel" (V.ii.325) devouring children. And it is this England to whom Pym would immediately "render up my charge" (V.ii.280). For although this is the inevitable encounter, it is not to be the anticipated meeting. Pym foresees that he is to die soon after Strafford, and both agree that the tryst so long awaited will be better postponed until heaven (V.ii.291-310). Yet at the end, when he thinks of Charles's fate at Pym's hands, Strafford begs that the king be spared: "No, not for England now, not for Heaven now.../ This is the meeting: let me love you well!" But in this life at least, Pym is relentless, and all the love sought from Strafford he now foregoes: "England,—I am thine own!" Strafford's final line—"O God, I shall die first"—is full of ambiguities: after him will follow not only the king and Pym but also thousands of Englishmen killed in the Civil War.

Almost certainly the conflict between Pym and Strafford was the germ of the play: which is to say, the play was conceived as an ironic drama of character. It is

of this, no doubt, that Browning speaks when in the preface he refers to *Strafford* as a play of "Action in Character, rather than Character in Action." At this point in his career, however, the young poet was unable fully to sustain or tolerate the openness and indeterminacy of ironic art soon to be displayed in the completed *Sordello*. He was still at the stage where he felt compelled to offer some approximation of reconciliation and harmonious resolution. The "meeting" of Pym and Strafford, given the countermovement of their characters outlined above, simply cannot take place; yet Browning permits the possibility of a resolution by postponing the meeting until an afterlife; which is to say, he allows a certain sentimental pretense, something totally alien to the nature of irony.

In addition, Browning attempted to provide a stable center for this drama of dialectical movement: on Lady Carlisle the "meaning" would focus.[7] Pym and Strafford were the historical données: the portraits of them are, Browning said, "faithful." "My Carlisle, however, is purely imaginary" (preface). Why is this so? Because the dramatist initially conceived of his play as a struggle between, in Thirlwall's words, "two contending parties" in which "the right and the truth lie on neither side exclusively." Then came the afterthought that the play perhaps needed not only something of a conventional romantic interest but also a moral center.[8] If everyone in the play were to be fickle, self-serving, or blindly deceived, at least in Lady Carlisle there would be one "good" character who was faithful, selfless, and aware of the deceptions about her. What results, alas, is an incredible character.

Carlisle's love for Strafford is both selfless and hopeless. She loves a man who does not love her but instead loves another—the king. And she constantly hides from him all evidence of the king's duplicity so as to assure his love for Charles: "One must not lure him from a love like that! / Oh, let him love the King and die!" (II.ii.243-44). To the last scene she keeps up this deception, pretending that it is the king and not she who had made plans for Strafford's escape from the Tower. She speaks no more after Pym is discovered at the door by which

---

[7] In his *Rhetoric of Irony* (Chicago: University of Chicago Press, 1974), Wayne C. Booth contends that beneath even the most ironic surfaces there is a stable center which permits the careful reader to reconstruct meaning. Paul de Man, on the other hand, maintains that irony's permanent parabasis denies us a stable center and hence the possibility of meaningful statement ("The Rhetoric of Temporality," in *Interpretation: Theory and Practice*, ed. Charles Singleton [Baltimore: Johns Hopkins University Press, 1969], pp. 173-209).

[8] One must not overlook the demands that W. C. Macready, the great actor-manager who commissioned *Strafford*, placed on Browning for an actable play with as wide appeal as possible. He may well have insisted on a larger role for Lady Carlisle. Certainly Helen Faucit, who acted the part of Carlisle, objected during rehearsal (and revision of the text) to the poverty of her part. See *The Diaries of William Charles Macready, 1833-1851*, ed. William Toynbee (London: Chapman and Hall, 1912), 1:354-94.

Strafford is to leave his prison, so that the last ninety-three lines are devoted to dialogue between the two antagonists, a fact which alone suggests her lack of centrality to the action of the play.

It is only by linking her to the major ironic theme of the play—deception— that Browning escapes making her totally extraneous. More than the other characters she is aware of the discrepancy between things as they are and things as they seem. With her various pretenses concerning the king, Carlisle is conscious of playing a role. Indeed, she regards herself and others as actors in a play, a notion which, as we shall see, other characters share. This self-consciousness on the part of the dramatis personae means that the characters become ironic observers and, as well, victims of irony to the extent that they doubt the meaningfulness of their actions in the play.

At the beginning the Puritans fancy that Wentworth has turned Ireland "to a private stage" (I.i.41), has superseded other Royalists "whose part is played" (I.i.151), and has tried to persuade Pym that "a patriot could not play a purer part / Than follow in his track" (I.i.115-16, as the passage reads in the 1863 revision). Strafford does indeed play a role, but not the one the Puritans envision. He perceives that the king wears a mask (II.ii.123) to hide his real self and that in order to save the monarch he too must do likewise. Thus, when members of the Parliamentary party arrive, just at the moment when Strafford discovers the king's double dealings, Strafford immediately drops to his knee before Charles in a gesture of hurried but loyal farewell. As Lady Carlisle says, "there's a masque on foot" (II.ii.260).

In this play-within-a-play conspirators teach their henchmen to recite to others "all we set down" with "not a word missed" and "just as we drilled" (III.i.8, 21). Strafford is to be kept "in play," ignorant of the real circumstances (III.ii.126). As in a theater the king and his party witness the impeachment proceedings against Strafford from a screened box, which "admits of such a partial glimpse" and whose "close curtain / Must hide so much" (IV.i.17-26). Their judgment of the trial is that it "was amusing in its way / Only too much of it: the Earl withdrew / In time!" (V.i.17-19). At the end Strafford wonders whether history will declare the chief part in this masque to have been played by an actor named "the Patriot Pym, or the Apostate Strafford" (V.ii.57).

The characters' sense of being observers and victims in a play is underscored by their reiterated belief that they are but puppets pulled by a master puppeteer. Pym and the Presbyterians feel, as good Calvinists should, that their actions are predestined. More than once Pym speaks of his fated course and of himself as "the chosen man" (IV.ii.159). Yet the Royalists also ascribe their actions to fate. Strafford says, "There's fate in it: I give all here quite up" (II.ii.195). And the king feels, "I am in a net / And cannot move" (IV.iii.82-83). But of course there is really no question of the irony of fate at all: there is only the irony of falsely

believing oneself trapped by a fateful irony. In actuality the characters are free to do as they choose.[9]

The actors in the masque are also very much aware of the superfluity of words which envelops the action. The opening scene, for example, is devoted to those of the Parliamentary party who "will speak out" (l.36) and those who say there has been "talk enough" (l.263). The Puritan who appears and reappears like a character in *Hellzapoppin* is forever quoting Scripture, only to be told to keep quiet: "Be you as still as David!" (l.20). What is needed is that "word grow deed" (l.243). The next scene shows Wentworth discovering the machinations of the Royalist party, who have "decried" his service (l.53) without ever uttering a "precise charge" (l.39) because they "eschew plain-speaking" (l.141). Wentworth believes that "one decisive word" on his part will put matters straight; surely the king "mistrusts...their prattle" (l.146). Pym argues, however, that even though Wentworth's letters to Charles "were the movingest" (l.159) and that the messages from the Scots were "words moving in their way," Wentworth can be sure that the king pays no attention to either (ll.162-63). Wentworth is nevertheless reassured by the king's profession of love for and confidence in him, although at the end of the scene Charles tells his queen that he does not confide in his newly-made earl (l.289).

The second act again presents parallel scenes. The first shows the Parliamentarians once more awash in a welter of words and divided in aim, until Pym brings news that Strafford will now be forced to take their part. The second scene shows Strafford reproaching the king for his duplicity but finally consenting to serve Charles in a new way. Lady Carlisle tries to convince Strafford that his enemies at court will again seduce the king, but Strafford does not want to hear: "In no case tell me what they do!" (l.198). Having warned him, Carlisle can do no more: she will be silent and allow Strafford to continue in his illusion concerning the king.

In the remaining acts Strafford is impeached and tried on trumped-up charges, to which he responds with countercharges. When the trial threatens to expose the machinations of the Puritans, Pym brings in a bill of attainder, which even his followers recognize as a "hideous mass / Of half-borne out assertions— dubious hints /...distortions—aye, / And wild inventions" (IV.ii.129-32). Never denying this, Pym justifies himself by claiming that "the great word went from England to my soul" (IV.iii.99). In his last moments Strafford, wanting "to

[9] Just before writing *Strafford,* Browning had satirized Calvinistic doctrines of election and reprobation in "Johannes Agricola in Meditation," published in *Monthly Repository,* 10 (January 1836): 45. It is salutary to remember this fact because it is often said that Browning's sympathies in the play are with Pym and the Puritans. See, for example, William Clyde DeVane, *A Browning Handbook,* 2d ed. (New York: Appleton-Century-Crofts, 1955), pp. 70-71.

hear the sound of my own tongue" (V.ii.83), begs Pym to spare the king, while Pym waits to hear "if England shall declare [her] will to me" (V.ii.353).

The characters not only see themselves as actors in a play whose words convey the action but also regard themselves and their circumstances as part of a text to be interpreted. The Parliamentary party are ever reading or about to read reports. Pym charges the king with attempting "to turn the record's last and bloody leaf" so as to record a new "entry" on a "new page" (I.i.153-59). Strafford conceives of himself as a figure in a romance in which "we shall die gloriously—as the book says" (II.ii.169-81). The text of every proposal is carefully scrutinized by both Puritans and Royalists. It is a set of notes which seals Strafford's fate (IV.i.65). Only time and fame, "the busy scribe," will provide the "curious glosses, subtle notices, / Ingenious clearings-up one fain would see" (V.ii.52-55).

Because words are only signs and not the thing itself, because men use words to rationalize their actions, the text which is life and living can never be interpreted in a wholly satisfactory way. One speaks truly only when one has nothing to hide, from oneself as well as from others. In the phenomenal world this never happens, even though one can delude oneself like Pym, who believes that "the great word went from England to my soul" (IV.iii.99). The only time when word and thing become truly one is that which Strafford foresees:

> Earth fades, Heaven dawns on me: I shall stand next
> Before God's throne: the moment's close at hand
> When Man the first, the last time, has leave to lay
> His whole heart bare.... (V.ii.204-7)

Until that time language will remain a deceptive veil through which it is impossible fully to penetrate. It is not the least of the ironies of the play that language, the medium by which man supposes he can know himself and communicate with his fellows, is shown to conceal more than it reveals.[10]

*Strafford* marks an important step in the development of Browning's artistic outlook and practice. Mainly it shows the poet's increasing awareness of the contradictions in life which cannot be reconciled and hence his determination

---

[10] In his consideration of language Browning is often remarkably prescient of Jacques Derrida and other modern French linguistic philosophers, who see interpretation of the "meaning" of language as an illusion left over from an outdated metaphysics. For the implications for irony of such a view see the essay by Paul de Man cited in note 7 and also his "Nietzsche's Theory of Rhetoric," *Symposium* 28 (Spring 1974): 33-51; and "Action and Identity in Nietzsche," *Yale French Studies* 52 (1975): 16-30. See also Morse Peckham's chapter on Browning in his *Victorian Revolutionaries: Speculations on Some Heroes of a Culture Crisis* (New York: George Braziller, 1970), pp. 84-129. Peckham remarks of Browning, "The mask of language, or language as a mask, is his theme." (p. 91).

that the only possible alternative for him was irony. The play reflects Browning's realization that a work of literature is both a communication and the thing communicated, pretending to be mimetic and yet drawing attention to itself at the same time. Friedrich Schlegel says of irony: "In it, everything must be jest and yet seriousness, artless openness and yet deep dissimulation. Irony originates in the union of a sense of an art of living and a scientific intellect, in the meeting of accomplished natural philosophy and accomplished philosophy of art. It contains and incites a feeling of the insoluble conflict of the absolute and relative, of the impossibility and necessity of total communication."[11] *Strafford* is Browning's first effort to dramatize this kind of irony. It offers even further evidence of the young poet's distance from Shelley and other English romantic predecessors during his apprenctice years.

---

[11] *Lyceum* fragment number 108, in Friedrich Schlegel, *Dialogue on Poetry and Literary Aphorisms,* trans. Ernst Behler and Roman Struc (University Park, Pa., and London: Pennsylvania State University Press, 1968), p. 131.

ROBERT L. OAKMAN

# *Frederick the Great:* Carlylese with a Difference

TRADITIONALLY, CRITICS HAVE seen Thomas Carlyle's long, late biography of his Prussian hero, Frederick the Great, as his final colossal failure. Even in this era of massive redicovery of the great Victorians, *Frederick* has in general received little favorable, suggestive comment. As the reviewer in the *Times Literary Supplement* rightly notes, Morse Peckham's article on *Frederick*, which appeared in *Carlyle Past and Present: A Collection of New Essays* (London: Vision, 1976), pp. 198-215, represents *the* major positive reevaluation of the work during the last twenty-five years. Peckham's "small gem" of an essay "is as likely to persuade people to try to read it [*Frederick*] as anything since John Holloway's study in *The Victorian Sage* (1953)." Peckham confronts a major issue, "the extent to which Carlyle's theme is itself the very nature of historical discourse."[1]

Peckham contends that *Frederick* is not Carlyle's final, strident failure of creativity but his last word on the role of historian. From 1852 to 1865, Carlyle struggled to assemble facts and evidence, to digest them, and to produce the massive biography; by 1859 he was calling it "that unutterable horror of a Prussian Book"[2] after publishing the first two of what would eventually be six volumes in the original editions. (The Centenary Edition breaks *Frederick* into eight volumes.) Given the author's misgivings and malaise, Peckham defines

[1] Adrian Poole, review of *Carlyle Past and Present: A Collection of New Essays,* ed. K. J. Fielding and Rodger L. Tarr, in *Times Literary Supplement,* 2 July 1976, p. 828.
[2] Letter to J. Marshall (28 November 1859), British Museum, Egerton MSS, quoted in Arthur A. and Vonna H. Adrian, *"Frederick the Great:* 'That Unutterable Horror of a Prussian Book,'" in *Carlyle Past and Present,* p. 184.

Carlyle's "radical difference of vision" by analysis of several peculiarities of the work: a mixture of large and small type on the page, the use of multiple invented narrators, and the uneven lengths of the sections of the life (more than one-third covering, for example, the years before Frederick's accession to the throne; about one-tenth for the last twenty years of his life). As Peckham reads *Frederick,* the work enacts the problems of the historian trying to recreate history through the interpretation of documents; he cannot relive the past, now accessible only through the language of records. In effect, "*Frederick,* then, rests upon an historian's alienation from his task of constructing an historical discourse" (Peckham, p. 212). The historian's linguistic directions for understanding history are based in his reading and assembling the evidence before him. Carlyle's intuition that history cannot be objective represents an important contribution about the nature of historical discourse. Peckham asserts that the unevenness and oddity that readers and critics have always sensed about *Frederick* embody Carlyle's most significant contribution in his last major work.

Issues implicit in Peckham's analysis raise questions about the extent of stylistic continuity and eccentricity in the work worth checking in more detail. My own research into the syntax of Carlyle's prose has involved computer-assisted parsing of a large, representative sampling of Carlyle's paragraphs selected at random, without critical bias in favor of certain passages, from the whole canon of works published in Carlyle's lifetime. Not the only computerized stylistic study of Carlyle, my work covers more of the whole range of prose in *Frederick* than any other: thirty-two paragraphs, 182 sentences, and 5,469 words drawn from all eight volumes of the Centenary Edition.[3] For each sentence the computer produces a diagrammatic parsing with phrases and clauses marked. I have collected from the analyses large amounts of information about particular features of the prose—such as types of verbs, occurrences of elements in a series, and uses of expressive punctuation—and analyzed them with statistical analyses. Finally these quantitative measures are combined with close textual analysis of the passages themselves so that traditional critical aspects of the style may not be lost in a pile of statistical tables.[4] In what ways does all this quantitative linguistic evidence, comprising probably the most detailed, close analysis of *Frederick the*

---

[3] Surprisingly, there have been two other computerized analyses of Carlyle's style with some samples from *Frederick*: Frederick L. Burwick looked at one long 10,000 word segment from book 13 ("Stylistic Continuity and Change in the Prose of Thomas Carlyle," in *Statistics and Style,* ed. Lubomír Doležel and Richard W. Bailey [New York: American Elsevier, 1969], pp. 178-96); whereas Robert Cluett examined six smaller samples (in *Prose Style and Critical Reading* [New York: Teachers College Press, Columbia University, 1976], pp. 178-205). Happily the three studies agree in essentials about the style of *Frederick.*

[4] For a description of my methodology with more results than those discussed here, see "Carlyle and the Machine: A Quantitative Analysis of Syntax in Prose Style," *Bulletin of the Association for Literary and Linguistic Computing* 3 (Summer 1975): 100-114.

*Great* set among Carlyle's whole work, help to explain and document the positive readings of Morse Peckham?

As I have noted, Carlyle worked for thirteen years on this biography, which in midstream (1859) Jane Welsh Carlyle thought might be a lost cause: "He... ought never to have tried to make a silk purse out of a sow's ear."[5] Nevertheless, Peckham, unlike most modern critics, sees the same basic Carlyle impulse in *Frederick* that had been around since the late 1820s: the urge to find order behind chaos by penetrating surface appearances to the divine realities that lie behind them. Stylistically there are many similarities between the prose of *Frederick* and the earlier works, especially the other historical and biographical writings—*The French Revolution, Heroes and Hero-Worship, Past and Present,* and *The Life of John Sterling*—with which it may reasonably be expected to compare. With the exception of *Past and Present,* these historical works have the most even spread of choice in all of Carlyle among the five basic sentence types—simple, compound, complex, compound-complex, and fragment. Only in the category of fragments (14.8 percent of its sentences) does *Frederick* stand out; in fact, this percentage is the highest for all of Carlyle's works. For the other types, the range in *Frederick* is fairly broad: 16.5 percent of simple sentences; 12.6 for compound; 17.6 for compound-complex; and 38.5 for complex sentences, always the most common sentence pattern in Carlyle. The figures for *Sterling,* written in 1851, just before *Frederick,* are comparable: 22.0 percent for simple sentences, 12.0 for compound, 38.0 for complex, 16.0 for compound-complex, and 12.0 for fragments. By contrast, the essays of the late 1820s and *Sartor Resartus,* written in the period of heaviest Germanic influence on Carlyle's prose, have more than 55 percent complex sentences with few fragments—3.3 percent (the lowest value in Carlyle) and 5.4 percent, respectively. The *Sartor* sample also has the lowest number of simple sentences in the whole canon, only 8.1 percent. The figures suggest that in the historical works written in his middle and late years, Carlyle's sentence structures got away from a dependence on any particular type; for *Frederick* and the other histories, the complete range of sentence patterns is one indication of the variety and fullness of Carlyle's mature style.

A more interesting similarity relates *Frederick* and other narrative works— *German Romance, Sartor Resartus, French Revolution,* and *Heroes and Hero-Worship*—the extent to which the verbs of independent clauses are active (as opposed to passives or copulars like *seem* and *be*). Except in the *Life of Schiller,* with a large number of passive verbs in the samples, Carlyle used active verbs in the majority of his sentences in all of his works. Granted that one expects the number of active verbs to outnumber passives and copulars, the overwhelming choice of active verbal vocabulary—61.5 percent of all verbs in the corpus—is one indication of that concrete particularity and fascination with the vibrantly

[5] *New Letters and Memorials of Jane Welsh Carlyle,* ed. Alexander Carlyle (London: John Lane, 1903), 2:201.

alive universe that have long been noted in Carlyle. Among all works, *Frederick* is fourth in active verbs at 65.5 percent (behind only those works listed above, excepting *Heroes*); when passives are added in, the total is 72.3 percent of main verbs, with only 27.7 percent of copular verb forms. In other words, Frederick, his family, friends, allies, and enemies act out their activities or have them acted out on them in Carlyle's version of the story. Carlyle's favored copular sentence structures used elsewhere—subject + *be* verb + predicate adjective or noun, as in "it is heartening" or "he is a competent leader"—are bypassed here for narrative action manifested in a plethora of specific verbs.

Corollary with this high incidence of action verbs is a relatively low index of nominal/verbal style, measured by dividing the number of series of nominal constructions by the number of verbal ones.[6] The nominal score counts the total number of noun, adjectival, and prepositional constructions in series, whereas the verbal score is the total number of series serving the functions of verbs, verbals, and adverbs. For the whole corpus, Carlyle's median index ratio is 2.19, an indication that he is twice as prone to make a nominal series as a verbal one. Yet *Frederick* shares the fourth lowest ratio with *Sartor* (1.81), behind only *Wilhelm Meister, German Romance,* and *French Revolution,* almost the same works with which it shares a strong tendency for action verbs. In other words, the verb structures are expanded into several elements more commonly than usual in *Frederick* and these other narratives as the percentage of action within their sentences increases. Carlyle's specificity and particularity of detail with verbs manifest themselves in these works in both a choice of active verbs and the tendency to use a compound series in place of a singular verbal structure.

Suggestive of the style of *Frederick* as typical Carlylese is a sample paragraph from a chapter on the battle of Kolin (18 June 1757) at the height of the Seven Year's War (book 18).[7] Peckham comments on the centrality of these war years and campaigns, which comprise about 60 percent of Frederick's whole history in Carlyle's version. In this section Carlyle as omniscient narrator presents Frederick's interior monologue dramatically as he weighs his military strategy before closing with orders to "March!":

> Friedrich, from his Inn near Planian, seeing how Daun deploys himself, considers him impregnable on the left wing; impregnable, too, in front: not so on the Kreczor side, right flank and rear; but capable of being rolled together, if well struck at there. Thither therefore; that is his vulnerable point. March along his front; quietly

[6] For discussion of the characteristics and effects of nominal versus verbal styles, consult Rulon Wells, "Nominal and Verbal Style," in *Style in Language,* ed. Thomas A. Sebeok (Cambridge: MIT Press, 1960), pp. 213-20.

[7] All Carlyle's passages discussed here are from my samples and are quoted from *The Works of Thomas Carlyle,* ed. H. D. Traill, Centenary Edition, 30 vols. (New York: Scribners, 1898-1901). The volume and page numbers from the edition follow each quotation.

parallel in due Order of Battle, till we can bend round, and plunge-in upon that. The Van, which consists of Ziethen's Horse and Hülsen's Infantry; Van, having faced to right at the proper moment and so become Left Wing, will attack Kreczor; probably carry it; each Division following will in like manner face to right when it arrives there, and fall-on in regular succession in support of Hülsen (at Hülsen's right flank, if Hülsen be found prospering): our Right Wing is to refuse itself, and be as a Reserve,—no fighting on the road, you others, but steady towards Hülsen, in continual succession, all you; no facing round, no fighting anywhere, till we get thither:—'March!' (XVII:175)

This is surely fully developed Carlylese: one compound sentence, two complex, and the long final compound-complex sentence of 101 words. Within the seven independent clauses alone, Carlyle uses six active verbs, including two in series in the last sentence: *considers, march, will attack, carry, will face,* and *fall-on;* in addition, the multiple dependent clauses and verbal phrases are filled with action verbs of military movements.

Syntactically the elliptical second sentence—"[Strike] thither therefore; that is his vulnerable point"—contrasts with the long, loosely accumulative last one. This latter sentence, especially, exemplifies a common Carlyle pattern, the addition of clauses, phrases, parentheses to load the basic structure with specific detail; here we find eight dependent clauses (including the final direct quotation, 'March!'), an appositive, and several verbals. The internal elaboration between the initial subject and verb ("Van ... will attack") gives the sentence a periodic character, a pattern used more frequently by Carlyle than one expects for a romantic writer. In addition, the distinctive additive structure explodes the sentence outward from the beginning with added phrases, clauses, and other grammatical elements that extend and expand the range of the sense and syntax. Perhaps Carlyle's most characteristic pattern, the loose accumulative sentence has been recognized for a hundred years; in 1857 Henry David Thoreau spoke enthusiastically of this style that "streams freely forth like a spring torrent. He does not trace back the stream of his thought, silently adventurous, up to its fountain-head, but is borne away with it, as it rushes through his brain like a torrent to overwhelm and fertilize."[8] In the current instance, the stream of thought springs from the king's mind as the prose enacts dramatically his calculations of military strategy and verbal orders to his generals. As Peckham reminds us, "the struggle to create order out of chaos" (p. 203) is a lifelong Carlyle theme; here Frederick is trying to impose some order prior to battle by strategic planning. Imperative verbs and the apostrophe to his officers ("you others") effectively verbalize his plans; the subjunctive clause, "If Hülsen be found prospering," appropriately embodies the uncertainty and hopeful desire about Hülsen's successful infantry campaign against Kreczor.

[8] Henry David Thoreau, "Thomas Carlyle and His Works," in *Thomas Carlyle: The Critical Heritage,* ed. Jules P. Seigel (New York: Barnes and Noble, 1971), p. 282.

The first sentence, another accumulative one, employs a series of predicate adjectives to suggest the whole sequence of Frederick's inner thoughts about how best to attack Daun, the Austrian field marshall. The final part contains two elliptical patterns: an antithetical construction, "not so…but capable," left irregularly parallel by omitting the adjective *impregnable* and an adverb clause lacking both subject and verb ("if [he is] well struck at there"). If he had preferred a simpler sentence, Carlyle could have presented this material in four independent clauses rather than one. Instead, in both accumulative sentences, Carlyle compresses a quantity of semantic information in the loose syntactic mold of the complex sentence of outward expansion.

Granted that the paragraph is readily recognizable, typical Carlylese, Carlyle in *Frederick* moves away from his conviction held through *Latter-Day Pamphlets* that pursuing realities underneath surface appearances is redemptive. As his faith began to disappear, Carlyle's prose becomes more irregular and exaggerated, full of effects that catch the reader's attention. Compared with the other major histories—*French Revolution, Heroes and Hero-Worship, Past and Present,* and *Sterling—Frederick* stands out clearly as exceptional in several characteristics of irregularity which mark it as eccentric: high percentages of fragments, appositives, absolute constructions, and disjunctive punctuation marks, as well as uncommonly few antithetical structures. More than its similarities, it is these deviancies that are of especial stylistic interest in *Frederick.*

Related in effect to the large number of fragments already noted are the increasing frequency of appositives, absolute constructions, and punctuation marks like the dash and parenthesis. In *Frederick* all these patterns substitute for independent clauses and enact Carlyle's struggle to assimilate a myriad of documents and witnesses in order to present a whole portrait of his hero and his century. Equally revealing of stylistic difference in *Frederick* is Carlyle's syntactic embodiment of rhetorical techniques such as parallelism, antithesis, and apposition; after 1827 more than four-fifths of all of Carlyle's sentences, on the average, contain at least one rhetorical construction. Excluding *Frederick,* the most common syntactic and rhetorical characteristics used by Carlyle are parallel structures, appositives, antithesis, and comparison, in that order, with absolutes a distant sixth. In *Frederick,* however, appositives lead the list (37 percent of all rhetorical structures, second only to the last works like *Early Kings of Norway*); and absolutes are third (15 percent, high for all Carlyle's works).

Although structural parallelism is the most common kind of syntactic patterning associated with rhetoric in Carlyle, comprising a third of all structures, in *Frederick* its frequency, second to apposition among patterns (21 percent), is, in fact, the least for all the works; all others have more syntactic parallelism than this work. In addition, parallelism often shows up in imbalanced form, as in the following syntactic fragment describing Frederick William's mansion in Reinsberg:

Architecture everywhere of cheerfully serious, solidly graceful character; all of sterling ashlar; the due *risalites* (projecting spaces) with their attics and statues atop, the due architraves, cornices, and corbels,—in short the due opulence of ornament being introduced, and only the due. (XIV:164)

To characterize the "cheerfully serious, solidly graceful" quality of the house, Carlyle has cleverly employed the adjective *due* not only to set up the two irregularly parallel phrases of architectural detail but also to summarize the effect of "due opulence...and only the due." The absolute construction ("opulence...being introduced") occurs noticeably in place of a clause with a finite verb at the end of the fragment; this kind of verb substitution, preferred only in *Frederick the Great* with any frequency, partially accounts for the high percentage of fragments in that work. In *Frederick,* Carlyle does not lose his touch with parallel constructions; he just applies them with less balance and frequency in his more elliptical and fragmented style.

Like the penchant for sentence fragments, Carlyle in *Frederick* especially favors apposition, the syntactic practice of adding a substantive (normally a noun phrase) behind another substantive to identify or clarify the first. In his early writings Carlyle's appositives are usually infrequent in appearance, short in form, and routine in function. By *Frederick,* he has adapted the technique to get more particularity and concreteness into the mold of a sentence, while dismembering his syntax into fragments. Although the syntactic connections are missing, Carlyle retains his characteristic specificity with collections of packed appositives, often in series of two or more elements. The sentence quoted above represents the common pattern; the skeleton of the fragment can, in fact, be analyzed as four appositional structures and a final absolute construction which fill out the details about the architecture of the Reinsberg mansion: "Architecture...all of sterling ashlar; the due *risalites*...the due architraves, cornices, and corbels...the due opulence...being introduced...." The appositional material does not just rename the opening noun phrase about architecture; instead it specifies the opulent ornamentation of the castle by cataloguing various features of the exterior.

Antithesis is the third most frequent rhetorical strategy employed in the syntax of the Carlyle corpus as a whole; yet *Frederick* has the lowest percentage of all the volumes. Antithetical structures rank sixth in frequency in *Frederick* among rhetorical devices and account for only 6 percent of the total number in the work. George Levine and other critics have noted the fundamental organizing principle of duality in Carlyle's work between good and evil, right and wrong;[9] syntactically this important dualism is often embodied in antithesis,

9 See George Levine, "The Use and Abuse of Carlylese," in *The Art of Victorian Prose,* ed. George Levine and William A. Madden (New York: Oxford University Press, 1968), pp. 101-26.

perhaps best exemplified in the famous antithetical, parallel sentences in the "Everlasting No" section of *Sartor Resartus*:

> The Everlasting No had said: "Behold, thou art fatherless, outcast, and the Universe is mine (the Devil's)"; to which my whole Me now made answer: "*I* am not thine, but Free, and forever hate thee!" (I:135)

In passages like this one, content and form work together to contrast effectively the forces of necessity and the individual, dual powers constantly at war in the universe.

By the time of *Frederick*, as Peckham notes, Carlyle's belief that penetration through sham to reality is redemptive "is now gone or at best has suffered a severe attrition" (p. 203). It is not surprising that antithesis had dropped off in popularity among rhetorical aspects of syntax. Those few instances that do occur illustrate formal antithesis without the overriding duality principle, as in the opening structure in the following sentence about Frederick's father:

> He was not yet Hereditary Prince, he was only second son: but the elder died; and he became Elector, King; and had to go with his spine distorted,—distortion not glaringly conspicuous, though undeniable;—and to act the Hohenzollern *so*. (XII:308)

The antithetical structure—"not yet Hereditary Prince... [but] only second son"—is now empty of the philosophical weight of duality and serves to clarify Frederick William's secondary role before his brother's death made him the Prussian heir. The antithetical relation is of time before and after, a conventional use of the "not this but that" syntactic formula. Here in the common sentence of outward syntactic elaboration are present other favorite rhetorical methods favored by Carlyle in *Frederick*: an appositive, "Elector, King," and a paren- thetical expression, "distortion not glaringly conspicuous, though undeniable," almost another appositive, delaying the completion of the sense of the sentence in the final parallel infinitive phrase. The antithetical structure is among the top three devices of all the earlier historical works, *French Revolution, Heroes and Hero-Worship, Past and Present,* and *Sterling,* written when Carlyle was surer of the reality behind surface appearance and sham. With *Frederick* the withdrawal or attrition of faith parallels the slackening off of the duality principle and its appropriate syntactic embodiment through antithesis.

Characteristic of the chronological development of Carlyle's prose style is a growing tendency to omit important syntactic elements or to introduce irregularities in standard syntactic formulations. As always, Carlyle stretched the capacities of English syntax to fit his own needs and to create some of his most unusual effects. To gauge the extent of these phenomena, an index of syntactic irregularity can be developed by combining the totals of fragments, inversions, absolute constructions, elliptical clauses, and irregularities in parallelism and seriation; only by lumping all these features together can a true measure of

Carlyle's odd syntax be taken. When compared with all of the other works, *Frederick* has the greatest index value, 88 percent, calculated by dividing the total number of irregularities by the number of sentences. By contrast, the median value for irregularities per sentence among all works is 58 percent, shared by two other historical works, *Heroes* and *Past and Present,* which resemble the late biography in other aspects.

The extent of irregularity in *Frederick* is matched by its variety. Instead of one particular type predominating in frequency, five different types occur about equally: fragments and adverb clauses with omitted syntactic elements (17 percent each), inversions and absolutes (15 percent each), and elliptical main clauses (12 percent). As noted earlier, the number of absolutes in *Frederick* exceeds that in all of Carlyle's other works. Inverted sentences, those in which the main verb precedes the subject out of expected order, have long been noted as peculiarly Carlylean—since John Sterling in 1835 complained of too many in *Sartor Resartus.*[10] After *Sartor* and *Latter-Day Pamphlets, Frederick* ranks third in frequency of inversion, a statistic which matches well its rank behind only these works and the *Life of Schiller,* in the occurrence of the periodic sentence structure, atypical of most nineteenth-century prose.

On the average, only about one sentence in ten lacks some form of fragmented, nonparallel, or irregular construction. Besides the fragment quoted above, two other examples will illustrate the kinds of irregularities abundant in the prose of *Frederick*:

> Our poor Kaiser will not 'retain Bohemia,' then; how far from it! The thing is not comfortable to Friedrich: but what help?(XV:406)

> Keith and baggage once safe in Leutomischl (July 8th), all goes in deliberate long column; Friedrich ahead to open the passages. (XVII:367)

In the initial sample, Carlyle constructs two compound sentences with omitted main elements in their final clauses (*is he* and *is there,* respectively); in doing so, he interrupts the straightforward flow of narrative with exclamation and question. By emphasizing the extent of the loss and questioning the possibilities of an alternative in the added elliptical clauses, Carlyle as narrator is dramatizing Frederick's uneasiness about losing Bohemia. Much the same effect of semantic compactness is achieved in the second passage by means of two absolute constructions, from which the participles—*being* and *going,* respectively—have been omitted. Carlyle has included in one simple sentence three ideas which could have been presented in separate clauses. As Frederick Burwick has noted, when Carlyle began relying on patterns of omission, verb substitutes such as the absolute, often took the place of predication.[11]

---

[10] Reprinted in *The Life of John Sterling,* in the Traill edition, XI:112.
[11] Burwick, p. 185.

The tendency of the syntax to become more disconnected in *Frederick* is again reflected in the favored kinds of expressive punctuation marks, especially the dash and the parenthesis. Among all the works, only *Past and Present* and *Latter-Day Pamphlets* have more expressive punctuation per sentence; yet in neither of these is the frequency so dominated by these marks, which reflect a lack of logical relationship between parts of a sentence. The dash accounts for 44 percent of all expressive punctuation in *Frederick,* more than in any other work; material set off by parentheses is also more frequent here than elsewhere. Often Carlyle conjoins a hurried collection of ideas and clauses with dashes in place of common transitions or connectives. For instance, in the following compound sentence, successfully capturing an interior monologue of the English prime minister William Pitt, the dash in the second independent clause marks the place of the omitted subject "Abercrombie," which in the first clause is the subject of the embedded quotation:

'Abercrombie may be better,' hopes he;—was better, still not good. (XVII:348)

It is not surprising that in this work, in which the percentage of fragments and syntactic omissions is high, Carlyle uses the dash more frequently than any other mark of expressive punctuation. Walker Gibson has identified breathlessness and lack of logical relationship between parts of a sentence as characteristic of a prose style full of dashes.[12] Similar to his use of absolutes, Carlyle's frequent dashes compress his vast materials into syntactic molds that do not require him to develop ideas into complete clauses. The fact that *Frederick* leads in fragments correlates well with its exceptional preference for dashes among expressive punctuation marks.

Taken in the composite, the style of *Frederick the Great* differs considerably from the earlier, more assured histories. In my analysis, the entire Carlyle canon grouped into fifteen works (or periods, for the essays) is eventually ranked in ascending order from 1 to 15 for the following stylistic variables: sentence length, complex sentence patterns, action verbs (active and passive), expressive punctuation, accumulation of both series and rhetorical devices, periodicity, and kinds of irregularity. Although sometimes the combination of ranks tends to equal them out, even a cursory glance at the final total over the eight variables shows up *Frederick* as Carlyle's most eccentric history in terms of style. The ranks for the five histories set among the fifteen works are as follows, in ascending order:

> *French Revolution,* 3rd from bottom
> *Heroes and Hero-Worship,* 5th

[12] Walker Gibson, *Tough, Sweet, and Stuffy* (Bloomington: Indiana University Press, 1966), p. 133.

*Life of John Sterling*, 7th
*Past and Present*, 8th, the medial rank
*Frederick the Great*, 12th

In the composite ranking, *Frederick* resembles *Sartor Resartus* (13th) and other late works, *Latter-Day Pamphlets* (15th) and the final group (*Early Kings of Norway* and other last essays, 14th) more than it does the histories, with which it may be expected to compare. As we have seen, it stands apart from the earlier histories in those qualities which especially typify an extravagant Carlyle style: fragments, clausal substitutes, disjunctive punctuation, irregularity.

In recent years Albert J. LaValley has restated the common critical view that *Frederick* looks "like notebook jottings, research that has not yet been controlled by any dominant theme or artistic ordering."[13] LaValley goes on to classify *Frederick*, and *Cromwell* before it, as gigantic failures:

> ... merely treadings of water, the futile heroism of the man of letters without a real appointed task or mission in the nineteenth century, totally alienated from his audience and forced into self-communication, now barred even from the oblique style of Teufelsdröckh.[14]

This idea about alienation in *Frederick* is not a new one; in his nineteenth-century assessment of the book, James Russell Lowell speaks of Carlyle as "the purely literary man ... no longer a voice with any earnest conviction behind it."[15] The main problem with LaValley's view as it applies to *Frederick* relates to the style. Peckham has convincingly shown that Carlyle skillfully uses at least three narrators in addition to his authorial voice to retain distance and obliqueness as he does with the Editor and Teufelsdröckh in *Sartor* (pp. 207-9). Moreover, in the composite stylistic analysis, *Frederick*'s style resembles that of Teufelsdröckh's *Sartor* in terms of a generally high ranking of numerous features distinctively Carlylean. Indeed, LaValley's summary judgment about *Frederick*, admittedly shared by almost all Carlyle scholars, seems to be more impression and rhetoric than is warranted by close examination of the texture of work and its implications.

Morse Peckham also notes in *Frederick* "an alienation more thorough-going than at any previous stage in Carlyle's life" (p. 210) and relates it to the style. The writing "forces on the reader an awareness of the narrator's struggle with documents and with previous histories on this and related subjects" (p. 210). My analysis certainly verifies the author's "struggle," embodied in a choppy,

---

[13] Albert J. LaValley, *Carlyle and the Idea of the Modern* (New Haven: Yale University Press, 1968), p. 253.

[14] LaValley, p. 255.

[15] James Russell Lowell, "Carlyle," in *My Study Windows* (Boston: Houghton Mifflin, 1892), p. 140.

irregular, elliptical syntax within a recognizable framework of "historical Carlylese," with strong reliance on action verbs and the loosely accumulative sentence pattern. In his most insightful observation, Peckham goes on to remind us that historians are not really objective recorders of past facts, which cannot be known except through documents and records:

> . . . the historian's task, is the interpretation of language before him, not of events in the past. The past is inaccessible; only language is accessible. The historian constructs a language discourse which is related, somehow or other, to a selected assemblage of discourses, a package of discourses held together by the wrappings of the package, not by internal affiliation. Their affinities are elected, but the historian does the electing. (p. 213)

"Here we do find a really major issue fully confronted," says the *Times Literary Supplement* reviewer in praise of Peckham; positive criticism like this has been absent too long in discussions of *Frederick*. Carlyle was fighting to create a coherent biography from great quantities of evidence; his style of "notebook jottings," fragments, and disjointed syntax is not surprising, and may even be justified. If, as Peckham says, "the drama of *Frederick* is the drama of an historian struggling to learn how to read his documents" (p. 214), the style of *Frederick*— Carlylese with a difference—bears appropriate witness to the struggle.

# A Checklist of the Writings, from 1946 to 1983, of Morse Peckham

This checklist represents the editor's correction, rearrangement, annotation, and slight expansion of a chronology of his writings, by date of composition, publication, or delivery, which Morse Peckham himself prepared in the fall of 1980. Custom has dictated the present arrangement into categories of publication: books, collected essays, editions, published essays and lectures, textbooks and anthologies, reviews, and unpublished essays and lectures. Within each of these customary categories, however, titles appear in the order in which they appeared on Peckham's original chronology, except for one review published in 1976, which was incorrectly listed (after an evident typographical error) as having been published in 1967. With this exception and with the addition of an item forgotten, the editor has tried to preserve a sense of the sequence of Peckham's authorial concerns by numbering the items according to their slots on his chronological list.

Happily, though retired, Morse Peckham is still hard at work, and we can expect this list to grow with the coming years.

## I. *Books*

3 "Guilt and Glory: A study of the 1839 *Festus,* A Nineteenth-Century Poem of Synthesis." Ph.D. dissertation, Princeton University, 1947.

21 *Humanistic Education for Business Executives: An Essay in General Education.* Philadelphia: University of Pennsylvania Press, 1960.

25 *Beyond the Tragic Vision: The Quest for Identity in the Nineteenth Century.* New York: George Braziller, 1962.

25 *Oltre la Visione Tragica: La Ricerca dell' Identità nel Secolo Diciannovesimo* [Beyond the Tragic Vision]. Translated by Leda Mussio Sartini. Milano: Lerici, 1965.

37 *Man's Rage for Chaos: Biology, Behavior, and the Arts.* Philadelphia and New York: Chilton, 1965. Reprint. New York: Schocken, 1967.

62 *Art and Pornography: An Experiment in Explanation.* New York: Basic Books, 1969. Reprint. New York: Harper and Row, 1971.

71 *Victorian Revolutionaries: Speculations on Some Heroes of a Culture Crisis.* New York: George Braziller, 1970.

145 *Explanation and Power: The Control of Human Behavior.* New York: Seabury, 1979.

## II. *Collected Essays*

70 *The Triumph of Romanticism: Collected Essays.* Columbia: University of South Carolina Press, 1970.

117 *Romanticism and Behavior: Collected Essays, II.* Columbia: University of South Carolina Press, 1976.

## III. *Editions, with Introductions and Notes*

19 Darwin, Charles Robert. *The Origin of Species by Charles Darwin: A Variorum Text.* Philadelphia: University of Pennsylvania Press, 1959.

61 Browning, Robert. "Paracelsus." In *The Complete Works of Robert Browning with Variant Readings & Annotations.* Roma A. King, Jr., gen. ed. Vol. 1, pp. 58-277, 285-306. Athens: Ohio University Press, 1969.

72 Swinburne, Algernon Charles. *Poems and Ballads, Atalanta in Calydon.* Indianapolis and New York: Bobbs-Merrill, 1970.

81 Browning, Robert. "Pippa Passes." In *The Complete Works of Robert Browning with Variant Readings & Annotations.* Roma A. King, Jr., gen. ed. Vol. 3, pp. 5-82, 343-51. Athens: Ohio University Press, 1971.

82 Browning, Robert. "The Return of the Druses." In *The Complete Works of Robert Browning with Variant Readings & Annotations.* Roma A. King, Jr., gen. ed. Vol. 3, pp. 263-341, 387-95. Athens: Ohio University Press, 1971.

98 Browning, Robert. "Luria." In *The Complete Works of Robert Browning with Variant Readings & Annotations.* Roma A. King, Jr., gen. ed. Vol. 4, pp. 273-351, 393-400. Athens: Ohio University Press, 1973.

125 Browning, Robert. *Sordello: A Marginally Emended Edition.* Troy, N. Y.: Whitston, 1977.

## IV. Published Essays and Lectures

2 "A Bailey Collection." *Princeton University Library Chronicle* 7 (June 1946): 149-54.

4 "American Editions of *Festus:* A Preliminary Survey." *Princeton University Library Chronicle* 8 (June 1947): 177-84.

5 "Selections form the Letters of Philip James Bailey." *Princeton University Library Chronicle* 9 (February 1948): 79-92.

6 "English Editions of Philip James Bailey's *Festus.*" *Papers of the Bibliographical Society of America* 44 (First Quarter 1950): 55-58.

7 "Blake, Milton, and Edward Burney." *Princeton University Library Chronicle* 11 (Spring 1950): 107-26.

8 "Toward a Theory of Romanticism." *PMLA* 66 (March 1951): 5-23. Reprinted in *Romanticism: Points of View,* pp. 212-27. Edited by Robert F. Gleckner and Gerald E. Enscoe. Englewood Cliffs: Prentice-Hall, 1962. Reprinted in *The Triumph of Romanticism: Collected Essays,* pp. 3-26.

8 "Beitrag zu einer Theorie der Romantik" [Toward a Theory of Romanticism]. Translated by Erna Dehring. In *Begriffstimmung der Romantik,* pp. 349-76. Edited by Helmut Prang. Darmstadt: Wissenschaftliche Buchgesellschaft, 1968.

9 "Dr. Lardner's *Cabinet Cyclopaedia.*" *Papers of the Bibliographical Society of America* 45 (First Quarter 1951): 37-58.

10 "The Triumph of Romanticism." *Magazine of Art* 45 (November 1952): 291-99.

11 "Constable and Wordsworth." *College Art Journal* 12 (Spring 1953): 196-209. Reprinted in *The Triumph of Romanticism: Collected Essays,* pp. 105-22.

12 "Is Poetry Self-Expression?" *Four Quarters* 2 (May 1953): 1-5. Reprinted in *The Triumph of Romanticism: Collected Essays,* pp. 394-400.

13 "Emancipating the Executives." *Chicago Review* 8 (Special Issue 1954): 104-14.

14 "Gray's 'Epitaph' Revisited." *MLN* 71 (June 1956): 409-11.

16 "What did Lady Windermere Learn?" *College English* 18 (October 1956): 11-14. Reprinted in *The Triumph of Romanticism: Collected Essays,* pp. 226-30.

17 "The Problem of the Nineteenth Century." In *The Cultural Heritage of 20th Century Man,* pp. 43-54. Philadelphia: Pennsylvania Literary Review and Philomathean Society, University of Pennsylvania, 1956. Reprinted in *The Triumph of Romanticism: Collected Essays,* pp. 87-104.

20 "Darwinism and Darwinisticism." *Victorian Studies* 3 (September 1959): 19-40. Reprinted in *Darwin: A Norton Critical Edition,* pp. 385-92. Edited by Philip Appleman. New York: W. W. Norton, 1970; 2nd ed., pp. 297-304. New York: W. W. Norton, 1979. Reprinted in *The Triumph of Romanticism: Collected Essays,* pp. 176-201.

23 "Toward a Theory of Romanticism: II. Reconsiderations." *Studies in Romanticism* 1 (Autumn 1961): 1-8. Reprinted in *The Triumph of Romanticism: Collected Essays,* pp. 27-35.

26 "Metaphor: A Little Plain Speaking on a Weary Subject." *Connotation* 1 (Winter 1962): 29-46. Reprinted in *The Triumph of Romanticism: Collected Essays,* pp. 401-20.

29 "Sign/Symbol in the New Bayreuth." *Connotation* 2 (1963): 70-97.

38 "The Dilemma of a Century: The Four Stages of Romanticism." Reprinted in *The Triumph of Romanticism: Collected Essays,* pp. 36-57. See below, section V, item 38.

43 "Romanticism: The Present State of the Theory." *The PCTE* [Pennsylvania Council of Teachers of English] *Bulletin* 12 (December 1965): 31-53. Reprinted in *The Triumph of Romanticism: Collected Essays*, pp. 58-83.

44 "Art and Disorder." *Literature and Psychology* 16 (Spring 1966): 62-80. Reprinted in *The Triumph of Romanticism: Collected Essays*, pp. 255-80.

45 "The Place of Architecture in Nineteenth-Century Romantic Culture." *Yearbook of Comparative and General Literature* 15 (1966): 36-49. Reprinted in *The Triumph of Romanticism: Collected Essays*, pp. 123-44.

46 "Literary Interpretation as Conventionalized Verbal Behavior." *Penn State Papers in Art Education* 2 (1967). Reprinted in *The Triumph of Romanticism: Collected Essays*, pp. 341-70.

47 "Aestheticism to Modernism: Fulfillment or Revolution?" *Mundus Artium* 1 (Winter 1967): 36-55. Reprinted in *The Triumph of Romanticism: Collected Essays*, pp. 202-25.

48 "Order and Disorder in Fiction." *Sage* 11 (Spring 1967): 225-43. Reprinted in *The Triumph of Romanticism: Collected Essays*, pp. 290-317.

49 "Can 'Victorian' Have a Useful Meaning?" *Victorian Studies* 10 (March 1967): 273-77. Reprinted in *The Triumph of Romanticism: Collected Essays*, pp. 145-52.

50 "Art and Creativity: Proposal for Research." *Art Education* 20 (April 1967): 5-8. Reprinted in *The Triumph of Romanticism: Collected Essays*, pp. 281-89.

51 "Theory of Criticism." In *The Triumph of Romanticism: Collected Essays*, pp. 371-93. Delivered April 1967.

52 "Discontinuity in Fiction: Persona, Narrator, Scribe." In *The Triumph of Romanticism: Collected Essays*, pp. 318-40. Delivered November 1967.

53 "Historiography and *The Ring and the Book*." *Victorian Poetry* 6 (Autumn-Winter 1968): 243-58. Reprinted in *Romanticism and Behavior: Collected Essays, II*, pp. 109-25.

54 "Hawthorne and Melville as European Authors." In *Melville and Hawthorne in the Berkshires*, pp. 42-62. Edited by Howard P. Vincent. Kent, Ohio: Kent

State University Press, 1968. Reprinted in *The Triumph of Romanticism: Collected Essays*, pp. 153-75.

55 "A Reply [to E. H. Gombrich's review of *Man's Rage for Chaos*, in *New York Review of Books*, 23 June 1966, p. 3.]." *New York Review of Books*, 17 November 1966, p. 42. Reprinted in *Innovations: Essays on Art and Ideas*, pp. 119-21. Edited by Bernard Bergonzi. London: Macmillan, 1968.

56 "The Current Crisis in the Arts: Pop, Op, and Mini." *Studies in the Twentieth Century* 1 (Spring 1968): 21-38. Reprinted in *The Triumph of Romanticism: Collected Essays*, pp. 231-51.

59 "Semantic Autonomy and Immanent Meaning." *Genre* 1 (July 1968): 190-94.

63 "An Introduction to Emerson's Essays." In Ralph Waldo Emerson, *Essays/ Essays: Second Series*, pp. v-xvi. Edited by Matthew J. Bruccoli and Joseph Katz. Columbus, Ohio: Charles E. Merrill, 1969. Reprinted in *Romanticism and Behavior: Collected Essays, II*, pp. 126-38.

64 "The Intentional? Fallacy?" *The New Orleans Review* 1 (Winter 1969): 116-24. Reprinted in *The Triumph of Romanticism: Collected Essays*, pp. 421-44.

65 "An Interdisciplinary Approach to Nineteenth Century Culture: Some Problems." *South Atlantic Bulletin* 34 (January 1969): 8.

67 "Signs, Verbal and Non-verbal." *Studies in the Twentieth Century* 3 (Spring 1969): 19-40. Two sections from chapter 3 of *Art and Pornography: An Experiment in Explanation.*

75 "Is the Problem of Literary Realism a Pseudo-Problem?" *Critique* 12 (November 1970): 95-112. Reprinted in *Romanticism and Behavior: Collected Essays, II*, pp. 179-95.

76 "Religion as a Humanizing Force." *Southern Humanities Review* 4 (Summer 1970): 214-22.

77 "The Collins Review of the Browning Edition." *The Browning Newsletter* 5 (Fall 1970): 3-5.

78 "Poet and Critic: Or, The Damage Coleridge Has Done." *Studies in the Twentieth Century* 6 (Fall 1970): 1-11. Reprinted in *Romanticism and Behavior: Collected Essays, II*, pp. 196-205.

79 "On Romanticism: Introduction." *Studies in Romanticism* 9 (Fall 1970): 217-24.

80 "The Deplorable Consequences of the Idea of Creativity." In *Romanticism and Behavior: Collected Essays, II*, pp. 206-21. Delivered October 1970.

83 "On the Historical Interpretation of Literature." In *Romantic and Victorian: Studies in Memory of William H. Marshall*, pp. 21-25. Edited by W. Paul Elledge and Richard L. Hoffman. Cranbury, N. J.: Fairleigh-Dickinson University Press, 1971. Reprinted in *The Triumph of Romanticism: Collected Essays*, pp. 445-50.

84 "The Virtues of Superficiality." *TriQuarterly* 20 (Winter 1971): 180-93. Reprinted in *Romanticism and Behavior: Collected Essays, II*, pp. 249-62.

85 "The Corporation's Role in Today's Crisis of Cultural Incoherence." *Innovation* 21 (May 1971): 30-40. Reprinted in *Romanticism and Behavior: Collected Essays, II*, pp. 263-84.

86 "Ernest Hemingway: Sexual Themes in his Writing." *Sexual Behavior* 1 (July 1971): 62-70. Reprinted in *Romanticism and Behavior: Collected Essays, II*, pp. 139-58.

87 "The Function of History in Nineteenth-Century European Culture." *Survey* 17 (Summer 1971): 31-36. Reprinted in *Romanticism and Behavior: Collected Essays, II*, pp. 32-39.

89 "The Arts and the Centers of Power." In *Critiques 1971/72*. New York: Cooper Union, 1972. Also in *Proceedings of the CCTE* [Conference of College Teachers of English of Texas] 37 (September 1972): 7-17. Reprinted in *Romanticism and Behavior: Collected Essays, II*, pp. 328-50.

90 "Afterword: Reflections on Historical Modes in the Nineteenth Century." In *Victorian Poetry*, Stratford-upon-Avon Studies 15, pp. 277-300. Edited by Malcolm Bradbury and David Palmer. London: Edward Arnold, 1972. Reprinted in *Romanticism and Behavior: Collected Essays, II*, pp. 40-66.

93 "Iconography and Iconology in the Arts of the Nineteenth and Twentieth Centuries." *The Structurist* 12 (1972-73): 26-31. Reprinted in *Romanticism and Behavior: Collected Essays, II*, pp. 90-108.

94 "Cultural Stagnation in American Universities and Colleges." In *Romanticism and Behavior: Collected Essays, II*, pp. 313-27. Delivered January 1972.

96 "Literature and Knowledge." In *Romanticism and Behavior: Collected Essays, II*, pp. 222-45. Delivered May 1972.

97 "Romanticism, Science and Gossip." *Shenandoah* 23 (Summer 1972): 81-89.

99 "Arts for the Cultivation of Radical Sensitivity." In *Educational Reconstruction;: Promise and Challenge,* pp. 201-21. Edited by Nobuo Shimihara. Columbus, Ohio: Charles E. Merrill, 1973. Reprinted in *Romanticism and Behavior: Collected Essays, II,* pp. 285-312.

100 "The Current Consequences of Romanticism in the Arts." In *Proceedings of the Seventh National Sculpture Conference,* pp. 53-68. Lawrence, Kansas: National Sculpture Center, 1973.

101 "Rebellion and Deviance." In *Romanticism and Behavior: Collected Essays, II,* pp. 67-89. Delivered January 1973.

102 "The Cultural Crisis of the 1970s." In *Romanticism and Behavior: Collected Essays, II,* pp. 362-79. Delivered March 1973.

103 "Humanism, Politics, and Government in the Nineteenth Century." In *Romanticism and Behavior: Collected Essays, II,* pp. 351-61. Delivered April 1973.

107 "Browning and Romanticism." In *Robert Browning,* pp. 47-76. Edited by Isobel Armstrong. London: G. Bell, 1974.

108 "The Place of Sex in the Work of William Faulkner." *Studies in the Twentieth Century* 14 (Fall 1974): 1-20. Reprinted in *Romanticism and Behavior: Collected Essays, II,* pp. 159-76.

109 "Romanticism and Behavior." *Philosophic Exchange: The Annual Proceedings of the Center for Philosophic Exchange* 1 (Summer 1974): 65-83. Reprinted in *Romanticism and Behavior: Collected Essays, II,* pp. 3-31.

112 With David R. King. "Editing Nineteenth-Century Texts." In *Language and Texts: The Nature of Linguistic Evidence,* pp. 123-46. Edited by Herbert H. Paper. Ann Arbor: Center for the Coordination of Ancient and Modern Studies, University of Michigan, 1975.

113 "A Doctor of Philosophy in the Humanities?" *South Atlantic Bulletin* 40 (January 1975): 29-47.

115 "Victorian Counterculture." *Victorian Studies* 18 (March 1975): 257-76.

116 "Notes on Freehafer and the CEAA Editions." *Studies in the Novel* 7 (Fall 1975): 402-4.

118 "Frederick the Great." In *Carlyle Past and Present: A Collection of New Essays,* pp. 198-215. Edited by K. J. Fielding and Rodger L. Tarr. London: Vision, 1976. New York: Barnes and Noble, 1976.

119 "Psychology and Literature." *Yearbook of Comparative Criticism* 7 (1976): 48-68.

126 "The Pleasures of the Po." *The Texas Arts Journal* 1 (1977): 1-12.

127 "Semiotic Interpretation in the Humanities." *Man in Seven Modes,* pp. 10-18. Southern Humanities Conference. Winston-Salem, N. C.: Wake Forest University Publications Office, 1977.

129 "Thoughts on Editing Sordello." *Studies in Browning and His Circle* 5 (Spring 1977): 11-18.

131 "The Infinitude of Pluralism." *Critical Inquiry* 3 (Summer 1977): 803-16.

134 "Edgar Saltus and the Heroic Decadence." In *Essays in American Literature in Memory of Richard P. Adams,* pp. 61-69. Edited by Donald Pizer. *Tulane Studies in English* 23 (1978).

135 "'Literature': Disjunction and Redundancy." In *What is Literature?,* pp. 219-30. Edited by Paul Hernadi. Bloomington: Indiana University Press, 1978.

137 "Romantic Historicism in Italy: Opera, Painting, Fiction." *Concept, The Texas Arts Journal* 2-4 (1978): 73-92.

138 "Perceptual and Semiotic Discontinuity in Art." *Poetics* 7 (April 1978): 217-30.

139 "The Evaluation of Art." *Arts Exchange* (January/February 1978): 13-15.

140 "An Explanation of 'Realism.'" *Denver Quarterly* 13 (Summer 1978): 3-10.

146 "The Problem of Interpretation." *College Literature* (1979): 1-17.

150 "Truth in Art? Why Not?" *The Structuralist* 19/20 (1979/1980): 15-19.

**152** "Three Notions about Criticism." In *What is Criticism?*, pp. 38-51. Edited by Paul Hernadi. Bloomington: Indiana University Press, 1981.

## V. *Textbooks and Anthologies*

**22** With Seymour Chatman. *Word, Meaning, Poem.* New York: Thomas Y. Crowell, 1961.

Peckham's contributions to the volume are "To the Instructor," the first two "Notes to the Student," the selection and editing of all poems, and twenty-five "interpretive hypotheses"—brief but exhaustive explications of single poems or passages by Arnold, Auden, Browning, Collins, Dickinson, Donne, Dryden, Eliot, Frost, Gray, Hardy, Herbert, Herrick, Hopkins, Jonson, Keats, Milton, Pope, Shakespeare, Shelley, Spenser, Stevens, Swinburne, Wordsworth, and Yeats.

**38** *Romanticism: The Culture of the Nineteenth Century.* New York: George Braziller, 1965.

The Introduction to this anthology is reprinted as "The Dilemma of a Century: The Four Stages of Romanticism" in *The Triumph of Romanticism: Collected Essays,* pp. 36-57.

**73** With George P. Elliott, Philip McFarland, and Harvey Granite. *Themes in World Literature.* Boston: Houghton Mifflin, 1970.

Peckham contributed brief commentaries, containing questions for high school students, on thirty-two pieces of visual artwork and their relationships to the literary art in the anthology. The artists treated are Albright, Blume, Botticelli, Bruegel, Bronzino, Cesar, De Chirico, Church, Courbet, Daumier, David, Delacroix, Dürer, Friedrich, Gropper, Gros, Lorenzetti, Massaccio, Munch, Picasso, Raphael, Rouault, Rousseau, Steen, Turner, Van Steenwijck, Vasarely, Cecchino da Verona, and Watteau. Two anonymous works are discussed: an illuminated manuscript colophon of Dante's Inferno, showing Lucifer, and a Japanese scroll depicting the burning of Sanjo Palace.

**88** With Philip McFarland, et al. *Moments in Literature.* Houghton Mifflin Literature Series. Boston: Houghton Mifflin, 1972.

**88** _____. *Explorations in Literature.* Houghton Mifflin Literature Series. Boston: Houghton Mifflin, 1972.

**88** _____. *Perceptions in Literature.* Houghton Mifflin Literature Series. Boston: Houghton Mifflin, 1972.

**88** _____. *Reflections in Literature.* Houghton Mifflin Literature Series. Boston: Houghton Mifflin, 1972.

**88** _____. *Themes in American Literature.* Houghton Mifflin Literature Series. Boston: Houghton Mifflin, 1972.

**88** _____. *Forms in English Literature.* Houghton Mifflin Literature Series. Boston: Houghton Mifflin, 1972.

Peckham's contributions to the Houghton Mifflin Literature Series are brief essays on "Ideas and Art." Each relates six reproduced examples of visual art and a piece of recorded music to the thematic and historical concerns of a section of anthologized literature.

A partial list of composers treated, some represented by more than one work, includes Beethoven, Bloch, Carpenter, Copland, Debussy, Delius, Franck, Handel, Haydn, Honegger, Ives, Liszt, Mendelssohn, Schoenberg, Schumann, Vaughan Williams, and Wagner.

A partial list of visual artists treated, some also represented by more than one work, includes Altdorfer, Archelaos, Barlow, Beard, Bingham, Brett, Brown, Bruegel, Burne-Jones, Caravaggio, Chagall, Ch'iu Ying, Constable, Copley, Cornell, Crawford, Dali, David, Degas, Delacroix, DeMorgues, Dossi, Durand, Dürer, Van Dyck, Eakins, Van Eyck, Field, Giorgione, Girodet-Trioson, Van Gogh, Gottlieb, Goya, Hamilton, Harnett, Henderson, Hicks, Hodges, Hogarth, Holbein, Homer, Hopper, Hunt, Ingres, Inness, Kane, Knight, Lambert, de La Tour, Lear, Lefranc, Lewis, McMillan, Magritte, Marsh, Millais, Miro, Motherwell, Mytens, Nash, O'Keefe, Patinir, Peale, Perugino, Peto, Piero della Francesca, Pollaiuolo, Rembrandt, Rivers, Rubens, Ryder, Shahn, Sheeler, Siberechts, Sickert, Spencer, Frank Stella, Tooker, Trova, Turner, Vasarely, Vermeer, Wang Chien, Warhol, Waterhouse, Wesselmann, Whistler, Wood, Wright of Derby, Andrew Wyeth, and Zurbaran.

These partial lists do not include anonymous works or miscellaneous musical recordings discussed; nor do they include the artists, composers, and works which Peckham treats in the *Explorations* and *Perceptions* volumes in the Houghton Mifflin Literature Series, which the editor was unable to lay his hands on.

## VI. *Reviews*

1 *The Portable Faulkner,* edited by Malcolm Cowley. *Foreground* 1 (1946): 185-87.

15 *The Metaphoric Tradition in Modern Poetry,* by Sister Mary Bernetta Quinn. *The United States Quarterly Book Review* 12 (June 1956): 174.

18 "A Survey of Romantic Period Textbooks." *College English* 20 (October 1958): 49-53.

24 *Regina vs. Palmerston,* by Brian Connell. *Saturday Review,* 2 September 1961, 20-21.

27 *The Image, or What Happened to the American Dream,* by Daniel J. Boorstin. *Annals of the American Academy of Political and Social Sciences* 344 (November 1962): 183.

28 *The Tangled Bank,* by Stanley Edgar Hyman. *Victorian Studies* 6 (December 1962): 180-82.

30 *The Hero of the Waverley Novels,* by Alexander Welsh. *Saturday Review,* 15 June 1963, 26.

31 *Mrs. Browning: A Poet's Work and Its Setting,* by Alethea Hayter. *Saturday Review,* 7 September 1963, 34.

32 *Scrutiny: A Quarterly Review, 1932-53,* edited by F. R. Leavis. *Saturday Review,* 2 November 1963, 27, 37.

33 *Christina Rossetti,* by Lona Mosk Packer. *Saturday Review,* 28 December 1963, 41.

34 "Recent Studies of Nineteenth-Century English Literature." *SEL* 3 (Autumn 1963): 595-611.

35 *Erasmus Darwin,* by Desmond King-Hele; and *Doctor Darwin,* by Hesketh Pearson. *Saturday Review,* 28 March 1964, 44-45.

36 *The Correspondence of Emerson and Carlyle,* edited by Joseph Slater. *Saturday Review,* 19 December 1964, 34, 39.

39 *Religious Humanism and the Victorian Novel,* by U. C. Knoepflmacher. *Saturday Review,* 22 May 1965, 78.

40 *The Artifice of Reality,* by Karl Kroeber. *JEGP* 64 (July 1965): 591-93.

41 *The Disappearance of God: Five Nineteenth-Century Writers,* by J. Hillis Miller. *Victorian Poetry* 3 (1965): 202-5.

42 *The Life of the Mind in America from the Revolution to the Civil War,* by Perry Miller. *Saturday Review,* 28 August 1965, 31, 48.

**57** *Victorian Minds,* by Gertrude Himmelfarb; *Feasting with Panthers,* by Rupert Croft-Cooke; and *Prince Albert and Victorian Taste,* by Winslow Ames. *Saturday Review,* 30 March 1968, 29.

**58** *The Sense of an Ending,* by Frank Kermode. *Modern Philology* 65 (May 1968): 434-35.

**60** *Life with Queen Victoria,* edited by Victor Mallet. *Saturday Review,* 26 October 1968, 50.

**66** "Robert Browning: A Review of the Year's Research." *The Browning Newsletter* 2 (April 1969): 3-9.

**68** *Carlyle and the Idea of the Modern,* by Albert J. La Valley. *Victorian Studies* 12 (June 1969): 485-86.

**69** *English Romantic Poetry,* by Albert S. Gerard. *The CEA Critic* 32 (December 1969): 15.

**74** *Music, the Arts, and Ideas,* by Leonard B. Meyer. *History and Theory* 9 (March 1970): 127-35.

**95** *Poetic Closure,* by Barbara Herrnstein Smith. *Genre* 5 (March 1972): 61-64.

**110** *Natural Supernaturalism,* by M. H. Abrams; and *Revolution and Romanticism,* by Howard Mumford Jones. *Studies in Romanticism* 13 (Fall 1974): 359-65.

**120** *The Transformative Vision,* by José A. Argüelles. *Journal of Aesthetics and Art Criticism* 34 (Spring 1976): 343-44.

**121** *Victorian Conventions,* by John R. Reed. *Novel* 9 (Winter 1976): 171-72.

**122** *The Romantic Progression,* by Colin Martindale. *American Literature* 48 (May 1976): 249-51.

**123** *The Letters of Henry James 1843-1875,* edited by Leon Edel. *Resources for American Literary Study* 6 (Spring 1976): 113-16.

**124** *The Stranger in Shakespeare,* by Leslie A. Fiedler. *Shakespeare Studies* 9 (1976): 320-24.

128 *The Classic,* by Frank Kermode. *JEGP* 76 (January 1977): 117-21.

130 *William Morris,* by Edward P. Thompson. *The Nation,* 9 July 1977, 53-55.

136 *The Romantic Will,* by Michael G. Cooke. *Studies in Romanticism* 17 (Winter 1978): 91-93.

142 *Progress in Art,* by Suzi Gablik. *Lone Star Book Review,* June 1979, 7.

143 *A History of the Oratorio,* by Howard E. Smither. *Lone Star Book Review,* July 1979, 9.

144 *Cultural Materialism,* by Marvin Harris. *Lone Star Book Review,* January/ February 1980, 13.

147 *The Walter Scott Operas,* by Jerome Mitchell. *Studies in Scottish Literature* 14 (1979): 277-80.

147 *The Scottish Enlightenment,* by Anand Chitnis. *Studies in Scottish Literature* 14 (1979): 299-300.

151 *Critical Understanding,* by Wayne C. Booth. *JEGP* 79 (July 1980): 429-31.

153 *On the Margins of Discourse,* by Barbara Herrnstein Smith. *Poetics Today* 2:1a (1980): 191-95.

## VII. *Unpublished Essays and Lectures*

*A History of the Ninth Bomber Command (USAF).* 1944-1946.

91 "The Gothic Novel: Some Observations on an Old Hat." November 1972.

92 "Humanists, Education, and Society." June 1973.

104 "The Thematic Studies Program of the John Jay College of Criminal Justice." April 1973.

105 "Methodology in the Humanities." October 1973.

106 "Philosophy and Art as Related and Unrelated Modes of Behavior." November 1973.

111 "Man's Use of Nature." October 1974.

114 "Literature, Ideology, and Society." February 1975.

132 "A Response to M. H. Abrams." August 1977.

133 "What is Affirmation?" December 1977.

141 "Romanticism, Surrealism, *Terra Nostra*." May 1978.

148 "Two Ways of Using 'Creativity.'" December 1979.

149 "Literature and Behavior." April 1980.

"Documents." May 1983.

The editor has not assigned numbers to Morse Peckham's history of the Ninth Bomber Command or to "Documents" because neither appeared on Peckham's 1980 chronology of his works. A number of these unpublished essays and lectures will appear in a third volume of collected essays, tentatively entitled *Romantic Ideologies of Art and Behavior,* to be published by the Penkevill Press, probably in 1984.